Harbor for the Poor

Harbor for the Poor

*A Missiological Analysis of Almsgiving
in the View and Practice of John Chrysostom*

ERIC COSTANZO

With Forewords by Wendy Mayer and Keith E. Eitel

PICKWICK *Publications* · Eugene, Oregon

HARBOR FOR THE POOR
A Missiological Analysis of Almsgiving in the View and Practice of John Chrysostom

Copyright © 2013 Eric Costanzo. All rights reserved. Except for brief quotations in critical publications or reviews, no part of this book may be reproduced in any manner without prior written permission from the publisher. Write: Permissions, Wipf and Stock Publishers, 199 W. 8th Ave., Suite 3, Eugene, OR 97401.

Pickwick Publications
An Imprint of Wipf and Stock Publishers
199 W. 8th Ave., Suite 3
Eugene, OR 97401

www.wipfandstock.com

ISBN 13: 978-1-62032-496-7

Cataloging-in-Publication data:

Costanzo, Eric.

    Harbor for the poor : a missiological analysis of almsgiving in the view and practice of John Chrysostom / Eric Costanzo, with Forewords by Wendy Mayer and Keith E. Eitel.

    xviii + 178 pp. ; 23 cm—Includes bibliographical references and indexes.

    ISBN 13: 978-1-62032-496-7

    1. John Chrysostom, Saint, d. 407. 2. Generosity—Religious aspects. 3. Christian Literature, Early. 3. I. Mayer, Wendy, 1960–. II. Eitel, Keith Eugene, 1954–. III. Title.

BR1720.C5 C777 2013

Manufactured in the USA

This book is dedicated to my beautiful wife, Rebecca, who continually finds new ways to support my calling. May the privilege of serving our Lord never cease to define the purpose of our marriage.

Contents

Foreword

Often studies of the past remain just that, studies of the distant past. They make interesting reading and further our knowledge of a part of human history, but in the end we set them aside and get on with our lives. The author of *Harbor for the Poor*, an evangelical pastor with a heart for the poor, is not content to let a Christian discipline of the distant past remain a curiosity. In the United States and around the developed world, urban poverty remains a compelling issue. It challenges Christians of all denominations to examine their hearts and respond. In this book Eric Costanzo draws to the attention of twenty-first century Protestants, particularly those of evangelical conviction, a long-neglected approach to caring for the poor. Drawing on the teachings on almsgiving of one of the most enduring preachers of eastern Christianity, he bridges the gap between past and present, persuasively presenting his case that in the thought of John Chrysostom there are sound principles that can be applied directly to addressing this issue in the contemporary urban setting in the developed world.

This book breaks new ground on several fronts. For scholars it presents the first detailed study of John Chrysostom's thought on almsgiving, adding to recent research that seeks to more deeply understand his approach to poverty and the poor. Almsgiving is not peripheral for John, but a central aspect of his theology. In this respect, *Harbor for the Poor* replaces the sole previous study on the topic by Otto Plassmann (*Das Almosen bei Johannes Chysostomus*, 1961), now much dated and no longer adequate. For pastors, lay people, and those interested in social justice or who work with the poor, it situates old ideas in a new context, contributing to contemporary discussions about poverty and how to respond. Such critiques of poverty, justice, and the church's response in both the early centuries and today are growing as the post-modern world grapples anew with these issues. In this regard, *Harbor for the Poor* joins a new wave in scholarship that seeks to bring patristic thought on these issues to the attention of the church in the world today. Here it sits side by side with the significant contributions of

Susan Holman (*God Knows There's Need: Christian Responses to Poverty*, 2009) and Helen Rhee (*Loving the Poor, Saving the Rich: Wealth, Poverty, and Early Christian Formation*, 2012).

John Chrysostom himself is unfamiliar to the majority of the Protestant Christian world. Yet his value extends well beyond the eastern churches for whom he is a venerated hierarch and the Roman Catholic church for whom he is a saint. His preaching is rich with teachings on social issues and Christian living that still resonate with us today. Both Luther and Calvin admired and cited his work, yet only rarely since the time of the Reformation has his thought been brought directly to the attention of Christians on that side of the divide. By bringing Chrysostom's teachings on almsgiving to the attention of fellow evangelicals Eric Costanzo follows in the footsteps of the great reformers, recognizing the value in what has gone before and connecting us to both a preacher and principles for Christian living that within the Protestant tradition would otherwise remain a forgotten part of the distant Christian past.

Wendy Mayer
Honorary Fellow,
Centre for Early Christian Studies,
Australian Catholic University

Foreword

The poor we always have with us, as Christ indicated. Yet, there are fresh needs to engage them with biblically driven motives and desired outcomes that touch their greatest needs not ours. This is another paradigm crossroad in Christian history. It behooves us to look back in order to see our way forward. John Chrysostom's life and work in fourth-century Antioch is informative, offers insightful parallels, and helpful instructions to the modern church.

Eric Costanzo keenly develops this historically oriented trend of thought for us against the backdrop of the modern dilemma and mixed set of motives for assisting the poor, especially by the specific act of almsgiving. Costanzo argues cogently that God designed almsgiving as a demonstration of his love and compassion for the world. Essentially, if done in keeping with biblical designs, it is an effective witness of life to both a lost world and even perhaps a church that has lost its way.

Costanzo develops Chrysostom's ideas regarding the practice of almsgiving and shows the points of separation between what the fourth-century "golden-tongued" pastor advocated and more modern renditions such as the Social Gospel and Liberation Theology movements that some are now reviving in new forms. Chrysostom stands apart, and beckons down the corridors of history to instruct in our time of urgent need for clear headed and biblically defined ways forward.

Costanzo takes the reader to fourth-century Roman Antioch and defines its myriad of social contexts. Then he exegetes Chrysostom's teachings and homilies regarding wealth, poverty, and the role of almsgiving as the sage of old developed these in the Gospels and Acts as well as the Pauline Epistles. These surveys are done against the backdrop of understanding both doctrinal ecclesiology and the role of rhetorical persuasion in the churches of Chrysostom's day.

Today there is specific need to develop a renewed sense of what constitutes right practices as we see the tragic faces of increasing numbers of the world's poor. Implications abound both for Christians living in the West and those throughout the non-western world. Biblical, missiological, ethical, and even historical factors for interpreting our twenty-first-century need are evident in this book. It provides insight from older days for deriving right responses in relation to the greater witness of the church as it still is learning to be both settled and on the move in a lost and dying world.

Keith E. Eitel,

Dean,

Roy Fish School of Evangelism and Missions,

Southwestern Baptist Theological Seminary, Fort Worth, Texas

Acknowledgments

I am indebted to many scholars for their contributions to this volume. First, to my doctoral supervisor Dr. Keith E. Eitel, who not only oversaw my dissertation but also helped me in countless ways to grow into a higher level of scholarship. Dr. Bill Goff and Dr. Matt Queen also contributed significantly to my dissertation. I appreciate all three of you for offering encouragement that I seek to publish my work. And to Dr. Wendy Mayer, of course, I offer sincere gratitude and admiration for your contributions to this volume in all stages.

To my wife Rebecca and our incredible children Adin, Noah, and Abigail. I continue to receive the best this life has to offer from within my own home. Each of you sacrificed a great deal in your own ways to help achieve these goals. I am blessed beyond measure to walk down this road of faith with the four of you as we seek to bring glory to our Lord among the nations.

To my parents, Bill and Terri, thank you for the countless investments you have made in my life, ministry, and family. It still amazes me that we all started our journey with Christ together more than twenty years ago.

To my other parents, Dr. Glenn and Carol Plum—thank you for loving me as one of your own and for being the example of a godly man and woman that we continue to follow. Glenn, thank you for being my first and only pastor and for giving me the greatest gift I've received on earth—the hand of your youngest daughter in marriage.

To my grandparents, Harold and Teresia (Mema and Bepa), thank you for always believing in me and always giving me the benefit of the doubt. Thank your supporting me in absolutely everything, for teaching me the joy of learning, and for incalculable amounts of cheesecake muffins.

The wrap-up music began to play a long time ago, but I would be remiss to not thank this final group of people. Since this book represents the culmination of my academic career as a student, I would like to thank several men and women of God who helped ignite a love for Christ and the study of God's Word along the way.

To the late Dr. Dick Rader—thank you for teaching me about Christian leadership by word and example. Thank you for skipping that important meeting with the university president to hear me preach in chapel. I will never forget you were there.

To Dr. Tom Wilks—thank you for teaching me that the most important part of ministry is loving people; and thank you for believing in me so much that you sent me to preach all over the state when I was still just a teenager!

To Dr. Bobby Kelly—thank you for having the courage to speak truth to me when I needed it most. Thank you for teaching me how to read Greek, how to study the New Testament with passion, and how to have a good time while doing it.

To Dr. Mack Roark—thank you for convincing me to change my major to Greek so I could learn to read the "real New Testament."

To Dr. Kevin Hall and Dr. James Hamilton—thank you for helping me find Christ in the Old Testament.

To Dr. Warren McWilliams and Dr. Bill Goff—thank you for teaching me how to study and apply biblical ethics and for being such great men of character at the same time.

To Dr. Karen Bullock—thank you for helping me discover the joy and enrichment that comes from studying church history.

To Dr. Deron Biles—thank you for being my teacher, supervisor, and friend. It is an honor to have served with your entire family in ministry.

To Bryan Reed and Kevin Laufer—thank you for helping me to discover Christ and my call to serve in ministry during my adolescent years. Sorry for all the headaches I caused you.

I would also like to thank Deron Spoo and First Baptist Tulsa, Dennis Hester and First Baptist Watauga, and all the loving folks at Blackburn Chapel Baptist Church for their constant support and encouragement during my studies. You all believed in me and I never heard you complain that I spent too much time on my schoolwork!

Eric Costanzo
Tulsa, OK
February 2013

Abbreviations

AF	*The Apostolic Fathers*. Edited and Translated by Michael W. Holmes.
ANF	*The Ante-Nicene Fathers*. Edited by Alexander Roberts and James Donaldson.
BDAG	*A Greek-English Lexicon*, 3rd ed. Edited by Walter Bauer, et al.
CCSL	Corpus Christianorum Series Latina. Brepols.
CSEL	Corpus Scriptorum Ecclesiasticorum Latinorum. Austrian Academy of Sciences.
LXX	The Septuagint
LCL	Loeb Classical Library
NPNF	A Select Library of the Nicene and Post-Nicene Fathers. Edited by Philip Schaff.
OP	*Six Books On the Priesthood*. Translated by Graham Neville.
ORA	*On Repentance and Almsgiving*. Translated by Gus George Christo.
OWP	*On Wealth and Poverty*. Translated by Catherine P. Roth.
PG	Patrologiae Cursus Completus: Series Graeca. Edited by J.-P. Migne.
PL	Patrologiae Cursus Completus: Series Latina. Edited by J.-P. Migne.
SC	Sources Chrétiennes. Cerf.

Prologue:
An Evening in Fourth-Century Antioch

In the late fourth century CE, the Syrian city of Antioch was at the pinnacle of its status in the Roman Empire. In the meantime, a polarity of affluence had developed resulting in a few who were supremely wealthy, a few who lived in utter destitution, and the vast majority living well above the poverty line. The wealthiest landowners enjoyed lavish lifestyles, hosting important guests in their homes on a regular basis, each being treated to the finest foods and entertainment available.[1]

Many evenings on the eve of the Sabbath, wealthy Jews and Christians would host such gatherings in their homes. The meals were perfectly prepared and scheduled, from the pre-meal festivities and garnishments to the entrees and desserts. Throughout the meal, each person would have limitless amounts of bread served with various dipping sauces. The breads were the best available, often kneaded with wine, honey, milk, oil, eggs, and other spices. As long as the bread baskets continued to be refilled, the guests could be confident that the dishes would keep coming.

The main course of the meal would consist of fruits and grains, followed by exotic meats including oxen and poultry. Typically, a person who lived at this level could serve meat in his home every day, equaling the cost of paying thirty employees their annual salaries. The dessert was often some variety of spongecake or grain, usually roasted and flavored with honey, with different types of nuts sprinkled strategically in various places. Throughout the evening, the finest wines available, which were first used to prepare the meal, would be served to the guests until they could take no more. Most of the guests would attend a worship service together in the next few hours, enjoying more fellowship with one another.

1. The descriptions of the contents and practices of Antiochene gatherings and meals in this introduction are adapted from the information on Jewish and Roman dietary practices in the later Roman Empire found in Hamel, *Poverty and Charity in Roman Palestine*, 31–41.

This type of lifestyle, enjoyed by more than a few Christians, was in stark contrast to that of the poor who lived in the urban center. In the marketplace, for example, a number of beggars, many who suffered from disabilities, would settle into their pallets each evening feeling hungry and dehydrated. This group of people, made up of men, women, and children, received food in very small amounts throughout the day. Most of what they ate was *cibarium*, low quality barley also known as "poor man's bread," which was frequently a few days old. The only exceptions to this diet came as the result of begging from door to door, if one were able, or receiving the leftover meat served at annual festivals and celebrations, such as the carnival of Dionysus, the Greek god of wine and celebration.[2] The poor who begged drank water from secondary sources, which was described as having a sour taste.

From a biblical and ecclesiastical standpoint, each of the three classes was meant to share life together. The practice of giving to the poor, known as almsgiving, had been a part of both Christian and Roman culture for more than three centuries. Throughout the empire, however, almsgiving had eroded to a symbolic act of perceived piety through which the wealthy and the middle class gave demonstratively, usually for the purpose of gaining praise and attention. John of Antioch,[3] the gifted preacher and rhetorician later given the name χρύσοστομος (*Chrusostomos*), or "golden–tongued," emerged as the fourth century's most renowned pastor and bishop to champion the cause of the poor in the Roman Empire. John's sermons in both Antioch and Constantinople remain some of the most influential ever delivered on the practice of almsgiving in the church.[4] John sought to incorporate the presentation of the gospel among Christians with a call to social mission on behalf of the poor. For this reason, John can be described as an "evangelist of the rich," as has often been said of the gospel writer Luke.[5] John preached to congregations that, for the most part, were filled with people who lived very comfortable lives. His preaching contained a beautiful symmetry of sound theological and practical teaching on the churches' responsibility to bring the good news of Jesus Christ to the poor.

2. Mayer and Allen, *John Chrysostom*, 13. See also Liebeschuetz, *Antioch*, 40–67.

3. It should be noted that throughout this book the given name "John" is used rather than "Chrysostom," since the latter was a nickname as opposed to a surname.

4. Baur, *John Chrysostom and His Time*, 1:30.

5. Bosch, *Transforming Mission*, 103; Schottroff and Wolfgang, *Jesus and the Hope of the Poor*, 117; Albertz, "Die 'Antrittspredigt' Jesu im Lukasevangelium," 203.

1

Introduction

The church has resources with which the state cannot compete.... Christian
self-esteem is grounded in God, and pride comes from living out one's vocation
within that doctrinal framework; ... one who understands herself to be baptized
into the death of Christ and given new life as a member of his body, the church,
will see the world differently than a person whose life and accomplishments
depend on his own merits.

—ELLEN T. CHARRY[1]

INTRODUCTION

A renewed Evangelical interest in ministry to the poor continues to
emerge in the twenty-first century. Issues such as benevolence, social
justice, and servant evangelism are gaining popularity in academic circles,
literature, and churches.[2] This study is intended to demonstrate that the

1. Charry, "When Generosity is not Enough," 269–71.

2. For examples of this renewed interest, see Brady, "A Burning Desire for Social Justice," 8–11; Lupton, *Toxic Charity*, 1–10; Lupton, *Compassion, Justice, and the Christian
Life*, 11; Hoag, "Everyday Benevolence," 60–61; Labberton, "A Mighty River or a Slippery
Slope," 20–25; Kinnaman, "Do We Give a Rip About the Poor?" 15–17. Kinnaman refers
to a recent study by The Barna Group which revealed that three out of four evangelical
Christians in the United States claimed to have some involvement in meeting the needs
of the poor in their community. While most purported to have given material resources
primarily, nearly half maintained they had actually donated personal time.

local church should bear the greatest responsibility for carrying out missions and ministry among the poor in urban areas of the developed world that are open to Christianity.[3]

Serious questions have surfaced, however, as to how effective the average believer and church can be in meeting the deepest needs of the poor in any culture.[4] This study takes a unique approach to addressing such deficiencies by applying what I consider to be sound principles from a patristic source which are to be applied to a twenty-first century, developed, and urban setting. This approach undoubtedly bears the challenges of historical, temporal, and cultural distances. Nevertheless, it is my contention that an increase in understanding and implementation of the biblical and historical practice of almsgiving, as modeled by John Chrysostom, will help bridge the gap between a desire to bring the gospel to the urban poor and a perceived inability to do so with success. John viewed almsgiving as the most important characteristic of authentic Christian living with the exception of humility.[5] For John, personal almsgiving was a matter of obedience to divine command and ecclesiastical almsgiving was an integral part of church doctrine.

John confronted the common teachings of his day by asserting that almsgiving was not meant for personal gain, but rather to be simultaneously confessional, ceremonial, and practical. Almsgiving was confessional in the sense that it represented a tangible expression of the Christian faith, which always brought with it the good news of Jesus Christ. A major weakness of John's teaching on almsgiving is found in his understanding of the

---

3. Sachs, *The End of Poverty*, 18–25. The term developed world, or developed countries, began to be used during the twentieth century to identify those nations who sit at the top of the "economic ladder" and control the majority of the world's wealth and resources. The vast majority of the population in these countries lives in urban areas. This includes the United States, Canada, Japan, Australia, New Zealand, and most of Western Europe. The term "developing" refers to the poorest nations which are mostly rural. This term is preferred to the more common designation "third world." Missiologists prefer the term "majority world" to describe developing countries. See Wan and Pocock, *Missions from the Majority World*.

4. Pope, "Aquinas on Almsgiving," 167. Pope argues that our modern approaches to giving charity are often in the form of "half-measures" which usually fail to bring about lasting results. He uses Thomist arguments that reflect an earlier pattern of almsgiving that saw the practice as a true "moral force" that would affect change not only in physical circumstances of the poor but also in the attitude of Christians regarding love and care for the poor.

5. *In John hom.* 33.3 (PG 59:192; trans., Goggin, *Commentary on St. John*, 1:329–31; NPNF 1.14:180).

confessional aspect of the practice, as he often described acts of mercy as a means to redemption. While it might be argued that John meant such statements as hyperbole, the ambiguity of these descriptions seems to contradict the more complete presentations of the gospel that he offered in other places.

John developed a method of almsgiving that was both ceremonial and practical in terms of ecclesiology, as the practice was meant to be a regular part of the church's mission and constantly in the process of refinement so that it would be effective. A missiological analysis of the practical aspects of almsgiving in Antioch, primarily, but also in Constantinople, will demonstrate that John and his churches were prodigious in their evangelistic activity. In terms of communication, John used a number of cultural symbols and contextual applications that brought the needs of the poor in front of the people in creative ways.[6] Because of the Jewish, pagan, and sectarian influences in both Antioch and Constantinople, John was careful to contextualize the message of the gospel and its content concerning the poor in ways that avoided syncretism.[7] John carefully "exegeted" his community and culture in such a way that he was familiar with the different types of poverty in the empire and historical approaches to meeting the needs of the poor.[8] He promoted shared forms of almsgiving that countered the typical top-down mentality of benevolence among the elite Christians of the day.[9] John used these evaluative skills to develop practical and effective strategies for reaching the poor with the gospel and meeting their needs.[10] The

6. *De Stat. hom.* 16.6 (PG 49:169–70; NPNF 1.09:515); Baur, *John Chrysostom and His Time*, 1:34–37; Krupp, *Shepherding the Flock*, 12.

7. Mayer and Allen, *John Chrysostom*, 4, 13. See also Lassus, "La ville d'Antioch," 67–74.

8. *In Matt. hom.* 66.3 (PG 58:630; NPNF 1.10:548–49); *In 1 Cor. hom.* 21.5 (Field, *Sancti Patris*, 253; Mayer and Allen, trans., *John Chrysostom*, 171; PG 61:176–77; NPNF 1.12:170); *De Eleem.* 1 (PG 51:261; trans., Christo, *ORA*, 131, xvi); *De Stat. hom.* 1.10 (PG 49:30; NPNF 1.09:369). For the idea of exegeting community and culture, see Stetzer and Putman, *Breaking the Missional Code*, 24.

9. *De Eleem.* 4 (PG 51:266–67; trans., Christo, *ORA*, 141); *In 1 Tim. hom.* 11.1–3 (PG 62:553–58; NPNF 1.13:590); Cardman, "Poverty and Wealth as Theater," 171; Leyerle, "John Chrysostom on Almsgiving," 42–43; 55.

10. *In Rom. hom.* 1.2, arg. (PG 60:393–94; NPNF 1.11:457–58). Here John uses the Apostle Paul as his primary example. He illustrates Paul's methods among different churches and in different contexts by discussing the methods of the common physicians and teachers of the fourth century. A physician, according to John, does not treat a patient the same in the earliest part of their treatment as used in later stages of treatment. In the same way, John said, a teacher does not instruct a beginner student with the same

churches in Antioch became increasingly diverse in terms of demographics under John's leadership, despite having been made up largely of the same kinds of people at the beginning of his pastorate.

The majority of this study's focus is limited to John's preaching and ministry in Antioch, because of its primacy in his homilies and literature that have survived. Within this context, John's ministry led to innovative developments in Christian charity which helped to establish the poor as a class characterized by dignity and advocacy. The changes that took place in Antioch affected the broader Christianized empire, in both the East and the West. As the imperial favor of Christianity extended, urban societies began to change. According to Peter Brown of Princeton University, who is a noted historian on the late Roman Empire and early Middle Ages, "Late antiquity witnessed the transition from one model of society, in which the poor were largely invisible, to another, in which they came to play a vivid imaginative role."[11]

The Problem

The practice of biblical forms of almsgiving, which played a substantial role in the *missio dei* from the time of Moses until the late Middle Ages, is all but absent within contemporary Evangelicalism. Ecclesiastical almsgiving reached a significant height in the late fourth century CE, as the Christian mission, which had turned inward as a result of more than half a century of relative religious freedom, contained a renewed focus on the needs of the poor. The Christianization of the West has been accompanied by a similar ethnocentricity among believers, which has likewise developed into the recent spike in interest toward ministry to the poor.[12] This has not, however,

---

methods used on a more advanced student. Likewise, neither should ministry be done in the same way to every person. On the contrary, the level of faith, spiritual maturity, and depth of need should all factor in to discerning the most appropriate pastoral response. This passage and illustration will be discussed again in chapter 8 regarding case management.

11. Brown, *Poverty and Leadership*, 74. Brown has since revised some of his thoughts on these issues by adding research which points to the influence of ascetic labor practices and their influence on invigorating the poor. See Brown, "A Parting of the Ways."

12. Two notable exceptions to this aspect of Christianization may be the two "great" Evangelical awakenings of the eighteenth and nineteenth centuries. Each contained new emphases on social activism and sought to "bridge the yawning cultural divide between blacks and whites." Missionaries and evangelists such as David Brainerd and Gilbert Tennent were active in bring the gospel to Native Americans and slaves. During the second

been followed by a rekindling of awareness concerning the significance of biblical forms of almsgiving. While most people who give to churches include the poor as likely recipients, almsgiving is meant to be identified with more than just the offering plate. As a habitude of the church, the practice of almsgiving should not be confused with a theology of the poor, such as Liberation Theology, or a Christian ethic in the same vein as the Social Gospel Movement. On the contrary, almsgiving is meant to be an applied ethic based upon biblical theology that is grounded in God's missionary concern for all people. Almsgiving should be practiced by believers of all demographics in order to facilitate direct access to the gospel of Jesus Christ for those suffering the effects of poverty. The contemporary ignorance regarding the practice of almsgiving has resulted in a lack of personal responsibility from churches and their individual members on behalf of the poor.

A general unawareness of the biblical, historical, and practical facets of almsgiving among evangelicals is displayed in at least three different ways. The first is a common failure on the part of a church or its membership with regard to giving consistent time, resources, and support to meet the needs of the poor. The second is a general ignorance, whether accidental or intentional, concerning the means and methods by which a church or organization currently offers care for the poor. This particular unawareness results in deficiencies in giving, evaluation, and progress concerning methods of almsgiving. The third, and most common, is a developing culture of evangelicals who lack sufficient education and training in terms of offering aid that is truly beneficial for the recipients.[13] Almsgiving should result in more than just the transfer of goods. The purpose of biblical almsgiving, and that which was modeled by John Chrysostom, is to provide practical acts of mercy to the poor, which stand as "an expression of justice," an affirmation of God's love for all humankind, and an illustration of his graciousness toward a sinful world.[14]

---

awakening, missionary activity increased not only among blacks and Native Americans but also on international fronts. See Noll, *A History*, 91, 105–8, 185–88.

13. Lupton, *Toxic Charity*, 1–2; Corbett and Fikkert, *When Helping Hurts*, 49–98.

14. Bosch, *Transforming Mission*, 103.

Background

In some ways, the story of almsgiving within Christian history is a tale of four hundred and fifty years. In the first four and a half centuries of faith, both charity and almsgiving clearly existed in the Christian community and were interwoven with the most significant ordinances of the church. However, the slow decline in personal and ecclesiological almsgiving was a pattern that existed even at the height of the practice. Near the turn of the fifth century CE, John Chrysostom joined the voices of other church leaders who were imploring their congregations to rediscover their responsibility to the poor. John and a few of his contemporaries, such as Augustine of Hippo, were successful in casting such a vision for a short time. From the late fifth century forward, however, almsgiving dwindled to a bare minimum with the notable exception of some monastic movements.[15] The near millennium that was the Middle Ages contained scattered amounts of church leadership who admonished their congregations to continue in almsgiving.[16] Both Augustine and Aquinas, the bookends of this period so to speak, affirmed the responsibility of churches and Christians to show mercy and give alms generously.[17] At the same time, however, almsgiving was largely institutionalized during this period and was used mostly for sacramental purposes. In some cases, church leadership "monopolized" the

15. Latourette, *A History of Christianity*, 1:428–40. Latourette mentions specifically the major mendicant orders, the Franciscans and Dominicans, who took up the missionary cause of caring for the needs of urban dwellers during the twelfth and thirteenth centuries through co-labor, caring for the sick, giving to the poor, and other tangible forms of ministry. Also see Pope, "Aquinas on Almsgiving," 167; Charanis, "Byzantine Monasticism," 456–59.

16. Perhaps the Islamic emphasis on almsgiving known as *zakat*, which became one of the five pillars of Islam during the Middle Ages, was a cause of decline in personal almsgiving by Christians who sought separation from Islamic theology and practice. See Haarmann, "Islamic Duties in History," 9–10; Johnson, *The Fear of Beggars*, 3–n; Yéor, *The Decline of Eastern Christianity Under Islam*, 78, 84. Yéor describes the situation of Muhammad al-Mudabbir who was placed in charge of finances in the Islamic-conquered part of Egypt in 861 CE. Mudabbir sanctioned the pillaging of churches in order to take the alms intended for Christian ministry. The alms were subsequently placed in the Islamic treasury. See also Caner, *Wandering, Begging Monks*. Caner discusses the monastic form of almsgiving known as *beneficia* which may have continued into the ninth century CE.

17. Augustine, *Ench.* 19.70–20.76 (CCSL 46:49–114; trans., Harbert, *Enchiridion on Faith, Hope, and Charity*, 315–18); Aquinas, "Question 32: Almsgiving," *Summa Theologiae*, 34:237–74; Munzer, "Heroism," 47–80.

practice in order to gain greater political and religious power. This, in effect, was the beginning of a fundamental demise in personal almsgiving.[18]

As the active observance of almsgiving continued to decline, it eventually evolved into a practice by which the papists of the Reformation era offered indulgences. According to the reformer Martin Chemnitz, almsgiving had become another avenue through which a number of religious leaders were acquiring wealth by promise of earned forgiveness.[19] For this reason, some have suggested that Reformation theology completely eradicated the idea of almsgiving, associating it with inauthentic sacrament. That is not completely accurate, however, as almsgiving played a minor role for several Protestant leaders and communities. The monastic traditions of philanthropy, care for the sick, and other benevolent ministries were not altogether abandoned by Catholics, Protestants, or other developing religious traditions.[20] Holman argues that John Calvin developed his diaconate based on John Chrysostom's teachings on almsgiving.[21]

In the four centuries that followed, however, almsgiving in Europe and the Americas became far less organized. Charity on the part of churches and the Christian community clearly existed, but not in the forms that characterized the church of the first four centuries following the advent of the Christian faith.[22] In North America, for example, missions and ministry

---

18. De Vinne, "The Advocacy of Empty Bellies," 88–91.

19. Chemnitz, *On Almsgiving*, 20–21.

20. Latourette, *A History of Christianity*, 1:174, 569; González, *The Story of Christianity*, 2:56. At the height of their success, the Anabaptists of the sixteenth century were "radical egalitarians," offering the same rights and privileges to men and women, rich and poor, educated and ignorant. The aforementioned reformer Chemnitz had a significant influence on the understanding of almsgiving. See also Mckee, "John Calvin on The Diaconate and Liturgical Almsgiving," 34–48; McKee argues that the Reformed tradition associated with John Calvin combined worship and benevolence through a practice of "liturgical almsgiving," and the training of lay ministers charged with care of the poor. Contrary to the idea that the reformers all but eradicated the practice of offerings and the giving of alms, Calvin was known to have instituted a somewhat sacramental form of almsgiving in Geneva. Calvin's intentional use of almsgiving as charity for the poor and not the clergy led to similar movements in other Reformed churches throughout Western Europe. See also the following essay: John Calvin, *La Forme Des Prieres*. More info on this essay can be found in Dorn, *The Lord's Supper In The Reformed Church*, 11–40. See also Oliphant, "Daily Prayer in the Reformed Church of Strasbourg," 125, 136–37. Oliphant discusses the combination of prayer and almsgiving that was a part of the Reformed church in Strasbourg and highly influenced by Calvin and Caspar Hedio. According to Oliphant, Hedio was a scholar who translated many works of John Chrysostom.

21. Holman, *God Knows*, 4.

22. In Western Europe, almsgiving was tied closely to feudalism and politics. It was

among the destitute, oppressed, and addicted have been carried out on the grandest scale by parachurch organizations and not churches themselves.[23] According to ethicist Kelly S. Johnson, Western Christian ethicists were nearly silent on the issue of almsgiving during the Modern Era. She describes such silence as a "gap in ethics," noting that "almsgiving has traditionally played a conspicuous role in Christian sanctity."[24]

---

often a means by which gubernatorial officials and wealthy individuals could boost their own standing. At best, many saw alms as a vehicle to receiving a more substantial quantity of grace on the account of good works. See Cole, "Royal Almsgiving in Medieval England"; Koch, "The Economy of Beggary." As colonialism took shape in America, many physical needs developed and were identified. In colonial New York City, the Dutch Reformed church took up the cause of distributing alms to legitimate residents of the city through the support of municipal taxes and contributions by church membership. A number of "almshouses" were also established in which juveniles were offered support which often created more problems and abuses than they solved. See also Carras, "The Poor in Colonial New York City"; Rothman, "Bad Girls/Poor Girls." For more information on the concept of almshouses, particularly with their European roots, see Goodall, *God's House at Ewelme*. Goodall chronicles in detail one particular European almshouse which, like most others, was catered to the elderly and disabled. As rapid urbanization transpired in the United States, a number of social action movements began, some of which still exist today. Two that stand out are the Salvation Army and World Vision. See Noll, *A History*, 304; McKinley, *Marching to Glory*, 1–350; Myers, *Walking with the Poor*, 43–50.

23. Mandryk, *Operation World*, 863.

24. Johnson, *The Fear of Beggars*, 3.

2

Precursory Issues

"Give to everyone that asks you"; for such generosity is truly of God.

—CLEMENT OF ALEXANDRIA

A BRIEF BIOGRAPHY OF JOHN CHRYSOSTOM

In the late fourth century CE, John Chrysostom became a pivotal Christian leader in the in the Eastern Roman Empire as a result of his preaching, teaching, and ministry in his birth city of Antioch. The epithet "Chrysostom," or "golden-tongued," was firmly applied to John in the sixth century because of his great skill as an orator in both Antioch and Constantinople.[1] John was born sometime between the years 347–349 and died on September 14, 407. His father, Secundus, was a prominent government official who, while not being supremely wealthy, had amassed an estate of some significance. Secundus died when John was very young. His mother, Anthusa, chose not to remarry and instead used the estate to help pay for John's education.[2]

---

1. The following biographical information is compiled from a number of sources including Roth, *OWP*, 7–10; Kelly, *Golden Mouth*, 4–6, 290–91; McGuckin, *Patristic Theology*, 190–91; Aquilina, *The Fathers of the Church*, 177–79; Baur, *John Chrysostom and His Time*, 2 Vols.; Mayer and Allen, *John Chrysostom*, 3–11; Krupp, *Shepherding the Flock*, 2–17.

2. Kelly, *Golden Mouth*, 4; Mayer and Allen, *John Chrysostom*, 5. Mayer and Allen

It has traditionally been held that John studied philosophy under one Androgathius and Greek rhetoric under the renowned Libanius of Antioch.[3] He later studied Scripture and theology under Meletius, the bishop of Antioch, who eventually baptized John at the age of twenty. Soon after his theological training, John committed his life to the service of the clergy. His calling and abilities were evident from the beginning. In 371, despite his youth, he was appointed lector for the Antiochene churches under the direction of Meletius. Like Meletius, John took a decidedly literal approach to the interpretation of Scripture.[4]

Despite strong opposition from his mother, John was compelled to pursue a life of ασχέσις (askesis), or self-denial, in a monastic community. For six years John lived as an ascetic under the tutelage of a Syrian monk. Traditionally, historians believed he spent two of these years in a cave where he committed the entire Old and New Testaments to memory.[5] His experiences with poverty and sickness gave him tremendous insight into the disciplines of simplicity which he would spend the rest of his ministry emphasizing in opposition to wealth, vanity, and arrogance. After his health began to deteriorate, he resumed his duties as lector in 377. When John returned to Antioch, he witnessed the ambivalence of his former churches toward the Christian mission, especially with regard to the poor.

point out that the level of John's education was a strong indication that his parents must have been of some status and the estate of significant value.

3. *De Sac.* 1.1 (PG 48:623; trans., Neville, *OP*, 37–38; NPNF 1.09:31-n). John addressed a friend named Basil throughout this treatise. This Basil, who has been confused with Basil of Caesarea and Basil of Seleucia, was rather a less known bishop from Syria. John referred to his teachers in this treatise, and they are identified as Androgathius and Libanius in NPNF by W. R. W. Stephens. Libanius also attracted large crowds with his rhetorical abilities, and was best known for his tutelage of the young Julian, who would become emperor of Rome known as "the Apostate." See also Baur, *John Chrysostom and His Time*, 1:20. According to Baur, Libanius was known for being a vocal adversary of Christianity. There are some contemporary scholars who have questioned whether or not Libanius was actually a teacher of John and whether or not certain early sources on the matter are trustworthy. See Malosse, "Jean Chrysostome," 273–80; Mayer, "The Making of a Saint," 39–59; Mayer, "Biography and Chronology."

4. Mayer and Allen, *John Chrysostom*, 26–27; Kelly, *Golden Mouth*, 17, 40–44.

5. Recent scholarship has raised several questions concerning the reliability of ancient sources, such as Palladius, who argue that John Chrysostom's ascetic experiences were primarily in seclusion. Such scholars argue that John's ascetic training, while being distinctly Syrian, might have taken place in an urban setting which allowed him to continue participating in church life. See Illert, *Johannes Chrysostomus und das antiochenisch-syrische Mönchtu*; Mayer, "What Does It Mean to Say That John Chrysostom Was a Monk?"

He immediately delivered the content of his messages in ways that contrasted earthly gain with the eternal fulfillment of participating in Christ's redemptive activity in the world.[6]

John was ordained as a deacon in 381 and then to the priesthood in 386. He became the most popular preacher in Antioch and his approach was both grounded and progressive. The Antiochene traditions of theology and rhetoric in which he was raised avoided the allegorical methods of interpretation of the rival Alexandrians, such as Clement and Origen, in favor of a more historical and literal use of the text. John's approach was unique, however, among the Antiochene clergy. For John, the academic and rhetorical purposes of theology were not nearly as important as their practical and moral applications to the Christian life among believers and churches. This style of preaching gave John the benefit of combining what he considered to be biblical and theological orthodoxy with meaningful orthopraxy that had transformative effects in the religious life and social structure of the cities in which he preached.[7]

In 398, John was appointed to the highest religious position in the Eastern Empire—the archbishopric of Constantinople—following the death of Nectarius.[8] John's relatively short tenure as archbishop garnered an enormous amount of public attention and intrigue as the result of his homiletical boldness and ecclesiastical practicality. He often faced the political turmoil that surrounded pagan and Christian controversies throughout the city. He also made great strides toward reforming the clergy, as many in the priesthood had become corrupt. This led to a rejuvenation of the disciplines and practices of ordained priests throughout the Eastern empire.

John's troubles in Constantinople began when his constant barrages against unnecessary vanity and ignorance concerning the needs of the poor were directed toward the Empress Eudoxia, the wife of Arcadius, son of

6. Among the most well-known of these original treatises and sermons are *De Sac.* and *De Stat.* which were directed toward clergy, deacons, and members of the Antiochene churches.

7. For more on the ethical aspects of John's teaching, see Murphy, "The Moral Doctrine of Saint John Chrysostom," 52–53.

8. It is likely that John had some reservations about this change of venue, but the choice was removed from his hands. He was brought to Antioch by force, and yet in secrecy, because of fears that the churches and community of Antioch would put up a fight to keep him in their city. See Roth, *OWP*, 10; Mayer and Allen, *John Chrysostom*, 7–8; McGuckin, *Patristic Theology*, 190; Aquilina, *Fathers of the Church*, 178. Mayer has questioned the authenticity of this account as well, which is steeped heavily in the tradition of Palladius. See Mayer, "John Chrysostom as Bishop," 455–66.

Theodosius I. His situation was complicated further by a scandal concerning a group of Alexandrian monks of Origen's school who had fled to Constantinople. When he refused to agree with the Alexandrian Archbishop Theophilus on the matter, Theophilus came to Constantinople and brought John to court on trumped up charges. In 403, John was found guilty and thus began two separate exiles that lasted more than three years from June 404 to September 407. He returned to Constantinople as a result of revolts among the people by whom he was beloved. After spending time preaching in Armenia, he was finally exiled to the eastern shore of the Black Sea, but he died in route.

Despite having died with some public disrepute among the Alexandrians and the elite of Constantinople, the legacy of John Chrysostom was one of righteousness and effectiveness in the centuries to follow. During the reign of Theodosius II, the son of Arcadius and Eudoxia, John's body was returned to Constantinople to be honored with a procession through the city streets. He was then buried with nobility near the places of imperial interment. Tradition holds that when John's body was returned, Theodosius II met his coffin and asked God to forgive his mother Eudoxia. In 451, John was honored as doctor of the church by the Council of Chalcedon.

ALMSGIVING DEFINED

Almsgiving, usually defined as giving financial or material resources to the poor, is a common practice within nearly every major Western and Eastern religious tradition. However, the contemporary understanding of almsgiving varies from one religious tradition to another, and between various sects within each religion. The Western word *alms* comes from the Greek ἐλεημοσύνη (*eleēmosunē*), which, in its simplest form, means charity or "that which is benevolently given to meet a need." The word's root and most traceable Greek etymology are traced back to the Septuagint use of ὁ ἔλεος (*ho eleos*) meaning "mercy, compassion, pity, or clemency." The Septuagintal usage of ὁ ἔλεος was loosely related to the Hebrew concept צדקה (*tzedakah*) which may be defined as "charity in the spirit of uprightness or justice."[9]

9. Kohler, "Alms," line 5; Heim, "Almsgiving," 267; Avery-Peck, "Charity in Judaism," 50–63; Cronbach, "The Me'il Zedakah," 503–67. See also Bosch, *Transforming Mission*, 103. According to Bosch, both Judaism and Islam have substantial emphases on charity and almsgiving. Almsgiving in its purest form is opposed to the modern view of charity

The word ὁ ἔλεος is used interchangeably in the Septuagint and New Testament to describe transactions among humans or between the divine and humans.[10] In the New Testament, the word ἐλεημοσύνη is used only a few times, all but once within the context of Lukan writings.[11] It is the same word used by the lawyer to describe the actions of the Samaritan in Luke 10:37 and Jesus' teaching on inauthentic righteousness among the Pharisees in Luke 11:41. As the missionary activity recorded in the New Testament expanded among the Jews and Gentiles, the word ἐλεημοσύνη was used to describe the good works of Tabitha (Acts 9:36–52) and Cornelius (Acts 10:2, 4, 31).

Though the word ἐλεημοσύνη is rare in the New Testament, the practice of almsgiving is referred to in many circumstances. In Matthew 25, Jesus' citation of the rabbinical tradition concerning "the least of these" is a direct reference to the Hebrew understanding of צדקה and, effectively, almsgiving.[12] In Luke 16:19–31, it is the lack of compassion and almsgiving that makes the actions, or lack of action as it were, of the rich man on earth so reprehensible.[13] Paul encouraged believers to give generously to their enemies (Rom 12:20). Paul also asked the Gentile churches to be generous in their collections, for much of what they gave went to help the needy in Jerusalem and beyond (1 Cor 16:1–2; 2 Cor 8:1–15). James, the half-brother of Jesus, implored believers to honor the poor and acknowledge their place of privilege in the kingdom of God (Jas 2).[14] Finally, the Apostle John

---

which Bosch describes as the "antithesis of justice." In Hebrew writings, the ideas of charity and justice are often used synonymously.

10. BDAG, 315–16. Examples of mercy distributed human to human are Matt 23:23 and Jam 2:13; Examples from divine to human are Luke 1:50 and Gal 6:16.

11. The sole non-Lukan use of the word ἐλεημοσύνη is found within the Sermon on the Mount, when Jesus implores his audience to practice their acts of mercy, or almsgiving, in secret (Matt 6:1–4).

12. Heim, "Almsgiving," 267; Avery-Peck, "Charity in Judaism," 50–63.

13. *De Laz. hom.* 1–2 (PG 48:963–992; trans., Roth, *OWP*, 19–56). The story of Lazarus and the rich man in Luke 16 is the focus of at least seven renowned homilies by John which will appear frequently throughout this study.

14. Hasselhoff, "James 2:2–7 in Early Christian Thought," 48–55. In Greco-Roman language, the poor were separated into two major categories: the πένητες (*penētes*), or working poor, and the πτωχοί (*ptōchoi*), also known as the beggars. The authors of the New Testament utilize both of these terms, but by and large use πτωχοί when referring to the poor. See Hamel, *Poverty and Charity in Roman Palestine*, 168–73; Parkin, "Poverty in the Early Roman Empire." These Greek categories will be discussed in chapter 3 along with the later additions of Roman categories for the poor.

exhorted Christians to demonstrate the internal love of God in an external manner, "with actions and in truth," by giving of their material possessions to those who are in need (1 John 3:17–18). The practice of almsgiving and caring for the needs of the poor served as a demonstration of Christ's love for all, Jew and Gentile alike, as the gospel continued to spread throughout the nations of the earth.

Among the Jews and Jewish Christians

Almsgiving was expected as an act of obedience in correspondence with God's missionary concern for the nations, as expressed in God's intentions for Abraham (Gen 18:18). The Hebrew concept צדקה is directly tied to the Torah and that which is considered to be central in Jewish faith and practice. According to distinguished Jewish scholar Jacob Neusner, "People cannot touch the treasure of *tzedakah*[;] . . . *tzedakah* is for eternity."[15] The Hebrew concept of righteous charity is demonstrated clearly in God's instructions to the prophet Isaiah on fasting. Fasting was meant to produce charity and resources for those in need as opposed to being only a spiritual discipline.

> Is not this the kind of fasting I have chosen:
> to loose the chains of injustice
> and untie the cords of the yoke,
> to set the oppressed free
> and break every yoke?
>
> Is it not to share your food with the hungry
> and to provide the poor wanderer with shelter—
> when you see the naked, to clothe him,
> and not to turn away from your own flesh and blood?[16]

The Hebrew usage of צדקה was tied closely to the idea of righteousness in terms of orthopraxy.[17] According to Jewish tradition, there are eight degrees of צדקה which correspond to the manner in which alms and charity are given to the recipient. Neusner summarizes these degrees by correlating them into three main principles:

15. Neusner, *Tzedakah*, 6; The concept of צדקה is also discussed in Holman, "Patristic Christian Views on Poverty and Hunger," 15–18. Both authors draw distinct connections between the Hebrew understanding of צדקה and contemprary charity.

16. Isaiah 58:6–7. All Scripture is quoted from the New International Version (NIV) unless otherwise noted.

17. Holman, "Patristic Christian Views on Poverty and Hunger," 17.

1. The way to deal with poverty is to help the poor help themselves.

2. When one gives (צדקה) to the poor, the way to do it is so that the left hand does not know what the right hand is doing, so to speak. The poor are respected; the donors remain anonymous.

3. The dignity of the poor must be respected.[18]

The Hebrew Scriptures represent perhaps the earliest writings in which the recipients of almsgiving are associated directly with God Himself, as seen in Jesus' teaching in Matthew 25. In the course of time, however, the Jewish concept of personal almsgiving offered directly to the poor gave way to organized forms of charity. One of these was known as the *ḳuppah*, or the "charity box," out of which the needy from within each town and those passing through could receive financial assistance.[19] As this type of organization developed, almsgiving took the form of collections within Jewish communities as opposed to individual acts of mercy.[20]

The vast majority of texts related to almsgiving in the Old Testament are presented in the Torah and refer directly to the Exodus. In both Leviticus 19 and Deuteronomy 15, God commands that the systems of צדקה are to be practiced with openhandedness and generosity toward one's neighbor. While this charity was intended to benefit the needy among the Hebrews directly, its scope more than likely included also those who were not Jews.[21] As a result, four major categories of recipients developed: the Levite, widow, fatherless, and alien. In the Torah, specifically, almsgiving was more formalized and structured and eventually developed into systems of provision.[22] These systems were in addition to the requirements of tithing and the temple tax, while remaining wholly dependent on both.

The poor were often given the same rights as priests regarding the regular harvest. The first right was the *peah*, or "corner", after which the Mishnaic tractate is named.[23] The corners of a harvester's field were to be

18. Neusner, *Tzedakah*, 10–12.

19. Brooks, "Peah," 8.7–9, 35; Kohler, "Alms," under "The Alms-Boxes"; Schwartz, *Imperialism and Jewish Society*, 229; Beeri, "Communal Amenities," 39–40.

20. Kohler, "Alms," lines 8ff.

21. Constantelos, "Hellenic Background", 197.

22. Kim, *Stewardship and Almsgiving*, 278.

23. Neusner, *Mishnah*, 14; Neusner, *Judaism and Christianity in the Age of Constantine*, 128–30. According to Neusner, the Mishnah became an essential part of the Jewish and Christian canons in most parts of the Eastern Empire during the fourth and fifth centuries.

left behind for the poor to find food. The second right was primary access to the heads of grain or grapes that had fallen to the ground and were to be left intentionally by the harvester. The third right was to items of produce that were left on the sheaf or branch after the first pass. These, too, were not to be collected by the harvester but rather by the poor. These commands were understood chronologically, corresponding to the order in which both harvesting and collection took place.[24] Tractate *Peah* also mentions a number of organized forms of Jewish charity that had emerged throughout the Roman Empire including a communal fund and soup kitchen designed for the resident and transient poor. The food and money collected were only to be distributed to those men, women, or families who could provide sufficient evidence regarding their need.[25] Among the Greek-speaking Jewish community in the later Roman Empire, almsgiving continued to play a significant role in spiritual development and covenantal obedience.

Among Ante-Nicene and Nicene Christians

Almsgiving of late antiquity represented the height of the practice among Christians. Exhortations to give alms permeated the teachings of later patristic leaders like the Cappadocians, John Chrysostom, Leo the Great, and Augustine. By the late fourth century CE, almsgiving had developed into new forms of resources for the poor including medical care, education, and hostels for the traveler.[26] At the turn of the fifth century, John Chrysostom and Augustine represented the most comprehensive writing on the subject. Both viewed almsgiving as more than just the redistribution or appropriation of material wealth. On the contrary, both taught almsgiving was best understood as a collective term encompassing the provision

24. Brooks, "*Peah*," 14–35; Brooks, *Support for the Poor in the Mishnaic Law*, vii, 211. Brooks argues that these grain laws were to be applied to the poor and the Levites equivocally. According to Brooks, both the poor and the priests owned no land and were reliant upon a share of the harvest each year.

25. Brooks, "*Peah*," 8.7, 35; Kim, *Stewardship and Almsgiving*, 279. For a discussion concerning the use of synagogue kitchens for community meals versus charitable purposes see Martin, "Communal Meals in the Late Antique Synagogue," 135–46.

26. Neil, "Models of Gift-Giving in . . . Leo the Great," 225–59. Holman, "Patristic Christian Views on Poverty and Hunger," 16–17; Holman, *God Knows*, 47–70. According to Holman, the most innovative of John's predecessors in the empire were Basil of Caesarea, Gregory of Nyssa, and Gregory of Nazianzus, also known as the three Cappadocian Fathers. See also Rhee, *Loving the Poor*, 112–31, 181–82.

of material goods and resources, physical or emotional care, spiritual guidance, or other general forms of help for those in need.[27] Before the Council of Nicea (325 CE), however, almsgiving was mostly a spiritual practice that was demonstrated in only a few ways.

The early patristic understanding of almsgiving was influenced heavily by the Hebrew, Septuagintal, and New Testament traditions mentioned above. In nearly every case, early Christian almsgiving was practiced as a unilateral gift to clergy, the poor, or persons facing some sort of distress.[28] Such gifts were a spiritual demonstration by the almsgiver of a Christian dualism in which good triumphed over evil and the eternal surpassed the temporal. This one-way approach to charity was highly advantageous to the giver, but often rendered the condition of the receiver secondary.

The early Christian document known as *The Didache* describes this dualistic view as "two ways, one of life and one of death, and there is a great difference between these two ways."[29] The way of death includes vices such as lust, immorality, idolatry, pride, jealousy, and greed.[30] The way of life, on the other hand, is exhibited by love for God and neighbor, blessing others, turning the other cheek, humility, and giving generously to "everyone who asks you."[31] Clement of Rome wrote about this dualism from an eschatological point of view. According to 2 Clement, the eschatological age will bring about a separation of this world from the next which will also include the dissolution of earthly wealth, adultery, corruption, greed, and deceit. As a result, the one who would follow Christ must be willing to both renounce and hate the things of this world.[32]

This dualism led to the patristic view of almsgiving as a means by which one could earn forgiveness of sins and salvation in the life to come.

27. *De Eleem.* (PG 51:260–72; trans., Christo, *ORA*, 131–46); McGuckin, *Patristic Theology*, 8; Heim, "Almsgiving," 266; Augustine, *Ench.* 19.72–73 (CCSL 46:49–114; trans., Harbert, *Enhiridion*, 315–17). For a more detailed look at almsgiving from the Latin perspective, including that of Augustine, see Ramsey, "Almsgiving in the Latin Church," 226–59.

28. Heim, "Almsgiving," 266.

29. *Didache* 1.1 (*AF*, 344–45). See also Rhee, *Loving the Poor*, 172. Rhee describes this dualism as antithesis, with Christian identity becoming solidified by embracing of virtues and abhorrence of vices. She also cites the *Epistle of Barnabas* and the *Shepherd of Hermas* as presenting a dichotomous view like that of the Didache. See *Epist. Barn.* 19-20 (*AF*, 434–39); *Shep. Herm.*, Mand. 6 (*AF*, 520–25).

30. *Didache* 5.1 (*AF*, 352–53).

31. Ibid., 1.1–6, 3.7–10 (344–49).

32. Clement of Rome, *Ep. II ad Cor.* 6.1–6 (*AF*, 144–45).

The Didache ascribes both innocence and "a ransom for your sins" to alms-giving.[33] The second and third century apologist Clement of Alexandria declared, "'Give to everyone that asks you;' for such generosity is truly of God. . . . You give the perishing things of the world and receive in exchange for them an eternal abode in heaven."[34] So also his contemporary Tertullian spoke of charity and eternal life in a discourse concerning the rich young man who refused to obey Jesus' command to avail himself of his wealth: "This vainglorious observer of the commandments was therefore convicted of holding money in much higher estimation (than charity). . . . [Jesus] declared that the name of God and of the Good belonged to one and the same being, at whose disposal were also the everlasting life and the treasure in heaven."[35]

Cyprian, the well-known bishop of Carthage in the third century, articulated a soteriological view of almsgiving that was echoed by many other patristic leaders including John Chrysostom:

> Be earnest in righteous works, whereby sins may be purged; frequently apply yourself to almsgiving, whereby souls are freed from death. What the adversary took from you, let Christ receive; nor ought your estate now either to be held or loved, by which you have been both deceived and conquered. Wealth must be avoided as an enemy; must be fled from as a robber; must be dreaded by its possessors as a sword and as poison. To this end only so much as remains should be of service, that by it the crime and the fault may be redeemed. Let good works be done without delay, and largely; let all your estate be laid out for the healing of your wound; let us lend of our wealth and our means to the Lord, who shall judge concerning us.[36]

This soteriological view of almsgiving is also known as redemptive almsgiving and will be discussed in more detail in chapter 7.

---

33. *Didache* 1.5–6, 4.5–8 (*AF*, 346–47, 350–51). It is worth noting that former reference also mentions a maxim for using discretion in choosing a worthy recipient for alms: "But it has also been said concerning this: 'Let your gift sweat in your hands until you know to whom to give it.'"

34. Clement of Alexandria, *Quis Dives Salv.* 31–32 (PG 9:637–38; text and trans., Butterworth, LCL 92:336–39).

35. Tertullian, *Adversus Marcionem* 4.36 (PL 2:449–51; ANF 3:589–92). For the story of the rich young man and Jesus, cf. Matt 19:16–30; Mark 10:17–31; Luke 18:18–30.

36. Cyprian, *De Lapsis* 35 (PL 4:492–93; ANF 5:733)

Secular Roots of Almsgiving

In Graeco-Roman culture, almsgiving was a known but much less prevalent idea. Neither Greek nor Roman traditions contained a common terminology that would indicate an established concept of almsgiving.[37] In his letter to one Arsacius around 360 CE, the emperor Julian argued that care for the poor was nearly absent with the exception of Jews and Christians who had taken responsibility to care for the poor among the pagans as well as their own.[38] This seems to indicate that, with the exception of individual relationships, the poor were not of much interest to the general public other than for the purpose of self-promotion.[39] The word ἐλεημοσύνη was all but absent in secular literature. The word was most often associated with the provision of grain, money, or other resources to a variety of recipients. Those receiving dispensation were not necessarily poor or victims of distress. On the contrary, almsgiving was often given from one to another along the same social plane. In many cases, alms were given to members of one's own family, circle of friends, or known members of their community.[40]

Antioch and Constantinople, the central cities of John Chrysostom's ministry, were heavily influenced by the pluralist and humanist culture of the Graeco-Roman world. John was, therefore, engaged in a polemic against the misuse of alms for the benefit of the givers and those closest to them. Because of these abuses, he was also tasked with defending the use of alms by the clergy. He sought to reclaim the biblical, moral, and practical uses of almsgiving among the Christian communities in which he taught and beyond. In Antioch, almsgiving became a familiar way to identify the church and its missionary activity.

37. Parkin, "'You Do Him no Service,'" 61.

38. Nagle and Burstein, *The Ancient World*, 314–15. According to Julian, "For it is disgraceful when no Jew is a beggar and the impious Galileans support our poor in addition to their own."

39. Garrison, *Redemptive Almsgiving*, 39–41. Garrison does argue, however, that the philosophical traditions of both Plato and Aristotle encouraged the wealthy to give to the poor for the purpose of developing virtue and character. In each successive case that Garrison mentions, the primary motivation for the giving of alms was self-interest.

40. Kim, *Stewardship and Almsgiving*, 280–81.

DEALING WITH THE SOCIAL GOSPEL
AND LIBERATION THEOLOGY

John Chrysostom's emphasis on almsgiving and its social implications are easily confused with two major Christian movements toward social justice during the twentieth century: the Social Gospel Movement and Liberation Theology.[41] Each of these movements developed from political and social trends dictated by the immediate context of the poor in the Americas. John's preaching and teaching concerning the poor began with the exposition of Scripture which was applied to healthy practices of individual and corporate giving as part of Christian mission. As a result, the political and social aspects of charity throughout the empire were redefined according to a biblical paradigm in Antioch. This enabled John to increase the social aspect of almsgiving already progressing as a result of the spread of Christianity throughout the Roman world.[42]

The Social Gospel Movement began with an ecclesiastical push for fair treatment, better wages, and improved working conditions for industrial employees.[43] Eventually, the movement would emphasize fair labor, social order, and the immanence of the kingdom of God as its primary facets.[44] The movement was also characterized by social progressivism, which paralleled the spirit of human and technological optimism. This progressivism culminated in a post-millennial eschatology that moved steadily away from a focus on spiritual transformation and added the idea that human progress would result in the kingdom of God on earth.[45] John Chrysostom did not preach or write with the same degree of millennial fervor. On the contrary, one will see that John's writing was focused on the dichotomy of this life and the afterlife, found most clearly in his homilies on the Gospels, in par-

---

41. Holman, *God Knows*, 4. Holman refers to John's teaching on the poor as a type of "social gospel," even though references to him were conspicuously absent as a part of the Social Gospel movement and its recorded influences. See also Rhee, *Loving the Poor*, 210–19. In her conclusion, Rhee discusses the movement known as the "Prosperity Gospel," which has ties to both the Social Gospel movement and Liberation Theology.

42. Brown, *Poverty and Leadership*, 74, 111–12.

43. Noll, *A History*, 305; Atherton, *Christian Social Ethics*, 157–58; Gladden, *Working People and their Employers*, 43.

44. Noll, *A History*, 306.

45. Rauschenbusch, *Prayers for the Social Awakening*, 121–22; Rauschenbusch, *Christianity and the Social Crisis*, 397; Mathews, *The Gospel and the Modern Man*, 36–54; for a more contemporary interpretation see Bowman, "Sin, Spirituality, and Primitivism," 95–126.

ticular those concerning the Parable of the Rich Man and Lazarus. John's concern for the poor had little to do with wages but rather the churches' ability to be an impetus for the πένητες to find work and more comprehensive care for the πτωχοί.[46] If the physical circumstances of the poor could be improved, the message of the gospel would be displayed with a greater degree of effectiveness. The poor were a direct representation of Christ on earth and were to be treated as such by Christians.

For Walter Rauschenbusch, the teachings and life of Christ were a means of living out the kingdom of God on earth through a just Christian society.[47] He argued the teachings of Jesus were primarily of moral character and concerned with humanity above any other doctrine.

For this reason, socialists, anarchists, fundamentalists, and others found "shelter in his great shadow."[48] In *Christianizing the Social Order*, he wrote,

> The purpose of all that Jesus said and did and hoped to do was always the social redemption of the entire life of the human race on earth. If we regard him in any sense as our leader and master, we cannot treat as secondary what to him was the essence of his mission. If we regard him as the Son of God, the revelation of the very mind and will and nature of the Eternal, the obligation to complete what he began comes upon us with an absolute claim to obedience.[49]

Another important figure in the Social Gospel Movement, Shailer Mathews, echoed the idea of the earthly kingdom purpose of Christ by advocating Christian living by the "Spirit of Christ." Mathews taught that the kingdom of God was attainable on earth through the moral efforts of man leading to an idealistic social order. For Mathews, Christianity was about following "the way of Christ" rather than subscribing to any particular Christian doctrine.[50]

46. See note 14 in this chapter.

47. Dorrien, *Soul in Society*, 27.

48. Rauschenbusch, *Christianity and the Social Crisis*, 47–51. Rauschenbusch made use of Marxist terminology, such as "Proletariat" and "Bourgeois," which resulted in a Marxist influence in some parts of the North American church.

49. Rauschenbusch, *Christianizing the Social Order*, 67.

50. Mathews, *The Social Teaching of Jesus*, 206–7; Dorrien, *Soul and Society*, 31, 35, 38.

John emphasized the importance of almsgiving and social improvement as a matter of salvation rather than morality. Almsgiving was itself a matter of virtue, but only in so far as it represented obedience to the divine mandate.[51] In other words, John considered almsgiving to be a Christian doctrine. To couch this idea in the terms of "Euthyphro's dilemma," God did not demand almsgiving because it was morally good in and of itself. On the contrary, almsgiving was morally good, or virtuous, precisely because God demanded it. Almsgiving was not a means to achieving the kingdom of God, but rather it was a clear responsibility for every believer who truly was a part of God's kingdom on earth.[52] Therefore, the commitment to ministry that provides social improvement must not preclude a softening of the gospel message. On the contrary, as Rhee aptly points out, such isolationist thinking can result in an "unwarranted and unfortunate wedge between these 'spiritual' and 'social'/'physical' ministries of churches . . . as though the churches have to choose either one or the other as their 'primary' mission, or as though the churches should devote their ministries entirely to 'spiritual life' rather than to paying attention to material needs."[53]

Those who might classify John as promoting a form of Liberation Theology do so erroneously for a number of reasons. First, John neither preached nor taught a theology of justice for the poor among the poor. The vast majority of those who made up John's audience in Antioch came from the middle and upper classes, and John's goal was to bring a new awareness concerning the needs of the poor to those who had opportunity to affect changes. Liberation Theology, on the other hand, is most popular among the rural poor in Latin America and its message is focused on the primacy of the poor. According to Gustavo Gutierrez, the most recognizable liberation theologian in Latin America, "the poor have a privileged place in the kingdom and should in the church."[54] The poor and oppressed are not a group neglected by God. They are "a gathered people animated by the power of the Spirit." By identifying himself with the poor, the Lord Jesus worked behind them, which means that the casting out of the poor is a denial of the kingdom.[55]

---

51. *In Matt. hom.* 47.3 (PG 58:485; NPNF 1.10:406).

52. *De Eleem.* 3 (PG 51:265–66; trans., Christo, *ORA*, 139).

53. Rhee, *Loving the Poor*, 204–5.

54. Gutierrez, *The Truth Shall Make You Free*, 157–60.

55. Ibid.

Second, John did not teach that the poor automatically have the eschatological advantage in terms of salvation over the wealthy which is a key tenet of Liberation Theology.[56] In his most famous sermons concerning the plight of the poor, those on the Parable of the Rich Man and Lazarus, John argued that even Lazarus was guilty of sin in his lifetime. He also asserted that the rich man did not have a greater quantity of evil than any other person. According to Cardman, "By showing that even Lazarus is not without some sin and the rich man not without some modicum of good, he can blunt the force of arguments about unjust suffering or undeserved prosperity in this world."[57]

Gutierrez also views social justice primarily in eschatological terms, with statements such as, "The elimination of misery and exploitation is a sign of the coming of the kingdom."[58] This view espouses a similar idea to that of the Social Gospel—the ability to usher in the kingdom of God with human moral efforts that are directed from the fortunate to the less-fortunate. For Gutierrez, "the apocalypse is not something that may happen in the remote future. It is the experience of the present, the future that has already begun."[59] John, on the other hand, taught that every believer, no matter his or her social status, was to participate in almsgiving in order to experience the blessings promised in the life to come. The eschatological age would come at the beckon of Christ himself, and the Christian doctrine of almsgiving would be a major factor in determining how one would experience the rewards or punishments of that age.

Third, John exhorted the wealthy and the poor to participate in a lifestyle of generous giving as obedience to God's command. Almsgiving was intended to be a shared practice, which meant the wealthy and the poor were not enemies. Liberation Theology lends itself to an adversarial relationship with regard to social status. Gutierrez describes the wealthy as "vultures" opposed to God, and argues they flourish as a result of the absence of God within government and the churches.[60] Such teaching has traditionally viewed the missionary ideal of the gospel as "oppressive."[61] John facilitated a healthy relationship between the rich and the poor within

56. Brown, *Gustavo Gutierrez*, 125; Nolan, "Theology in a Prophetic Mode," 437.

57. Ibid.

58. Gutierrez, *Essential Writings*, 199.

59. Brown, *Gustavo Gutierrez*, 125.

60. Nolan, "Theology in a Prophetic Mode," 437.

61. Escobar, *Changing Tides*, 165.

the churches while also placing responsibility on both groups to practice right Christian living for the benefit of others.[62]

SUMMARY

The biblical practice of almsgiving, as modeled by John Chrysostom and the ministry of his churches in Antioch, has significant implications for the Christian mission in the developed world of the twenty-first century. A renewed emphasis in social justice and ministry to the poor has all but ignored important aspects of this practice as it has been modeled throughout Christian history. Almsgiving is a matter of obedience to divine command as given in the Torah, reaffirmed by Jesus, and continued by the writers of the New Testament. Almsgiving, as an act of virtue, is more than moral action. Almsgiving is an illustration of God's mercy toward humankind that, when practiced correctly, is a highly effective form of missional living,[63] and an essential element of the presentation of the good news of Jesus Christ in a world full of suffering.

John faced the challenge of preaching and practicing almsgiving within a context that was exceedingly diverse. Antioch, like other major cities in the empire, had developed into a multi-cultural center where multiple faiths, traditions, and demographics competed for consideration. The first area of consideration for missiological analysis is the setting of John's ministry. Within the later Roman Empire and the cities of Antioch and Constantinople, respectively, a wide variety of opinions existed concerning wealth, poverty, and almsgiving. Many of these opinions would develop into definitions of poverty, explanations of the causes of poverty, and presuppositions with which many people viewed the poor.

---

62. On the topic of liberation theology and the use of John Chrysostom see the dissertation, Mulheron, "La opción por los pobres . . . San Juan Crisóstomo."

63. Guder, et. al., *Missional Church*, 4, 11–12. These essays define missional living as "The essential nature and vocation of the church as God's called and sent people." This term has been used frequently among missiologists and church leaders since these essays were published. Citing Lesslie Newbigin and John 20:21, the authors describe the impetus for the term missional: "We have learned to speak of God as a 'missionary God.' Thus, we have learned to understand the church as a 'sent people.'" See also Stetzer and Putman, *Breaking the Missional Code*, 3. Missional living is "*doing* missions everywhere . . . Scripture teaches that the church is God's missionary in the world. If we are going to join God in his mission, we have to recognize that we are missionaries . . . wherever he places us—just like the first disciples."

3

A Pastor of the Later Roman Empire

The poor are not primarily a class; the poor are people.

—RUBY BARCELONA[1]

Antioch, the city in which John Chrysostom spent the majority of his life and ministry, was one of the most important urban centers in the Roman world as the fourth century began. During the century, the empire underwent religious and political changes that left an indelible mark on Western world history. The most significant changes took place during and after the reign of Constantine I (306–337 CE),[2] which was accompanied by the advent of an increasingly Christianized empire. These developments set the fourth century apart from the previous three. The issues of wealth and poverty were multifaceted during the century, and influenced heavily by voluntary poverty through asceticism and a rising influence of the poor on society as a whole. It will be demonstrated that the greatest impact on the identity of the poor in the fourth century came as a result of the Christian

1. Barcelona, "The Face of the Poor," 3.

2. Constantine I, who came to be known as Constantine the Great, ruled as co-Emperor from July, 306, until October, 312. He became sole-Emperor in the West after defeating Maxentius of Rome at the Battle of the Milvian Bridge on October 28, 312. He became sole-Emperor of the entire Roman Empire after deposing Licinius at Chrysopolis on September 18, 324. See Eadie, "Constantine," 1966–67; Barnes, *Constantine and Eusebius*, 277–78; Brown, *The World of Late Antiquity*, 204–7. For an alternative contemporary view of the often vilified Constantine and his role in the formation of the Imperial church, see Leithart, *Defending Constantine*, 15–342.

mission and its rapid expansion throughout the empire. Not every aspect of the Constantinian legacy was positive, but the increasing dissemination of the gospel message brought a hope to the poor that, as a group, they had never experienced in the Greek and Roman eras. The developing emphasis on the practice of almsgiving in an increasingly Christianized empire led to new forms of charity toward the poor among Christians, Jews, and pagans. The city of Antioch, as it grew in its worldwide influence, followed the traditional Roman patterns concerning poverty and provided an ideal setting for John Chrysostom's innovative teaching and leadership regarding almsgiving. Almsgiving became an essential part of the Christian mission of the churches in Antioch as well as a part of the missional lifestyles of some individual believers. As noted in chapter 1, the practice of almsgiving in fourth century Antioch would remain a standard in Christian churches for centuries.

IMPERIAL ROME IN THE FOURTH CENTURY

The political climate of the Roman Empire was forever altered by the expansion of Christianity during the fourth century CE. The growing influence of Constantine and his leadership caused the empire and its government to come under Christian rule. According to Sozomen, a church historian of the fifth century CE, Constantine was "always intent on the advancement of religion, [and] erected the most beautiful temples to God in every place, particularly in the metropolises."[3]

A decade before, Christians had endured one of the most terrible persecutions the church had ever known at the hands of Diocletian. By the end of the third century, the Christian faith had come into view as a formidable movement in the Empire. According to Rhee, churches of the second and third centuries were characterized by "Numerical growth, increasing penetration into the upper echelon of Roman society, and the emergence of a distinct material culture and collective property by Christians."[4] Many churches had become professionalized to the extent that a "fixed salary" was arranged for some members of the clergy.[5]

---

3. Sozomen, *Hist. Eccl.* 2.3 (PG 67:936; NPNF 2.02:368). Note to readers: As NPNF is used as the English translation of note throughout this book I have likely rendered it as a modernized version.

4. Rhee, *Loving the Poor*, 47–48.

5. Ibid., 147, 150; Hillner, "Clerics, Property and Patronage," 59–68.

Following the Edict of Milan in 312, Christianity became woven into the fabric of Roman society. Constantine's sons, Constantine II, Constantius II, and Constans, each inherited the imperial throne for a time and were major proponents of the church. They took extreme measures to squelch the influence of paganism throughout the empire and put more ecclesiastical authority into the hands of the Emperor.[6] Roman society and culture was saturated with Christian literature and ideas, but the most influential bearers of the gospel remained the local churches and their clergy.[7] With a few exceptions, which will be discussed in chapter 8, the bishop remained a highly respected figure in Roman society and maintained important social, political, and economic roles.

When the Emperor Julian, also known as "the Apostate," came to power in 361, a renewed interest in paganism developed and Christianity was denigrated in various power circles.[8] Julian's attempts to reform and subvert Christianity, other organized religion, and pagan philosophy to his political preferences brought about major effects to the Roman religious landscape throughout his reign (361–363), and the reigns of Valentinian I and Valens (364–378). Valens was responsible for a renewed effort of persecution against the Christians in Antioch, particularly the Nicene Christians.[9] It was not until the reign of Theodosius I (379–395), who came to power very near the restoration of John Chrysostom to the pastorate in Antioch, that those who adhered to the older pagan rituals faced legal consequences.[10] John's ministry, therefore, took place near the end of a tumultuous century for the Christian faith in which it had endured persecution and won the day. Nevertheless, his ministry took place before the times when Christianity was mandated throughout the empire and its constituencies. Christianization still followed traditional patterns of movement based on the missionary activity of churches and individual believers. As Wilken has noted, it was not yet possible to "force people to accept the Christian truth; one had to convince them of it."[11]

6. Neusner, *Judaism and Christianity*, 15.

7. Brown, *Poverty and Leadership*, 1.

8. Sozomen, *Hist. Eccl.* 5.8 (PG 67:1236; NPNF 2.02:474). Sozomen mentioned the plundering of the churches in the Eastern Empire, and in Antioch specifically, under the command of Julian. A number of costly items were taken from the churches in Antioch and the Christians grieved their losses.

9. Wilken, *The Christians*, 32–33.

10. Neusner, *Judaism and Christianity*, 16.

11. Wilken, *The Christians*, 17. See also Maxwell, *Christianization and Communication*, 10. Maxwell argues, during the reign of Theodosius and immediately after,

When John resumed his duties as lector in Antioch in 377, there were an estimated five or six million Christians in the Roman Empire, representing nearly a tenth of the population.[12] In the two decades that followed, however, the Christian population grew to represent nearly half of the assimilated empire in both the East and West.[13] During this time of rapid expansion, the practice of Christian faith existed in a number of semi-private forms including eremitic and cenobitic monasticism, as well as more public forms represented by the churches. Public Christianity included sectarian groups such as the Arians, Marcionites, and Montanists, each fighting for standing against the majority view dominated by the Alexandrian Christians.[14] As the Christian population grew numerically, its influence grew as well. The church was identified with wealth as a result of its large cathedrals and the prestige of the bishop within the power structures of the community.[15] Libanius mentioned noticeable decline in Hellenistic philosophy and practice throughout the Eastern Empire and specifically in Antioch during the century.[16] In his early ministry, however, John preached frequently against the influence and effects of paganism in Antioch and throughout the empire. As Krupp stated, "John could not bring himself to believe that he was living in a Christian era and that the pagans would not rule again."[17] The identity of the poor, for example, was influenced significantly by paganism.

Christianity expanded through methods that were "gradual, interactive, and communicative," as opposed to force applied by the imposition of powerful leaders.

12. Hopkins, "Early Christian Number," 191–92; Harnack, *The Expansion of Christianity*, 321, 454; Finn, *Almsgiving*, 6.

13. MacMullen, *Christianity and Paganism*, 151; MacMullen, *The Second Church*; Frend, *The Rise of Christianity*, 749–50. Frend argues that both the influence of John in Constantinople, as brief as his position there might have been, was highly influential during the "Rise of Christianity." John's death was perhaps the most influential aspect of his archbishopric.

14. It is interesting to note here that giving alms to the poor became a point of distinction between mainline and sectarian groups associated with the Christian movement. Some considered caring for the poor to be a mark of "orthodoxy." Likewise, lack of commitment to meeting the needs of the poor became a mark of heresy. See Rhee, *Loving the Poor*, 173.

15. Mayer and Allen, *John Chrysostom*, 3–4; Finn, *Almsgiving*, 14–16; Brown, *Poverty and Leadership*, 1.

16. Libanius, *Orat.* 64. Isabella Sandwell has argued the declines pointed out by Libanius and others were more likely in public worship as opposed to private religious activities. See Sandwell, *Religious Identity in Late Antiquity*.

17. Krupp, *Shepherding the Flock*, 7. See also Swain, "Sophists and Emperors,"

IDENTITY OF THE POOR IN THE ROMAN EMPIRE

Salvian, a fifth-century priest in both Lyons and Marseilles, asserted just after John Chrysostom's death: "There is no single form of poverty shared by all those who number among the poor."[18] The Greek categories for the poor, which had various definitions depending on context, had become increasingly vague when applied to the Roman situation.[19] The rising popularity of voluntary poverty, which included a number of ascetics, virgins, and widows, confused the situation even further. These individuals could be classified as a part of the general categories of Greco-Roman poverty and yet they also represented something wholly different. Despite such ambiguity, categorization and segregation of classes was still a priority in the empire. As Rhee remarks, "Indeed, Roman society was obsessed with maintaining social distinctions and hierarchy."[20]

The Greeks had separated the poor into two major categories which they utilized to classify poverty in the Roman Empire. The first, the πένητες (*penētes*), worked primarily in agrarian settings during seasons when work opportunities were abundant.[21] Those who belonged to this category lived according to a much lower standard of living, but only experienced extreme poverty in short-term, temporary quantities. Perhaps greatest challenge for the πένητες was advancement. No matter how hard they worked, status was ascribed and not achieved in Greco-Roman culture. For this reason, many of the πένητες relied on the charity of others.[22] The second category, the πτωχοί (*ptōchoi*), were those forced to beg for the most basic necessities on a regular basis. When referring to the poor, the authors of the New Testament most often spoke of the πτωχοί.[23] The difference between the two categories was not only employment, but truly life and death.

355–400. Swain argues Libanius' use of Greek religion and rhetoric signaled a lack of homogenization as a result of the Christian mission immediately after the time of Constantine. Libanius' pagan practices surely influenced the pessimism of John regarding the end of paganism, since Libanius was his teacher.

18. Salvian, *Ad Eccl.* 4.21 (CSEL 8:307; trans., O'Sullivan, *Writings of Salvian*, 324).

19. Osborne, "Roman Poverty in Context," 15.

20. Rhee, *Loving the Poor*, 6.

21. Finn, *Almsgiving*, 22.

22. Hamel, *Poverty and Charity in Roman Palestine*, 168; Rhee, *Loving the Poor*, 10.

23. Hamel, *Poverty and Charity in Roman Palestine*, 168–73; Rhee, *Loving the Poor*, 11; Sider, *Rich Christians*, 41. Sider also discusses the Hebrew terms for the poor which were the basis for the Judeo-Christian usage of the Greek terminology for the poor. See also Parkin, "Poverty in the Early Roman Empire"; Knight, "Luke 16:19–31," 279.

As these categories developed in the later Roman Empire, new forms emerged with Latin appellations. Those of the first category, the *paupertas*, were more often victims of circumstantial poverty. These individuals were afforded various opportunities to improve their conditions. The second, the *egestas*, were poor as a result of resource shortages which, in some cases, perpetuated for long periods of time. The third, the *mendicitas*, were severe cases of poverty that often forced the person to resort to begging. The first two categories usually applied to citizens whose status gave them the potential for progress. While most of these individuals would never experience true wealth, they often experienced seasons where plenty of resources were available to them. The *mendicitas*, on the other hand, were mostly unsupported minor citizens, non-citizens, and slaves. In nearly every case, the *mendicitas* had irreparable status and would be confined to poverty for most if not all of their lives.[24]

Robin Osborne has described these ranges of poverty using contemporary categories. The first category, "conjunctural poverty," describes those who have fallen into poverty for a myriad of reasons but could have the opportunity to change their circumstances at some point in the future. The second category, "structural poverty," refers to those who are "trapped by the structure of economic system" and will most likely live in permanent poverty as long as the system remains unchanged.[25] In terms of the Greek categories listed above, the πένητες were more often characterized by conjunctural poverty while the πτωχοί often fell victim to structural poverty.[26] In nearly all major cities, the poor and under-resourced of every kind gathered at the most public gates daily in hopes of receiving work or charity.[27] The leaders of the Christian mission, the ascetics and the clergy, sought to improve each form of poverty in the empire.

Lazarus is described as a πτωχός in Luke 16:19–31. According to Knight, Luke intended for the reader to understand that Lazarus was dependent on others and that his state of poverty was severe. For these reasons, the Lazarus in Jesus' parable was a major part of John's teaching on the state of poverty in the empire and the importance of almsgiving.

24. Finn, *Almsgiving*, 19.
25. Osborne, "Roman Poverty in Context," 1.
26. Finn, *Almsgiving*, 22; Rhee, *Loving the Poor*, 10–11.
27. Brown, *Poverty and Leadership*, 12.

Voluntary Poverty

Voluntary poverty, as it applied to monasticism, was based on the Greek idea of ἀποτάσσω (*apotassō*), a verb used to describe "renunciation of the world."[28] These acts of denial were most often carried out by the rejection of property ownership and possession of any kind. As monasticism transitioned from early Egyptian Christian forms into the more centralized parts of the Roman Empire, two major forms of asceticism developed. Anchoritic, or hermitic, ascetics lived in solitude both inside and outside of cities. Cenobitic, or communal, ascetics lived together in settings that were usually well outside of the urban center.[29] Both ascetic forms were classified as states of poverty, and yet in most cases being a member of a monastic society or way of life afforded the individual protection from destitution. Even though the ascetic owned no property or possessions of his or her own, the sharing of common necessities that were the property of the monastic community helped to meet the needs of the ascetics and those to whom they gave alms of various kinds.[30]

In many ways, Byzantine forms of monasticism were derivative of Stoic philosophy, which sought to disassociate with various forms of attachment, including that which resulted from all types of ownership.[31] The Eastern Empire saw a renewed interest in Greek philosophy, literature and culture, which has been described as "the Second Sophistic," seen most in the areas of religion, politics, and entertainment.[32] Libanius, John Chrysostom's alleged instructor in rhetoric at Antioch, was one of the most influ-

28. Bagnall, "Monks and Property," 13.

29. At times, both anchoritic and cenobitic ascetics vacillated between the desert and certain pockets of the urban centers. As a result, the relationship between those of the monastic persuasion and church leadership was strained by competiveness. For the most part, however, the relationship between ascetics and the church was "generally harmonious" in Syria. See Sterk, *Renouncing the World*, 23; Harmless, *Desert Christians*, 401–2; Brakke, "Care for the Poor . . . Evagrius Ponticus," 76; Mayer, "Monasticism at Antioch and Constantinople," 275–88. See also Brown, *Power and Persuasion*, 124–25. Brown argues that some monastic groups had resorted to violence in order to accomplish their purposes, prompting some bishops to align with government officials in keeping monks outside of the city. These types of ascetics appear to be the minority.

30. Brakke, "Care for the Poor . . . Evagrius Ponticus," 76; Mayer, "Poverty and Generosity," 154.

31. Caner, "Wealth, Stewardship, and Charitable 'Blessings,'" 221–22; Brown, *Power and Persuasion*, 123.

32. Maxwell, *Christianization and Communication*, 12.

ential voices of this movement. According to Sozomen, John was highly skilled in the content and presentation of Second Sophistic philosophy and might have inherited Libanius' position as a philosopher had he not chosen to enter the ministry instead.[33] John's experiences as an ascetic and philosopher did not fulfill the burden of his adolescence to follow the call of God.

Voluntary poverty evoked different reactions from one level of society to the next. Those who made up the Roman aristocracy frowned on such a lifestyle, while the majority of the common people viewed this self-sufficient lifestyle as pious and admirable.[34] Some ascetics reduced their lives to the same means as the πτωχοί. Others, including many of the once wealthy widows who were a part of John's churches in Antioch and Constantinople, committed themselves to an impoverished life of prayer, fasting, and almsgiving which drained their wealth significantly.[35] There were also a number of women in Antioch who had chosen an ascetic form of virginity which also resulted in a lifestyle of poverty.[36]

John often used those who had chosen the path of voluntary poverty to counter the glorification of luxurious living. The ascetic lifestyle, as he had experienced it, was an eschatological contrast to an earthly life of vanity and luxury. Those who had chosen asceticism had also chosen to embrace the hardships of poverty by personal identification, which represented an eternal investment that resembled the life to come.[37] John classified the lifestyles of both the cenobitic monks who lived in the deserts and mountains and the anchoritic monks who lived in cells as "virtuous." The ascetics, both male and female, were living examples of the selfless act of giving away, which led to new forms of giving to others.[38] He also praised the lifestyle

33. Sozomen, *Hist. Eccl.* 8.2 (PG 67:1513; NPNF 2.02:572). Concerning Libanius, Sozomen wrote: "When this sophist was on his deathbed he was asked by his friends who should take his place. 'It would have been John,' replied he, 'had not the Christians taken him from us.'" See also Kelly, *Golden Mouth*, 8; Ameringer, *Second Sophistic*, 20–28.

34. Lunn-Rockliffe, "A Pragmatic Approach . . . Ambrosiaster's *Quaestio* 124," 116; Mayer, "Poverty and Generosity," 154; Rhee, *Loving the Poor*, 189.

35. Mayer, "Poverty and Generosity," 148.

36. For more on ascetic virgins, see Dunn, *The Emergence of Monasticism*, 42–58. The Cappadocians had promoted a style of monastic virginity through which women altered their appearances to become "like men". This type of language is contrary to the teaching of John Chrysostom, who confronted those participating in roles that were not gender appropriate. See also Mayer, "John Chrysostom: Extraordinary Preacher, Ordinary Audience," 103–36.

37. *In Matt. hom.* 15.9, (PG 57:234–35; NPNF 1.10:142–43).

38. *In Eph. hom.* 13.3 (PG 62:97–98; NPNF 1.13:166).

of a number of young girls who had chosen to forsake the comfort of their inheritance in order to live a life of service. These young women had chosen the way of poverty as they ministered to the poor and those in the church through cooking, caring for the sick, and living like the servants they once called their own.[39]

John taught the commitment to voluntary poverty and asceticism was one part of God's larger evangelistic concern for the world. Monasticism was only successful from a biblical standpoint so long as it accompanied the mission of the church to bring the gospel to those who had not yet received it. He rejected any form of asceticism that was found to be consistently at odds with the churches. According to Sterk, John saw the purpose of monastic life "only with reference to the life and mission of the church as a whole. It may be precisely because of the failure of monks to serve the broader Christian community that John became slightly disillusioned or at least sobered with respect to the monastic vocation."[40]

Temporary Poverty

Conjunctural poverty, which was often only temporary, usually affected the able-bodied most of all. In some cases, the temporary poor were those who arrived in the major urban areas of the Roman Empire only to find them overcrowded and resources exhausted. On the one hand, the marketplaces were the only source of sustenance for many of these individuals. On the other hand, those locations offered goods and services based on status, which most migrants did not have. The poor and their needs did not seem to be of much consequence to those citizens with means in the urban centers. As Osborne has noted, "the poor were more often a topic for thinking with than a practical problem to be solved . . . there was only a discourse of wealth, not a discourse of poverty."[41]

As a result, the non-elite usually found themselves powerless to change their circumstances in the political arena. Those who resided in urban areas for long periods of time often experienced temporary poverty as a result of

39. Ibid., 13.3–4 (62:97–99; 1.13:166–67). See also Holman, *God Knows*, 64.

40. Sterk, *Renouncing the World*, 147. John dealt with the issues of priesthood and asceticism thoroughly in *De Sac*. See also Davis, "Chrysostom on Ministry, Discernment, and Call," 408–13.

41. Osborne, "Roman Poverty in Context," 5–7, 15. See also Morley, "The Poor in the City of Rome," 33–35.

legislative measures that levied significant expenses on the working poor, including labor taxes, lease expenses, and various types of debt.[42] Many laborers faced insurmountable debt to the wealthy and powerful who would loan them large sums of money in order to secure votes for themselves or the candidates they supported. These rich benefactors would intentionally loan amounts that could never be repaid so that the fear of punishment would provide leverage for gaining votes in important elections from the emerging poor social class.[43] Such relationships have been called patronage, which may be defined as "a voluntary, continuing exchange relationship between men of unequal power or status."[44] According to Saller, relationships of patronage went up all the way up to the Emperor. The beneficiaries of imperial favor were, as a matter of ethics, expected to offer some form of reciprocity to the Emperor, though perhaps such returns were not quite so voluntary.[45] Whereas most beneficiaries of imperial patronage were among the elite, the lower classes also entered into such relationships with those of more prominent social standing. In many cases, patronage added to the inability of the working poor to accumulate savings or enough resources to own land and home. As a result, according to Finn, many moved to rural areas and joined "bands of robbers who preyed on travelers."[46]

A final cause of temporary poverty was the lack of long-term employment available to those who failed to establish an indelible profession. In such cases, many of the working poor appeared to be lethargic when in reality the work opportunities were sparse. John rebuked his congregations for accusing the unemployed of being lazy or mislabeling them as runaway slaves as an excuse for failing to give alms:

42. Hamel, *Poverty and Charity in Roman Palestine*, 162.

43. Smith, *An Inquiry*, 5.3.62; Morley, "The Poor in the City of Rome," 22. See also *In Col. hom.* 8.1 (PG 62:351; NPNF 1.13:401). John mentioned that those who owed debts in Constantinople were put in the stocks as a form of public humiliation. See also Krupp, *Shepherding the Flock*, 17. Krupp indicates that John often fought against corruption in politics and leadership.

44. Saller, "Status and Patronage," 838; Rhee, *Loving the Poor*, 14. Both Saller and Rhee refer to a Seneca, *De Benef.* 1.4.2 (*Dial. Lib.* 2:1ff; trans., Griffin and Inwood, *On Benefits*, 22). See also Wallace-Hadrill, "Patronage in Roman Society," 63–87; Whittaker, *Frontiers of the Roman Empire*, 258–78.

45. Saller, "Status and Patronage," 842. The patron/beneficiary relationship will be discussed later in this chapter from an ecclesiastical standpoint.

46. Finn, *Almsgiving*, 19. See also Parkin, "'You Do Him No Service,'" 74. Parkin describes mobs of beggars who waylayed carriages of the rich and motivated almsgiving by fear of violence or humiliation.

When therefore you see a poor man, and say "It stops my breath that this fellow, young as he is and healthy, having nothing, would be willing to be fed in idleness; he is surely some slave and runaway, and has deserted his proper master": I bid you to speak these same words to yourself; or rather, permit him freely to speak them to you, and he will say with more justice, "It stops my breath that you, being healthy, are idle, and practice none of the things which God has commanded . . ."[47]

Finn and Mayer argue that it was common throughout the Roman Empire to think of the unemployed, yet able-bodied poor according to these terms. For this reason, many refused to give alms because they seemed to be healthy enough to work.[48] John implored the wealthy in his congregation to empathize with those suffering from temporary poverty and to show mercy to them without distinction.[49]

The Destitution of Beggars

For those who were physically, emotionally, or socially disabled, poverty was vastly structural. If a disabled person had little or no support from a network of family, friends, or organizational aid, he or she was completely dependent upon strangers for support. This was also true for those aliens who had very little chance of gaining citizenship.[50] With the exception of that which was received from almsgiving, these individuals would remain destitute.[51] Many who were sick, elderly, blind, or crippled were distributed along the main roads and near the city gates, baths, cathedrals, and palaces in hopes that the high volume of traffic might yield charity for those with the greatest need. The diet of most beggars was generally different types of bread and sometimes, albeit rarely, small amounts of cooked foods or meat.[52] Many slept on rough ground under shelter when available and usually in public places. John portrayed beggars who lived outside as lacking enough clothing to keep warm and near the point of death.[53] In his homilies

47. *In Matt. hom.* 35.3 (PG 57:409; NPNF 1.10:325).

48. Finn, *Almsgiving*, 21; Mayer, "Poverty and Generosity," 150.

49. Maxwell, *Christianization and Communication*, 72.

50. Finn, *Almsgiving*, 260.

51. Osborne, "Roman Poverty in Context," 5–6; Mayer, "Poverty and Generosity," 150.

52. Finn, *Almsgiving*, 19–21.

53. *In Heb. hom.* 11.3 (PG 63:93–94; NPNF 1.14:606–7).

concerning the Parable of the Rich Man and Lazarus, the location, clothing, and diet of the beggar Lazarus are representative of these same conditions as they applied to the poor throughout the empire.

In order to illustrate the desperation and hopelessness of the lifestyle, John used vivid descriptions of the destitute in Antioch. He described some who begged on the streets accompanied by children. According to John, some parents felt compelled to blind or disfigure their children in order to gain sympathy from those who passed by so that the children might receive food or be clothed during the winter.

> . . . some people have been compelled to blind their children at an early age, in order for them to touch our insensibility. The point is that, since while having sight and walking around naked they were able to win over the merciless neither on the grounds of their youth nor on the grounds of their plight, the parents added to ills of this magnitude another tragedy which is more painful. Their purpose is to put a stop to their hunger, because they think that it's easier to suffer deprivation of that common light, that sunlight which is given to all, than to struggle with continual hunger and undergo the most pitiful death.[54]

He mentioned others who had become deeply impoverished as a result of giving alms themselves. Many of these individuals gave freely but were never able to recoup losses. Others had lost their livelihood through fire or shipwreck. Still others were victims of unjust legal injuries and false accusations from enemies. According to John, "[many] have fallen into the extremes of poverty, sickness, and disease, and have obtained no help from anyone."[55]

Ambrose, writing near the end of the fourth century, revealed another situation that made the begging lifestyle more difficult. A number of counterfeit beggars had infiltrated the city of Milan and, "with lies about their lives," were asking greedily for larger amounts of money. As a result,

---

54. *In 1 Cor. hom.* 21.5 (Field, *Sancti Patris*, 253; trans., Mayer and Allen, *John Chrysostom*, 171; PG 61:176–77; NPNF 1.12:170). In the paragraph that follows this section, John mentioned many who performed painful and sometimes dangerous acts of "street theater" in order to gain alms above those who ask in humility.

55. *De Stat. hom.* 1.10 (PG 49:30; NPNF 1.09:369). See also Brown, *Poverty and Leadership*, 15. Brown argues that poverty in Antioch and other cities of the empire was caused by "ill-health, from the deaths of spouses, parents, and children, from economic and fiscal oppression, and from violence of every kind."

they were taking alms from those who truly needed them.[56] These types of deceptions added to the negative stereotypes of beggars among the general population. Beggars were treated with contempt and even hostility. Their actions were often considered socially immoral or even criminal. Those beggars who offered entertainment or a service as a part of their requests for alms were treated better, primarily because they gave the appearance of exchanging goods for services as opposed to taking something for nothing.[57] Because of these attitudes, John regularly reminded his audiences that the Christian mission to the poor should not include these inherent presuppositions concerning those who receive alms. While alms should be given responsibly, as will be demonstrated in Chapter 8, they should also be given freely. This interpretation of the Christian mission is presented particularly in John's homilies on Matthew 25, the Parable of the Rich Man and Lazarus, and *De Eleem*.

THE GOSPEL BRINGS A FRESH COMPASSION FOR THE DESTITUTE

As has been demonstrated, both the working poor and beggars found themselves without representation throughout the Roman Empire during the larger part of the fourth century CE unless they received charity from others. As the century came to a close, the influence of Christian leaders such as John Chrysostom helped the poor to develop a new identity in urban society. The church, through its continued mission to the poor, brought the multifaceted needs of the impoverished to the front of the public sphere. This included the πένητες, πτωχοί, and also many widows, orphans, travelers, and sick who were taken in by churches.[58] According to Osborne,

> Rome thus gives a case study in the sustenance of a population that is extremely unequally distributed in a world where communications were slow and uncertain. But Rome is also of particular interest because the arrival of Christianity gives an opportunity to

---

56. Ambrose, *De Off. Min*. 2.16.76 (PL 16:123; NPNF 2.10:104). Ambrose went on to say that many of these false beggars had well-crafted stories, disguised the true condition of their clothing, and made up stories about being robbed. The truth, according to Ambrose, was that they were in fact "empty[ing] the purses of the poor."

57. Mayer, "Poverty and Generosity," 150–54.

58. Constantelos, "The Hellenic Background," 198; Sitzler, "Identity," 477.

examine the impact of changing systems of belief upon the classification of and attitudes toward the poor.[59]

Brown produced the incipient argument for the elevation of the poor as a direct result of the Christianization of Rome in the fourth century. He is often credited with creating "the field of study referred to as late antiquity (250–800 CE)."[60] He argues that social attitudes toward the poor underwent both informal and formal changes following the conversion of Constantine I in 312 CE. These changes developed slowly in most places until late in the century as Roman society began to adjust to the new, burgeoning religion of the state. By the time of Theodosius I, Rome had transitioned from a classical, or "civic," model of social structure to a Byzantine model based largely on the Christian faith. As Christianity and the Roman world moved toward a medieval perspective, the division between "rich" and "poor" became more pronounced and the rich were "constantly challenged to bridge that division by 'acts of mercy' to the poor."[61] The result was a fundamental shift in the identity of the poor as individuals, from overlooked to prominence.[62]

Brown argues that Roman Christianization in the fourth century was accompanied by the emergence of the office of bishop as a position of social leadership.[63] What began as discourse on morality between the bishops and the Christian community concerning the plight of the poor resulted in both societal and governmental influence.[64] New levels of representation on behalf of the poor materialized in part because the Emperor began to seek counsel from bishops, as opposed to philosophers, and the former made the cause of the poor a first priority.[65] The church and its leadership, accord-

---

59. Osborne, "Roman Poverty in Context," 2–3.

60. Princeton University, "Peter Brown," lines 1-2.

61. Brown, *Poverty and Leadership*, 111. See also Patlagean, *Pauvreté*.

62. Brown, *Poverty and Leadership*, 74, 111–12; Brown, *Power and Persuasion*, 152–58. Brown believes this transition was highly influenced by a change in language as Near Eastern religious influences began to affect the growing class distinctions. This language reminded the rich that they were to be compassionate toward the suffering of the poor just as God had chosen to become involved with the suffering of mankind through His own experience.

63. Brown, *Poverty and Leadership*, 1.

64. Liebeschuetz, *Barbarians and Bishops*, 251; Maxwell, *Christianity and Communication*, 170.

65. Brown, *Power and Persuasion*, 119, 157; Brown, "The Rise and Function," 353–76. Brown attributes the preaching of the Cappadocians and John as a major part of this transformation. As Archbishop of Constantinople from 398–404 CE, John fulfilled such

ing to the biblical mission set forth by Isaiah 61:1–2, and by Jesus in Luke 4:18–19, helped bring "good news to the poor" throughout the empire.

By the end of the fourth century, the poor gained new access to the power structure of Roman society. This afforded them hope of social improvement that previously seemed impossible. Through the process of emerging thought and political action the poor in the later Roman Empire became a social force and materialized into a distinct social group.[66] The interest in a strict interpretation of Roman law, which favored the elite, had lessened and the advantages of the legal system were accessible to the lower classes of the empire in new ways.[67] This led to new forms of giving, as acts of philanthropy that had previously been directed toward architecture, entertainment, and public programs intended to benefit prominent citizens of the empire, had now shifted toward public, demonstrative almsgiving and charity toward the poor.[68] Brown suggests the effects of the emerging personal philanthropy were not all positive. The increase in the number of those who practiced almsgiving may have resulted in a decrease in the overall philanthropy of the wealthy citizens who were able to provide charity on a larger scale. According to Brown, "local almsgiving, by believers of every class, may have considerably reduced the impact of the occasional large sums provided by the great—by the rich and the emperors."[69] As a result, the practice of personal almsgiving took on certain unhealthy characteristics that had negative effects on the nature of the practice as it related to missions and evangelism in the cities. Almsgiving, among both Christians and pagans, was often used to further the status and reputation of the giver. John Chrysostom, therefore, sought to clarify the biblical and ethical

---

a role for the emperor Arcadius and the empress Eudoxia. See Mayer and Allen, *John Chrysostom*, 8–16; Kelly, *Golden Mouth*, 128–63; Sitzler, "Identity," 477. Sitzler argues the preaching and leadership of John helped to raise the status of the poor in order to make them "acceptable and desirable clients of the poor." Sitzler uses this to support her assertion that John's main goal was to increase the identity of the wealthy, as opposed to the rich, for the good of congregational health in Antioch and, later Constantinople.

66. Osborne, "Roman Poverty in Context," 2–3; Holman, "The Entitled Poor," 479.

67. Honore, "Roman Law AD 200–400," 109–32.

68. Mayer, "Poverty and Generosity," 141; Constantelos, "The Hellenic Background," 208. Constantelos argues that the new patterns of almsgiving and charity developed by Christians during this period lasted until the fourteenth century. While almsgiving declined in terms of volume in the East and West, the nature of its practice closely resembled that which was developed during this period as the poor were given a new identity in the empire.

69. Brown, *Poverty and Leadership*, 78.

nature of almsgiving so that its significance for the Christian mission would not be confused with personal profit and gains.

THE PRACTICE OF ALMSGIVING AMONG CHRISTIANS AND PAGANS

As John rose to prominence in Antioch, the Christian practice of almsgiving was already familiar to the rich and poor, citizens and non-citizens. The giving lifestyle that had characterized many ascetic movements was now a part of the everyday language and activity of the churches. The challenge within the churches, however, was to maintain a focus on almsgiving based on a Christian ethic and motivated by a desire to spread the gospel among people of all demographics. It will be demonstrated that there is seemingly no clear evidence of a structured emphasis on personal almsgiving outside of Christian settings. Nevertheless, the philanthropy of the secular Roman elite, which was promoted by pagan philosophy, impacted the Christian practice of almsgiving in significant ways.

Among Christians

As the fourth century came to a close, the church, and not the monastery, had emerged as the central location for resourcing the poor. By the time of John Chrysostom, most churches throughout the empire had created a space where members of the clergy could interact with the needy who came en masse during times of hardship. This type of atmosphere became a "public stage" for almsgiving from the church toward the poor.[70] The bishop became the key person to connect the poor with different forms of alms to meet their needs. Brown describes the bishops as "guardian[s] of the poor," which elevated the role of the bishop to the positions of societal leader and imperial liaison.[71]

---

70. Finn, *Almsgiving*, 14, 263.

71. Brown, *Power and Persuasion*, 119; Brown, *Poverty and Leadership*, 1. See also Finn, *Almsgiving*, 209–10, 219. Finn argues that John's public reputation for defending the poor and promoting personal almsgiving helped him to garner support from the populace and even the authorities during certain periods of his ministry. He also argues that almsgiving in and of itself could help a candidate to earn appointment to the bishopric. Finn also cautions that Brown's statements about the role of the bishop should not omit the fact that a number of bishops failed in their responsibilities concerning the poor and the practice of almsgiving. For a specific example from the fourth century, see Casey, "The Apocalypse of Paul," 1–32.

The bishop's position as intermediary on behalf of those receiving alms became an ecclesiastical form of the patronage relationship. Under Constantine, imperial patronage towards the churches and their leaders became common practice. Churches were shown imperial favor in return for their budding support of the empire. According to Rhee, "The most well-known support for Christianity is Constantine's extraordinary church buildings throughout the empire, . . . for example . . . the Golden Church in Antioch [and] the Church of the Twelve Apostles in Constantinople."[72] As beneficiaries of patronage, churches received imperial acknowledgement of "ownership of buildings, cemeteries, gardens, and other movable and immovable properties," as well as "financial assistance . . . that would turn into regular support and clerical exemption from all compulsory public services and personal taxes so that they could devote themselves to worship their God on behalf of their communities and the empire."[73] Since the church functioned as "mediator between the rich and the poor of the society," the Emperor continued to provide support which included finances, food, clothing, and other resources.[74] Since churches now served as local distribution points for imperial goods, the practice of almsgiving became more pronounced and professionalized.

Like other forms of philanthropy, the Christian promotion of almsgiving was not free from selfishness and exploitation. The Greek idea of εὐεργεσία (*euergesia*) or "the urge to 'do good,'" had been adopted by the Romans with regard to generosity on behalf of the poor.[75] For the most part, εὐεργεσία was understood only in philanthropic terms on behalf of the *polis* and its official citizens.[76] Nevertheless, both Jewish and Christian leaders promoted the ideas associated with εὐεργεσία, the only difference being the Christian inclusion of outsiders. Euergetism, according to Finn, developed into unhealthy forms of competition between Jews and Christians that were aimed more at political standing than true care for the poor.[77] As a result, some members of the clergy were accused of abusing their manage-

72. Rhee, *Loving the Poor*, 180. See also Mayer, "Patronage," 58–70; Hillner, "Clerics, Property and Patronage," 59–68.

73. Rhee, *Loving the Poor*, 179. Here Rhee cites the often capricious Eusebius, *Hist. Eccl.* 10 (PG 20:841–906; trans., Maier, *The Church History*, 308–32).

74. Rhee, *Loving the Poor*, 180–81; Finn, *Almsgiving*, 32, 108–15.

75. Brown, *Poverty and Leadership*, 4.

76. Finn, *Almsgiving*, 19, 217.

77. Ibid., 268.

rial authority regarding alms, which became an issue that John confronted directly.[78]

Many preachers like John took on the responsibility of making poverty visible to their congregations and in the public sphere. These Christian leaders used the Scriptures to promote action on behalf of those who were experiencing conjunctural poverty and generosity toward those who still suffered from structural poverty.[79] The bishop remained the primary benefactor of the poor in terms of almsgiving, but members of the congregations were also encouraged to give generously. John, along with other Christian leaders throughout the empire, exhorted the clergy and laypeople to be faithful in giving alms personally, or "with one's own hands," as they encountered needs during their daily lives. In such cases, personal almsgiving could be done without the mediation of the church.[80] In this sense, bishops and pastors like John served as the primary missionaries to the poor. They were not only responsible for presenting the gospel and administering alms directly, but also with charging others in the community of faith to become involved in this missional practice as a part of their everyday lives. Without the influence of the bishop, the Christian mission could have easily led to an elite religion made up only of Roman citizens. The practice of almsgiving modeled in the fourth century, which was evangelistic in its nature, became the standard for the next millennium in the Eastern churches, despite patterns of decline similar to those seen in the West after Augustine.[81]

Among Pagans

Despite the rapid Christianization of the Roman world during the fourth century, paganism maintained its prevalence and remained in tension with Christianity throughout the empire. In Antioch, for example, the civic calendar still functioned according to its pagan roots as did the many festivals that took place annually.[82] In Constantinople, most of the pagan temples remained active and operated as they had for centuries.[83] As with Judaism,

---

78. See Chapter 8.

79. Finn, "Portraying the Poor," 144.

80. *In 1 Tim. hom.* 14.6 (PG 62:578–79; NPNF 1.13:612–13); Finn, *Almsgiving*, 184, 214.

81. Constantelos, "The Hellenic Background," 208.

82. Mayer and Allen, *John Chrysostom*, 15.

83. Ibid.; Dagron, *Naissance d'une capitale: Constantinople*, 378–79.

the Christian practice of almsgiving, as a part of missions and evangelism throughout the empire, found itself in competition with pagan forms of charity. This does not mean, however, that Christian charity in the empire developed out of pagan philanthropy.[84] On the contrary, Christian forms of charity in the form of almsgiving included the πτωχοί as emphasized in the New Testament, which was a group all but ignored by those with means in secular culture.[85]

Tertullian, in his work *Apologeticus*, described what he perceived as duplicity and dishonesty in the pagan temples of the empire. The priests and servants of the Roman temples were always entreating the people for more money for their insatiable gods and goddesses to the detriment of human need around them. According to Tertullian,

> "At any rate," you say, "the revenues of the temples are breaking down daily, how many are they who toss their coins in there?" We cannot cope with both men and your gods begging together; and do not think alms should be given to others than those who ask. Come, let Jupiter hold out his hand and receive! In the meantime, our compassion spends more street by street than your religion temple by temple.[86]

Tertullian went on to say that even if people gave more to the Roman temples, their resources would likely be used fraudulently.[87]

According to Parkin, the most significant evidence for a lack of pagan almsgiving toward the destitute is an argument made from silence. Pagan sources from the Roman Empire offer details on little, if any, charity among the destitute during the fourth century. The mention of beggars is all but absent, and any details concerning pagan almsgiving among the poor come from Christian sources that displayed a higher level of interest in the helpless. For the most part, beggars were to be ignored and charitable aid was only to be offered if it benefited citizens who, in turn, could benefit the

---

84. Parkin, "'You Do Him No Service,'" 60; Bolkestein, *Wohltätigkeit und Armenpflege*, 337–40. The rejection of pagan roots for Christian almsgiving was first espoused definitively by Bolkestein. See also Francis, *Subversive Virtue*, 6–10; Downing, *Cynics and Christian Origins*, 115–42. Both Francis and Downing argue that almsgiving was not a part of pagan philosophical practice, even among the ascetic types, but was unique to Christianity.

85. Parkin, "'You Do Him No Service,'" 60; Finn, *Almsgiving*, 217.

86. Tertullian, *Apol.* 42.8 (PL 1:494; ANF 3:64–65).

87. Ibid.

polis.[88] To date, specific details of pagan almsgiving in the Greco-Roman world simply do not exist in a noteworthy quantity. Perhaps this is the strongest argument that almsgiving was not commonplace among pagans as it progressed in the developing Christian traditions.

One of the main reasons for this lack among pagan society, according to Parkin, was the influence of Stoic philosophy on the learned elite. Because the Stoics frowned upon making decisions made by compassion, or emotion of any kind, many educated citizens simply saw no value in almsgiving.[89] Syncretism in terms of philosophy was a major issue during the fourth century. This took place within philosophical traditions themselves, which often merged one or more philosophies with others, and also between such traditions and Byzantine Christianity. The latter syncretism was not necessarily popular among pagans or Christians, but its existence is well documented.[90]

The Greco-Roman idea of φιλανθρόπια (*philanthropia*), which was the civic virtue of offering charity to the needy throughout the empire, has been suggested as a form of pagan almsgiving on behalf of beggars. Constantelos, for example, argues for civic φιλανθρόπια toward the destitute, citing works from Hesiod and Homer which speak of offering assistance to those in "tribulation."[91] Both Finn and Holman, however, question the true nature of the content cited by Constantelos. In each case, it can be argued that the φιλανθρόπια offered was in fact a form of political capital, based on strategic advantage rather than compassion or virtue.[92]

88. Parkin, "'You Do Him No Service,'" 61, 65.

89. Ibid., 63, 70. Parkin does leave open the possibility that a number of non-elite citizens might have participated in almsgiving because their lack of education in Stoicism caused compassion to be less denigrated in their mindsets.

90. Colish, *The Stoic Tradition*, 2–5. Colish mentions, among others, the Apostle Paul, Cyprian, Lactantius, Ambrose, Jerome, Salvian, and Augustine. See also Ierodiakonou, *Byzantine Philosophy*, 9–11. Ierodiakonou mentions specifically Clement of Alexandria and the Cappadocians with regard to Stoicism. See also Verbeke, *The Presence of Stoicism in Medieval Thought*, 7–20. Verbeke argues that this syncretism continued into the Middle Ages. For a comparison of first-century correlations between the writings of the New Testament, Clement of Rome, and Stoic philosophy see Thorsteinsson, *Roman Christianity and Roman Stoicism*, 207–9.

91. Constantelos, *Byzantine Philanthropy*, xii, 4–5. Constantelos cites Hesiod's *Works and Days* and both the *Illiad* and *Odyssey* by Homer. He argues for a tradition of charity among pagans toward the less-fortunate, including the destitute, until the twelfth century.

92. Finn, *Almsgiving*, 216; Holman, "The Entitled Poor," 479. Finn suggests that the Hesiod example was most likely "royal" philanthropy which was given toward those who were defeated or guilty of a crime. In the second, the recipients were most likely poorer

The apparent lack of almsgiving to beggars does not indicate a complete philanthropic failure among pagans in the empire. Brown and Constantelos have demonstrated that the Greco-Roman idea of φιλανθρόπια was considered admirable, even when compared to the Christian emphasis on almsgiving. φιλανθρόπια was praised to the point that the Emperor himself was expected to participate in charitable action toward the empire and its citizens.[93] By the end of the fourth century, bishops had such a strong influence on the Emperor that Christian almsgiving was also one of his most important emphases.[94] Generosity through philanthropy, therefore, was considered a Roman virtue and taught as one of the most important applications of education in the humanities.[95] The Emperor and bishops were able to use almsgiving cooperatively to improve the status of the Imperial seat and the Holy See, both of which resided in Constantinople.[96]

The Greco-Roman understanding of φιλανθρόπια, not unlike contemporary approaches to philanthropy, was often used by the wealthy to create more opportunities for profit and personal gain.[97] According to Brown,

---

citizens and not beggars. Holman refers to the praise of Theodosius I as giving for the purpose of appeasing the social power groups that had developed among the poor.

93. Brown, *Poverty and Leadership*, 1; Constantelos, "The Hellenic Background," 203.

94. Holman, "The Entitled Poor," 479.

95. Parkin, "'You Do Him no Service,'" 62; Finn, *Almsgiving*, 217; Brown, *Poverty and Leadership*, 4.

96. Finn, *Almsgiving*, 210.

97. Bremner, *Giving*, 121–34, 159–68. The nineteenth and twentieth centuries in the United States represent perhaps the most comparable contemporary example of secularized philanthropy. In the secular arena, many of the United States' largest charities that received the largest percentage of donations developed into powerful leaders in modern business. Many of the wealthiest Americans, such as Carnegie and Rockefeller near the turn of the twentieth century, helped to pioneer significant philanthropic pursuits out of their massive excesses. As a result, many of the largest charitable organizations "represented" the needy more than they offered direct assistance. This entrepreneurial spirit eventually thrust the nation toward the inception of a welfare state. The inception of federal funding for "faith-based" social organizations, which became prominent in the mid-twentieth century, has raised a number of questions among evangelicals. See also Martin, *Virtuous Giving*, 94–127; Pipes and Ebaugh, "Faith-Based Coalitions," 66; *Christian Century* Religious News Service, "Federal Faith-Based Grants Doubled in 2004," 13. In 2004, it was estimated that more than $2 billion in federal funding was given to groups or organizations in the "faith-based" category. Many fear that autonomy could be in jeopardy if certain conditions, which might limit the mission and message of such organizations, are not met. Because many organizations have both federal and private funding, questions of financial impropriety and the true nature of "non-profit" also raise a number of questions.

A εὐεργετές (*euergetes*) might be no altruistic philanthropist, but a rich landowner who had decided that the time was ripe to offer his grain upon the market, thereby reaping for himself both a handsome profit and the additional glory of being known to have saved "his city from imminent famine." ... The rich thought of themselves as the "fellow citizens" of a distinctive community— *their* city. It was their city they were expected to love. A rich man was praised for being a φιλοπάτρις (*philopatris*), a "lover of his home-city," never for being a φιλοπτόχης (*philoptochēs*), a "lover of the poor." The εὐεργετές showed his "love of his city" by lavishing gifts upon it so as to increase the glory of its urban fabric and the comfort and overall vigor of its citizens.[98]

In this sense, the rich throughout the urban empire had molded the practice of charity into a model that was almost completely "civic." Churches that chose to participate in municipal forms of charity could expect some remuneration from the state. On the other hand, any church that did not officially align with an association that was a part of the local community government would receive far less support from city leadership.[99]

A Developing Syncretism

The aforementioned argument against the development of Christian almsgiving from pagan philanthropy remains intact. Nevertheless, by the time of John Chrysostom's pastorate, the two were not easily discernible from one another. The social benefits of philanthropy had reduced many forms of pagan and Christian charity to less than altruistic motivations. A tension of necessity emerged between the masses that made up the lower and middle classes[100] and the elite regarding philanthropic activities. Jill Harries, a scholar at St. Andrews University noted for her work in Roman law and society, describes this tension: "While it was true that the *populus* could be exploited as pawns in elite status-games, the elite needed the popular support to support their status and could be themselves forced into concessions."[101]

98. Brown, *Poverty and Leadership*, 4–5.
99. Ibid., 54.
100. See note on the appropriateness of the term "middle class" in chapter 4.
101. Harries, "Favor Populi," 139.

Brown argues the emergence of grand Christian basilicas throughout the empire during the time of Constantine led to a synthesis of almsgiving and political impulse that was veiled as organized charity. He offers an example from Carthage in 310 CE, when a particular widow gave a large gift to the church in order to secure votes for a political candidate whom she supported. This money was supposed to be given to the poor, but was distributed among the bishops instead. When the Emperor found out about this, he sent an even larger gift in order to secure votes for his candidate instead of his opponent supported by the widow. The supposed gifts were now being used to gain political clout with no benefit to the poor.[102] As a result of these circumstances, civic forms of philanthropy toward Roman citizens and the Roman state merged with the Christian emphasis on the poor, resulting in forms of charity practiced mostly for the purpose of public display.[103]

On the other hand, the Christian understanding of almsgiving remained in contrast to pagan philanthropy. John demonstrated this separation in one particular homily concerning Matthew 25:

> For tell me, should you see one at a loss for necessary food and omit appeasing his hunger, while you first overlaid his table with silver; would he indeed thank you, and not rather be indignant? What, again, if seeing one wrapped in rags, and stiff with cold, you should neglect giving him a garment, and build golden columns, saying, "I am doing it to your honor," would he not say that you were mocking, and account it an insult, and that the most extreme? Yet this then is your thought with regard to Christ also, when He is going about a wanderer, and a stranger, needing a roof to cover Him; and you, neglecting to receive Him, instead deck out a pavement, and walls, and capitals of columns, and instead hang up silver chains by means of lamps; but Himself bound in prison you will not even look upon.[104]

Perhaps the best illustration of the difference between Christians and pagans in terms of almsgiving and compassion for the poor is found in language. According to Finn, pagans continued to describe the poor with negative connotations such as ἄδοξοι (*adoxoi*) and ταπεινοί (*tapeinoi*), meaning "base" and "ignoble," respectively. Christians, alternatively, used

---

102. Brown, *Poverty and Leadership*, 26–27.

103. Mayer, "Poverty and Generosity," 141.

104. *In Matt. hom.* 50.4 (PG 58:509; NPNF 1.10:428–29).

terms like οἱ δεομένοι (*hoi deomenoi*) and οἱ θλιβόμενοι (*hoi thlibomenoi*), meaning "the needy" and "the afflicted," respectively.[105]

---

105. Finn, *Almsgiving*, 183. See also Patlagean, *Pauvreté*, 28; Holman, "The Entitled Poor," 483.

4

A Pastor in Antioch

A city that has not pious citizens is meaner than any village,
and more ignoble than any cave.

—John Chrysostom

ANTIOCH

The majority of recorded history concerning John Chrysostom's ministry, sermons, and writings comes from the eminent Syrian city of Antioch. John's prominence in Antioch provided a platform for his renowned reputation throughout the Roman Empire. In terms of the Christian movement, the See of Antioch was compared closely to that of Alexandria.[1] Antioch was located at the "nexus" of trade routes of the eastern Mediterranean, Egypt, and Constantinople, which resulted in a considerable rate of produce and trade. This, in turn, brought a larger number of visitors to the city requiring the growth of hospitality services. Antioch was a major component of Roman culture and politics. It had an imperial

1. Brown, *Poverty and Leadership*, 50; Kelly, *Golden Mouth*, 2; Mayer and Allen, *John Chrysostom*, 7–12. Brown adds both Antioch and Alexandria to Constantinople to make up the three most important cities of the Eastern Empire. Mayer and Allen contend that over 900 of John's sermons have survived, with the majority having been preached in Antioch. During his twelve years of pastoral ministry in that city, it is likely that the number of his sermons was far higher than the total that has survived.

palace, military stations, and significant sacred sites. The city also hosted a number of important religious synods. The Olympic Games took place regularly in Daphne, a suburb of Antioch, beginning in second century CE during the reign of Commodus.[2] John described the city of Antioch as a budding metropolis with magnificent structures and landscape. In addition, according to John, the abundance of goods in the Antiochene marketplace was of such a large volume that the area buzzed with people "even to midnight," which was a further indication that materialism had become rampant among the masses.[3]

For John, Antioch gained its greatest significance from its early church history as told in the book of Acts. He argued the city was "dignified" not because of its size, architecture, porticoes, or any other ornamentation. The dignity of Antioch was tied directly to "the virtue and piety of its inhabitants."[4] John described the first Christians in Antioch in terms of generosity toward their own community and those in other lands. This virtue and piety was seen most clearly in three separate biblical accounts. 1) The disciples were first called "Christians" at Antioch (Acts 11:26). 2) When Jerusalem and its people suffered during the famine, the church at Antioch sent aid (Acts 11:28–29). 3) When false teachers came to Antioch from Judea, the church at Antioch sent Paul and Barnabas to Jerusalem to plead the case of the Gentile believers (Acts 15:1).[5] Antioch was made great by its people, for, according to John, "a city that has not pious citizens is meaner than any village, and more ignoble than any cave."[6]

The city of Antioch featured poverty on a scale consistent with that of other urban centers in the empire. Sometime between 386–388 CE, John estimated one-tenth of the city's 300,000 inhabitants were very poor, another tenth were supremely wealthy, and the rest made up the middle class.[7] Brown affirms the accuracy of John's estimates and their similarities to urban demographics for the next few centuries:

---

2. Downey, *A History of Antioch*, 641–50; Mayer and Allen, *John Chrysostom*, 11–12; Kelly, *Golden Mouth*, 1–3; Baur, *John Chrysostom and His Time*, 1:39; Liebeschuetz, *Antioch*, 59.

3. *De Stat. hom.* 17.2 (PG 49:179; NPNF 1.09:523). See also Baur, *John Chrysostom and His Time*, 1:34–37; Krupp, *Shepherding the Flock*, 12.

4. *De Stat. hom.* 17.2 (PG 49:176–77; NPNF 1.09:521).

5. *De Stat. hom.* 17.2 (PG 49:179; NPNF 1.09:523); Krupp, *Shepherding the Flock*, 11; Kelly, *Golden Mouth*, 2.

6. *De Stat. hom.* 17.2 (PG 49:176–77; NPNF 1.09:521).

7. *In Matt. hom.* 66.3 (PG 58:630; NPNF 1.10:548); Maxwell, *Christianization and*

John Chrysostom's proportion of one-tenth indicates a poverty level not dissimilar to that of late medieval European cities and of early modern societies which have fragmentary statistics. The tolerance level of such societies appears to have wavered between accepting 5 percent to 10 percent of the population as permanently "poor" and in need of relief, while being prepared to help between 20 and 25 percent of the population for short periods in times of crisis.[8]

Roth also concurs with John's estimates concerning economic differences as well as his commendation of the city's prosperity and importance in the Eastern Empire and beyond. According to Roth, "Antioch prospered because of its position on the trade routes; some families were very rich, though others were very poor, and a majority were in adequate financial condition."[9]

Among those considered poor in Antioch, as in the rest of the empire, poverty was both conjunctural and structural. Brown describes each form of poverty as "shallow" or "deep," respectively. Most of the poor would experience shallow poverty throughout their lives. Shallow poverty was often a condition to which those submerged in deep poverty aspired to return. Deep poverty could be fatal and was a danger for all who lived below middle class standards throughout the city.[10] As a result, John continually urged the wealthy to redistribute their resources among the poor in order to alleviate their suffering.

John was convinced that many of the rich had gained wealth through exploitation of the poor, in similar ways to those who are condemned in James 5:1–11 and the rich man in Jesus' parable (Luke 16:19–31). In the first homily of *De Laz.*, John described the rich who were guilty of such oppression as "robbers lying in wait on the roads, stealing from passers-by, and burying others' goods in their own houses as if in caves and holes."[11]

Communication, 86. The contemporary understanding of an urban middle class does not accurately describe the middle class of the Eastern Empire of late antiquity. Recent scholarship has emphasized such distinctions, so that the middle class might be understood not as an independently recognized social group but rather the vast majority of people whose social standing and economic level fell somewhere in between the elite and the chronically poor. See Garnsey and Saller, *The Roman Empire*, 107–25; Rhee, *Loving the Poor*, 8.

8. Brown, *Poverty and Leadership*, 14.

9. Roth, *OWP*, 7.

10. Brown, *Poverty and Leadership*, 15; Mayer, "Poverty and Society," 465–84.

11. *De Laz. hom.* 1.12 (PG 48:980; trans., Roth, *OWP*, 36).

Many among the rich stood in the way of the poor and their opportunities for improvement, but this was not to be the case among Christians. John was not only contending with the rich on behalf of the poor, but also the public including the marketplace, theater, race-course, festivals, and other entertainment venues.

The Public Sphere

The fourth-century Antiochene religious landscape was pluralistic and three major belief systems were dominant: paganism, Judaism, and Christianity.[12] Within each religious tradition, however, various factions had developed and most areas were infiltrated heavily by more than one faith system.[13] A large contingency of Jewish leaders competed with Christians and pagans "for the souls of the city," resulting in a developing syncretism between and within the three traditions.[14] A Hellenized form of paganism continued to permeate the religious life of Antioch and had influences in each religious movement. Statues of Tyche, the Greek goddess of prosperity for cities, could be seen throughout the public arenas along with statues of the "deified Trajan" and many other gods and goddesses. Many pagan celebrations and festivals were practiced with fervor and the pagan priesthood of Antioch remained active in their daily practices.[15] According to Baur, the temples of Apollo, Jupiter, and Hecate were of major significance in the religious history and everyday life of Antioch.[16]

---

12. Maxwell, *Christianization and Communication*, 118; Walsh, "Wealthy and Impoverished Widows," 183. Walsh estimates the number of adherents in each of the three groups to be 100,000, each making up a third of the Antiochene population.

13. Mayer and Allen, *John Chrysostom*, 13; Wilken, *John Chrysostom and the Jews*, 16–36; Krupp, *Shepherding the Flock*, 215. Wilken and Krupp argue that there was not one truly dominant religious tradition in Antioch. The influence of the Emperor Julian the Apostate over the empire actually led to more pluralism. Julian sought to revitalize the state religions in his continual attempts to disavow Christianity. Wilken describes Antioch's multiple religious traditions, each with various factions, all vying for prominence in the Syrian cities of the empire.

14. Krupp, *Shepherding the Flock*, 215; Sandwell, *Religious Identity in Late Antiquity*, 3–33.

15. Mayer and Allen, *John Chrysostom*, 4, 13. See also Lassus, "La ville d'Antioch," 67–74.

16. Baur, *John Chrysostom and His Time*, 1:39.

The Marketplace

For John, the picture of the poor was clearest when set against the backdrop of the extraordinary marketplace of Antioch and its wealthy patrons. The marketplace of fourth-century Antioch, filled with a wide variety of items for sale, was arguably the main reason for the city's growing popularity. Many items were meant to indulge the senses through different forms of debauchery. The marketplace itself was a forum for the rich to flaunt their wealth, possessions, and entourage.[17] This popularity led John to describe Antioch as a "common harbor" for poor transients and migrants through-out the empire.[18] The budding population resulted in less than adequate access to food, necessities, housing, clothing, and resources to help obtain social advancement.[19] In the midst of the superfluous spectacle that was the marketplace were a large number of beggars. Among them were home-less men, women, and children who entreated citizens and travelers for aid daily. The extent of destitution paralleled with the callousness of the rich had created such a dire situation that many, as has been mentioned, had resorted to disfiguring themselves or their children in order to gain sym-pathy.[20] The homily *De Eleem.*, which was perhaps John's most influential sermon concerning almsgiving, was likely delivered in the winter of 387 CE after having walked through the marketplace where he saw many poor and beggars being neglected during the cold of the season.[21]

The marketplace benefited in many ways from the presence of beggars, especially in terms of entertainment. Conversely, the poor lived in a tension between having to rely on the marketplace for sustenance, competing with members of the other social strata, while often being excluded from areas of the marketplace or being treated shamefully while there.[22] For John,

---

17. Leyerle, "John Chrysostom on Almsgiving," 29–32.

18. *De Eleem.* 6 (PG 51:270; trans., Christo, *ORA*, 148).

19. Osborne, "Roman Poverty in Context," 7.

20. *In 1 Cor. hom.* 21.5 (Field, *Sancti Patris*, 253; trans., Mayer and Allen, *John Chrys-ostom*, 171; PG 61:176–77; NPNF 1.12:170).

21. *De Eleem.* 1 (PG 51:261; trans., Christo, *ORA*, 131, xvi). See also Maxwell, *Christianization and Communication*, 71. For more discussion concerning the homilies of John in general, see Mayer, *The Homilies of St. John Chrysostom: Provenance.*

22. Morley, "The Poor in the City of Rome," 33–35. This situation is not dissimilar to current treatment of many homeless Americans sleeping on the streets in cities across the United States. In a number of cities, such as San Francisco, Philadelphia, and Ft. Worth, laws and ordinances have been put into place to regulate the movement and activity of beggars in certain areas. See Johnson, *The Fear of Beggars*, 2; Fagan, "New Panhandling

however, the marketplace revealed more about the spiritual condition of Antioch than the physical. On the one hand, the marketplace and the church were meant to be in opposition to each other. The poor were to be treated with dignity and respect in the churches. On the other hand, John saw the marketplace as the setting for the drama of almsgiving and the relationship between the rich and the poor to be played out. What happened in the marketplace in terms of Christian living and meeting the needs of the poor had severe eschatological applications.[23]

The Theater

The Theater of Caesar in Antioch was among the most visited attractions in the Eastern Empire. It was likely a stone theater, renowned for its architecture and featured entertainment.[24] John described the theater in similar terms to the houses of the wealthy, containing "tables covered with hangings and couches inlaid with silver," with a haughtily displayed stage.[25] The theatrical venue in Antioch had been a mainstay of festivity, display, and leisure in the urban center from the earliest eras of Roman ascendancy.[26] By 354 CE, as Libanius confirmed, the popularity of the theater in Antioch had risen to the point that there were shows nearly every other day during a calendar year.[27] Along with being the primary setting for entertainment in the city, the theater also hosted some of the most renowned rhetoricians of the day as it had for several decades.

For John, the theater was both licentious and advantageous. He constantly warned his congregation to beware of the theater's immorality while also using its style and rhetoric to contextualize his messages in a manner that was provocative and relevant. From a negative standpoint,

---

Law."; Fagan, "Success in the City of Brother Love."; Hall, Moore, and Vincent, *Same Kind of Different as Me*, 82–85.

23. Sitzler, "Identity," 472; Cardman, "Poverty and Wealth as Theater," 161. The eschatological aspects of almsgiving will be dealt with in Chapter 6.

24. Retzleff, "Near Eastern Theatres in Late Antiquity," 115. Retzleff mentions other important Syrian theaters in the cities of Apamea, Laodicea, and Seleucia. She compares the Syrian theaters to those in Caesarea, Damascus, Sidon, Jerusalem, and Wadi Sabra, and Petra. See also Downey, *A History of Antioch*, 659–64.

25. *In Matt. hom.* 83.4 (PG 58:750; NPNF 1.10:672).

26. Slater, *Roman Theater and Society*, 29–48, 166; Cardman, "Poverty and Wealth as Theater," 160.

27. Libanius, *Orat.* 64; Leyerle, *Theatrical Shows*, 14.

the theaters throughout the Eastern Empire often caused major drops in church attendance when the two had conflicting schedules.[28] In addition, John warned his congregation to stay away from the theaters because of their propensity for sexual immorality and pagan mythology.[29] The women of the Constantinopolitan theater, for example, were known to "place their soft voluptuousness on display, contort their limbs, sing indecent songs, and carry on suggestive conversations; in short, they offer all that could fluster a man."[30] The absence of congregants in John's churches was worsened by their carelessness in terms of temptation.

In a homily on Titus, John described the style of Greek dramas that took place in the theaters and the behavior of the patrons who attended. He clarified that this description was true of the Greeks before Christ and the theaters of the fourth century.

> [Athenian] dramas were replete with adultery, lewdness, and corruption of every sort. In their indecent nocturnal assemblies, women were admitted to the spectacle. There was seen the abomination of a virgin sitting in the theater during the night, amidst a drunken multitude of young men madly reveling. The very festival was the darkness, and the abominable deeds practiced by them. On this account he says, "For we ourselves also were sometimes foolish, disobedient, deceived, serving divers' lusts and pleasures." One man loved his stepmother, a woman her step-son, and in consequence hung herself. For as to their passion for boys, whom they called their "Pædica," it is not fit to be named. And would you see a son married to his mother? This too happened among them, and what is horrible, though it was done in ignorance, the god whom

---

28. *Cont. Lud.* 1 (PG 56:263; trans., Mayer and Allen, *John Chrysostom*, 119); Slater, *Roman Theater*, 175; Leyerle, *Theatrical Shows*, 13; Harries, "Favor Populi," 133; *De Stat. hom.* 15.1 (PG 49:153–54; NPNF 1.09:498). According to John, an exception to the lack of attendance took place for a time after the imperial statues were destroyed in Antioch. The city saw a period of spiritual renewal during which the theaters and other entertainment venues that were known for immorality were less frequented. Eventually, the influence of John and others led to civic enactments, such as that of Theodosius I in the 390s, banning theatrical shows and other pagan events on Sundays and other holy days.

29. *In Acts hom.* 44.3 (PG 60:312; NPNF 1.11:375); *De Stat. hom.* 15.1 (PG 49:153–54; NPNF 1.09:498); Leyerle, *Theatrical Shows*, 20; Slater, *Roman Theater*, 175; Harries, "Favor Populi," 133; Libanius, *Orat.* 41. The magnitude of the theater's immorality was such that even Libanius discussed its detriment from a non-Christian perspective.

30. *Cont. Lud.* 2 (PG 56:266; trans., Mayer and Allen, *John Chrysostom*, 121); Brändle, *John Chrysostom: Bishop, Reformer, Martyr*, 60. See also *In Matt. hom.* 7.6–7 (PG 57:79–82; NPNF 1.10:73–76).

they worshiped did not prevent it, but permitted this outrage to nature to be committed, and that though she was a person of distinction. And if those, who, if for no other reason, yet for the sake of their reputation with the multitude, might have been expected to adhere to virtue; if they rushed thus headlong into vice, what is it likely was the conduct of the greater part, who lived in obscurity? What is more diversified than this pleasure? The wife of a certain one fell in love with another man, and with the help of her adulterer, slew her husband upon his return. The greater part of you probably know the story. The son of the murdered man killed the adulterer, and after him his mother, then he himself became mad, and was haunted by furies. After this the madman himself slew another man and took his wife. What can be worse than such calamities as these?[31]

In terms of contextualization, John added to his description of the Athenian dramas:

But I mention these instances taken from the Heathens, with this view, that I may convince the Gentiles, what evils then prevailed in the world. But we may show the same from our own writings. For it is said, "They sacrificed their sons and daughters unto devils" (Ps 106:37). Again, the Sodomites were destroyed for no other cause than their unnatural appetites. Soon after the coming of Christ, did not a king's daughter dance at a banquet in the presence of drunken men, and did she not ask as the reward of her dancing the murder and the head of a Prophet? "Who can utter the mighty acts of the Lord?" (Ps 6:2).[32]

John's efforts to use the theater for communication and contextualization went beyond correlating the nature of sin among Jews, Gentiles, and Christians. The theater was not only the main venue for dramatic entertainment but was also a forum for discourse on philosophy, education, and politics.[33] Politics were a major component of everyday conversation in Antioch. As a result, many political issues became the content of entertaining

31. *In Tit. hom.* 5.4 (PG 62:693; NPNF 1.13:722–23).

32. Ibid. (62:693; 1.13:723)

33. Maxwell, *Christianization and Communication*, 12, 42; *In Matt. hom.* 69.3 (PG 58:658–53; NPNF 1.10:571–73). Maxwell mentions this homily on Matthew where John mentioned the constant, casual conversation of his congregants regarding politics and rhetoric. See also Kelly, *Golden Mouth*, 1. Kelly describes Antioch as a city that was well known throughout the Eastern Empire for having a burgeoning intellectual heritage and culture with renowned schools, educators, and rhetoricians.

plots and songs in the theaters. Because of the growing interest in rhetoric as a form of entertainment, John's use of cultural images and masterful homilies made preaching attractive to nearly every social group, from the elite to the ordinary.[34] John also preached in such a way that his rhetorical style would be provocative and entertaining in order to provide a virtuous and edifying alternative to the immorality of the theater.[35]

Other Venues

There were a number of other exhibitions throughout Antioch that vied for the attention of the masses on a regular basis. The race-course, built originally in 67 BCE, was similar to the Hippodrome of Constantine I in Constantinople. The track offered chariot and horse races nearly as often as shows were in the theater.[36] According to Libanius, the public bath houses were so frequented during the day that they had become a popular place for the destitute to beg for bread and alms.[37] There were also a number of smaller venues for public speaking where philosophers, politicians, preachers, and comedians offered rhetorical arguments and engaged in participatory dialogues with the public.[38] Sozomen mentioned a prominent figure named Aëtius, a physician turned rhetorician who attracted large crowds on numerous occasions. He was nicknamed "Atheist" because of his well known orations which questioned the existence and nature of God.[39]

Antioch also celebrated a number of important festivals, both religious and non-religious, throughout the year. On these occasions, church attendance saw attrition similar to what occurred on days of important events at the theater and racetrack.[40] During the larger festivals, which took place in the marketplace and other parts of the city, dialogical contests were held. In

---

34. Maxwell, *Christianization and Communication*, 42.

35. Hartney, *John Chrysostom and the Transformation of the City*, 140; Cardman, "Poverty and Wealth as Theater," 159–75. Cardman's essay on John's homiletical use of theatrical images and style will be revisited in Chapter 6 when discussing John's sermons on the Parable of the Rich Man and Lazarus.

36. Libanius, *Orat.* 64; Humphrey, *Roman Circuses*, 439–61; Brändle, *John Chrysostom*, 60; Leyerle, *Theatrical Shows*, 14; Harries, "Favor Populi," 133.

37. Libanius, *Orat.* 1.

38. Maxwell, *Christianization and Communication*, 42.

39. Sozomen, *Hist. Eccl.* 3.15 (PG 67:1084–85; NPNF 2.02:421). Sozomen mentioned Aëtius in later chapters as one who was involved in the Arian controversy.

40. Harries, "Favor Populi," 133.

many cases, awards were given to those who excelled rhetoric. The elite and the common people would attend, celebrating the rhetoricians as if they were winning battles in the Coliseum.[41] John warned against the festivals because many were prone to drunkenness, carousing, and obscene displays of immorality, including public nudity.[42]

The Churches

Fourth-century Antioch had at least four active Christian churches, each of which played an important role in the urban Christian experience. The Constantinian Great Church, or Golden Church, was the most influential in Antioch.[43] It was situated in the newer part of the city on the island which sat in the middle of the circular path of the Orontes River. The other three churches, the Old Church, also known as Palaia, the Church of the Maccabees, which was the meeting place of a Christian cult derived from an older Jewish cult, and the Church of St. Babylas, were all located in older parts of the city.[44] Most often, John preached in the Great Church, but he was also a regular at the Old Church and preached at the Church of St. Babylas on

---

41. Maxwell, *Christianization and Communication*, 43–44.

42. *In 1 Cor. hom.* 27.5–28.1 (PG 61:231–33; NPNF 1.12:223–25). One example of public nudity was the "water festival" of Maiumas, during which in which the orchestra pit of the theater was filled with water so that women who were either naked or scantily clad could swim while playing the part of "water nymphs." See Leyerle, *Theatrical Shows*, 32. John appeared to confront those who attended this very show during the festival in *In Matt. hom.* 7.6 (PG 57:79; NPNF 1.10:73–74). See also Segal, *Theatres in Roman Palestine*, 11; Kolbe, "Nur eine Metapher?," 567–76.

43. Rhee, *Loving the Poor*, 180. See note in chapter 3 concerning imperial patronage and Constantine's cathedrals.

44. Sozomen, *Hist. Eccl.* 2.3 (PG 67:936; NPNF 2.02:368); Mayer and Allen, *John Chrysostom*, 17–18; Mayer, "John Chrysostom: Extraordinary Preacher, Ordinary Audience," 126; Kelly, *Golden Mouth*, 2–3; Eltester, "Die Kirchen Antiochias," 254–70. Sozomen listed these churches as a part of the grand cathedrals that were commissioned by Constantine I. Kelly describes the Great Church as an octagon-shaped structure that was originally set to be built by Constantine in 327 CE and brought to completion by his son Constantius II in 341 CE. The Old Church was built between 312 and 324 CE, replacing a past cathedral structure that had been demolished in the persecutions of Diocletian earlier in the century. Some claimed that the Old Church was, in fact, a direct descendant of the church planted in Antioch by the Apostles. For a more contemporary reappraisal of data regarding the churches of Antioch, see Mayer and Allen, *The Churches of Syrian Antioch*.

occasion.[45] A number of martyrs' chapels and graves were said to have encircled Antioch, which John saw as one of the more positive aspects of the city.[46] The churches in Antioch had come a long way since the first century, but believers had not forgotten the missionary foundations of the Apostles and Christians of earlier centuries.

Several scholars argue that John Chrysostom, as an "evangelist of the rich," preached to audiences that were primarily upper class. Their argument is based on historical demographics, the emphasis on wealth and poverty in John's preaching, and the rhetorical styles with which he preached, likely developed from his training in the Second Sophistic style.[47] John has also been accused of misogyny and anti-Semitism because of his emphasis on male clerical leadership in the church and his strong statements against the Jews in Antioch.[48] Cunningham and Allen have argued that most Christian preachers in late antiquity, including John, did not address "the poorest sectors of society," in their recorded sermons.[49]

Finn offers three reasons why the absence of the poor in fourth century sermons and church descriptions might not necessitate their absence in the church. First, many of the poor might have remained outside during the church service in order to remain in their begging locations. Second, the lack of addressing the poor could have been a result of their low status. Third, it is possible that the more sophisticated uses of the Latin and Greek

45. Mayer, "John Chrysostom: Extraordinary Preacher, Ordinary Audience," 126; Kelly, *Golden Mouth*, 2–3, 57; Mayer and Allen, *John Chrysostom*, 140. At least one of John's recorded homilies was preached from the Old Church and seems to indicate that John preached there somewhat regularly for a time. There exist only two recorded sermons of John from the Church of St. Babylas.

46. Baur, *John Chrysostom and His Time*, 1:34.

47. Maxwell, *Christianization and Communication*, 12-n, 66. Maxwell describes the origins of Second Sophistic descriptions: "Philostratus (c. 230 CE) coined the term 'Second Sophistic' and emphasized eloquence over philosophical tendencies." See also Sitzler, "Identity," 472; MacMullen, "The Preacher's Audience (AD 350–400)," 504; Ameringer, *Second Sophistic*, 20–28.

48. *Adv. Jud.* (PG 48:843–945, trans., Harkins, *Discourses*, 1–244); Parkes, *Conflict of the Church and the Synagogue*, 163–66; Krupp, *Shepherding the Flock*, 1; Neusner, *Judaism and Christianity in the Age of Constantine*, 61; Wilken, *John Chrysostom and the Jews*, 10–20. Neusner argues that John, rather than speaking against the Jews as a people or religious tradition, was in fact speaking Christologically against Judaizers and backslidden Christians. Wilken also argues that John's principle issue was against aggressive Judaizers who rejected the divinity of Christ. See also Grissom, "Chrysostom and the Jews"; Meeks and Wilken, *Jews and Christians in Antioch*.

49. Cunningham and Allen, *Preacher and Audience*, 14.

languages in the churches were unintelligible to the uneducated poor.[50] It will be demonstrated, however, that John addressed the poor on numerous occasions concerning their role in almsgiving. John displayed a keen awareness of the emotions and circumstances of the poor, which is evidence of the considerable amount of time he spent with the poor as their pastor and missionary in Antioch.

Other scholars, however, argue that John's emphasis on wealth and poverty, along with his rhetorical styles, were merely representative of his social concern for the plight of the poor as opposed to any numerical majority within the congregations. Mayer and Walsh, for example, argue that the Antiochene congregations of the late fourth century included poor men and women, children, and slaves.[51] Maxwell adds to this list the unemployed, those who worked as artisans or laborers, and various demographic groups that all made up very diverse congregations.[52] The most persuasive argument for the inclusion of the poor in the churches of Antioch comes from John himself, who mentioned more than three thousand poor widows and virgins who were supported by the church, as well as those who had been imprisoned, sick, homeless, orphaned, crippled, and hungry.[53] If the poor were welcomed anywhere in fourth-century Antioch, it was certainly in the churches.

The Great Church, from which John did the bulk of his service and preaching in Antioch, was also the local epicenter for social ministry in the city. As has been demonstrated, the bishop in such settings was seen as the major social advocate for the poor in the Eastern Empire. To facilitate the growing number of needs that the church was addressing, the Great Church utilized four separate dining areas, a hostel for travelers, a hospital for the sick, and specific areas and resources designated for widows, orphans, and

---

50. Finn, *Almsgiving*, 141–43. A fourth option, not mentioned by Finn, could be that the poor were not mentioned because of their high status in the kingdom. The poor were honored in the church as a result of the preaching of Ambrose, the Cappadocians, and John Chrysostom, and therefore needed no spiritual direction.

51. Mayer, "John Chrysostom: Extraordinary Preacher, Ordinary Audience," 123–26; Mayer, "Who Came to Hear John Chrysostom Preach?," 73–87; Mayer and Allen, *John Chrysostom*, 34–40; Walsh, "Wealthy and Impoverished Widows," 183. See also Rousseau, "'The Preacher's Audience," 391–400.

52. Maxwell, *Christianization and Communication*, 65, 68.

53. *In Matt. hom.* 66.3 (PG 58:630; NPNF 1.10:548–49); Walsh, "Wealthy and Impoverished Widows," 183; Finn, *Almsgiving*, 73, 88–89, 630.

virgins.[54] Both the Great Church and the Old Church had developed regular collections of alms for the poor during scheduled times of the year, often a first-fruits type of offering. These offerings were supplemented by special collections in times when alms were not accumulating in sufficient quantities or specific needs had arisen.[55] In *De Sac.*, John mentioned a specific offering set aside for those who cared for widows in order to meet their expense requirements.[56] At times, it was also possible for the churches to receive the aid of Imperial resources through tax receipts or other funds that were set aside specifically for almsgiving for the benefit of the πτωχοί.[57]

Despite the convolution of religion and poverty in Antioch, John's attitude toward the churches and their responsibility to the poor never seemed to waver. He believed the church itself had the resources and potential to alleviate poverty without assistance from outside sources. If the tenth of the city that was comprised by the rich and the 80 percent that made up the middle class would redistribute their time and resources among the tenth that were poor, John believed "there would be no poor."[58] If the wealth with which God had blessed the majority in Antioch was spent on the poor, as opposed to "prostitutes, drink, fancy food, expensive clothes, and all the other kinds of indolence," poverty would certainly subside.[59]

As one scholar has aptly said, "John believed that wealth would be regulated almost automatically if men and women began to behave in a truly Christian manner."[60] Despite his impassioned pleas, John felt like most of his congregation remained unmoved. They had a tendency to respond to his preaching by applauding wildly and at times for long periods of time. Nevertheless, many failed to put his teaching into practice.[61] Poverty persisted on a grand scale, and the masses did not seem overly concerned. According to John, "For who from these discourses has become more forward in the giving of alms? Who has cast down his money? Who

54. Brändle, "This Sweetest Passage," 131; Mayer and Allen, *John Chrysostom*, 47; Brown, *Power and Persuasion*, 78–103. For more on the emergence of hospitals in Antioch and throughout the Eastern Empire, see Miller, *The Birth of the Hospital in the Byzantine Empire*, 69–74.

55. Finn, *Almsgiving*, 39, 46–56.

56. *De Sac.* 3.16 (PG 48:654–55; trans., Neville, *OP*, 94–97; NPNF 1.09:60).

57. Finn, *Almsgiving*, 56–58.

58. *In Matt. hom.* 66.3 (PG 58:630; NPNF 1.10:548–49).

59. *De Laz. hom.* 2.4 (PG 48:988; trans., Roth, *OWP*, 50).

60. Hartney, *John Chrysostom and the Transformation of the City*, 152.

61. Roth, *OWP*, 9; Finn, *Almsgiving*, 4.

has given even half of his substance? Who even a third part? No one."[62]
In areas where his preaching was applied, however, the churches' mission
to the poor achieved new levels of success in meeting needs. As will be
demonstrated, people of all demographics converged to participate in the
ministry of the Antiochene churches and the missionary transmission of
the gospel message was increasingly successful through the cooperative
practice of almsgiving.

SUMMARY

John Chrysostom's sentiments on the church's ability to reach the poor,
while admirable, were perhaps also unreasonable. As the contextual study
of Antioch and the Eastern Empire above has revealed, poverty was a com-
plex issue necessitating more than just the appropriation of resources. The
roots of poverty in the Roman Empire and the Hellenized world ran very
deep and Antioch was no exception. Brown affirms this idea by asserting
that John overestimated the extent to which his congregation might affect
the full measure of poverty felt by the tenth of the population that was the
poorest. Brown argues that many of John's congregants who belonged to
the middle class experienced shallow, or conjunctural poverty themselves,
making sacrificial giving on their part dangerous. If they in fact responded
as John suggested, they too might have become a part of the poorest 10
percent.[63] On the matter of the unlikelihood that the Antiochene churches
could do away with poverty by their ministry alone, perhaps the most convincing argument comes from Jesus himself, who reiterates the teaching of
the Torah that there will always be poor in the land (Matt 26:10; Mark 14:7;
John 12:8; Deut 15:11).

John may have been somewhat overzealous. I believe his fervor, however, was the result of a passionate belief that the churches' mission efforts
toward the poor began with evangelism and discipleship among the rich. If
the wealthy and middle class in his congregations would continue to deliver
the good news of Jesus Christ to the poor through almsgiving, the churches
could evangelize the city from the "bottom up."[64] I am convinced that John

62. *In Matt. hom.* 88.3 (PG 58:779; NPNF 1.10:703).

63. Brown, *Poverty and Leadership*, 14–15.

64. Hartney, *John Chrysostom and the Transformation of the City*, 6. See also pp. 30,
191, where, contrary to Brown, Hartney argues that John did not try to replace civic
virtues with Christian ethics or try to create a new, esoteric, Christian sect. She argues,

believed the entire city of Antioch would be changed through evangelism and meeting the needs of the poor. This would in turn alter the direction of the entire Eastern Empire and the known world. In order to accomplish this mission for the benefit of all types of people, a number of important theological beliefs had to be addressed. In his commentaries and homilies, John presented a sound biblical foundation for his developing missions and ministry among the poor.

---

instead, that John tried to use the existing Antiochene social framework as an entry point for the gospel into the city.

5

Counter-Cultural Generosity

Spend abundantly your goods upon the needy.

—JOHN CHRYSOSTOM

PROLEGOMENA: *MISSIO DEI* AND JOHN'S USE OF BOTH CANONS

Justo L. González, noted historian, theologian, and authority on Christianity in Latin America considers John Chrysostom's biblical perspectives on almsgiving to be the "fullest and most cohesive" of any church leader of late antiquity.[1] For John, the practice of almsgiving started with Scripture. He believed almsgiving to be a primary facet of God's missionary intent for the world, beginning with the Abrahamic covenant, continuing through the end of the church age, and culminating with eschatological ramifications.[2] Gerhard von Rad echoed John's interpretation of the *missio dei* in his commentary on Genesis: "What is promised to Abraham reaches far beyond Israel; indeed, it has universal meaning for all generations on earth."[3] In the same way, John believed the Hebrew Scriptures regarding almsgiving were foundational for all New Testament teaching on the subject.

1. González, *Faith and Wealth*, 211.
2. *In Gen. hom.* 31 (PG 53:282–92; trans., Hill, *Homilies on Genesis*, 2:245–48).
3. Rad, *Genesis*, 150.

John's interactions with the Old Testament were completely from the LXX and displayed tension in numerous areas. On the one hand, John commented and utilized the LXX regularly throughout his preaching career. His thoughts concerning cosmology, virtue, and holy living relied heavily on the LXX and other important Jewish writings. On the other hand, he targeted a number of "Judaizing" Christians in his sermons who were, in his view, committed more to the Old Covenant than to the Messiah.[4] As a result, John's exegesis and usage of the LXX were nearly always, and intentionally, from an Christological standpoint.[5] His Christological emphases were evangelistic, and therefore meant to combat the growing pluralism of the Eastern Empire by asserting: 1.) There was only one heaven and 2.) Jesus Christ alone had provided the way to get there.[6]

For John, the Pentateuch included some of the most important Judeo-Christian texts regarding God's concern for the needy and the responsibility of His people to join in the mission to the poor. The Christian idea of love for the poor was influenced by centuries worth of canonical teaching, from the Torah to the Apostle Paul, calling for the identification of every follower of God with human beings who are in need.[7] As God began shaping Abraham into the person who was to represent God's desire for His people, Abraham grew in faith and virtue. As his character improved, Abraham was to use his character to bless the world.[8]

John believed the Abrahamic covenant went far beyond the missionary call to leave one's country. The command was in fact eschatological: leaving earth for heaven. There is nothing gained by amassing possessions, living in luxury, and indulging the sinful nature with pleasure. On the contrary, the practice of almsgiving brings about eternal results that center on salvation and not selfishness.[9] John's interpretations of sacrifices and offerings, as presented throughout the Torah, are applied directly to the Christian practice of almsgiving. In Exodus 35:20–29, for example, John connects the offerings God expected for the tabernacle with almsgiving; specifically the offerings of yarn, linen, hair, and skins. These types of offerings, given by those who could not afford to bring jewelry, precious metals, or livestock,

4. Neusner, *Judaism and Christianity*, 62.

5. Ibid., 63; Grissom, "Chrysostom and the Jews," 3.

6. Maxwell, *Christianization and Communication*, 122.

7. Brown, *Poverty and Leadership*, 17–18.

8. *In Gen. hom.* 31 (PG 53:282–92; trans., Hill, *Homilies on Genesis*, 2:251).

9. Ibid. (53:282–92; 2:252–53).

were in the same vein as the widow's mites in Luke 21:1–4.[10] John often pointed out the Pauline uses of the Torah, especially concerning the rights of the clergy and their rightful claim to a share of alms that were received.[11]

In terms of the writings, John used a number of illustrations. Job, for instance, was commonly used as an example of a virtuous man of God who was generous before and after tragedy struck his household. Job was an example of God's expectation of almsgiving and His ability to bring about positive results in tragic circumstances.[12] John preached a number of homilies on the Psalms while in Antioch, which have been compiled into two English volumes translated by Robert C. Hill.[13] In his commentary on Psalm 110, John expounded on the practice of almsgiving by stating that God has commanded it as a result of injustice. He used the illustration of a large fish that swallows many smaller fish, reminding his congregation that the accumulation of wealth almost always comes at the expense of others, especially the poor.[14]

John also illustrated the biblical command to practice almsgiving from nearly all of the Major and Minor Prophets. On more than one occasion, he used the poor widow of Sidon who extended alms in the form of hospitality to the prophet Elijah (1 Chr 17:10).[15] He linked the prophets

10. *In Heb. hom.* 32.3 (PG 63:224; NPNF 1.14:744).

11. *In Matt. hom.* 30.2 (PG 57:365; NPNF 1.10:279); *In 1 Cor. hom.* 21 (Field, *Sancti Patris*, 241–58; trans., Mayer and Allen, *John Chrysostom*, 168–76; PG 61:169–80; NPNF 1.12:167–73); Brown, *Poverty and Leadership*, 17–18. In these examples, John connected the idea of "muzzling the ox" with its originating reference in Deuteronomy 25:4.

12. *De Stat. hom.* 1.9–10 (PG 49:29; NPNF 1.09:368); *In Matt. hom.* 13.4 (PG 57:213–14; NPNF 1.10:121); *In 1 Cor. hom.* 24.4 (PG 61:204; NPNF 1.12:196). Job provided John with a unique example, for Job was able to live a life that was pleasing to God in wealth and in poverty. Job was able to maintain the virtues of humility, moderation, and generosity in almsgiving in spite of his economic situation. His virtue made him a prime target for Satan, and yet Job emerged victorious, maintaining his faithfulness to God.

13. Hill, *On the Psalms*, 2 vols. In Hill's translation, volume one contains homilies from Psalms 4–13 and 44–50. Volume two contains homilies from Psalms 109–50, but excludes Psalm 119. John did preach and teach from Psalm 119, and many of his famous liturgies included references to Psalm 119. See *In Phil. hom.* 15.5 (PG 62:294; NPNF 1.13:347), *In Col. hom.* 9.2 (PG 62:363; NPNF 1.13:413); *In 1 Tim. hom.* 14.4 (PG 62:576; NPNF 113:611); *In 2 Tim hom.* 9.3 (PG 62:656; NPNF 1.13:687).

14. *In Ps. hom.* 110.3 (PG 58:281; trans., Hill, *On the Psalms*, 2:12–35); Kelly, *Golden Mouth*, 98.

15. *In Rom. hom.* 7.9 (PG 60:453; NPNF 1.11:519); *Eleem. et Dec. Vir.* 2 (PG 49:294; trans., Christo, *ORA*, 33); *De Incomp. hom.* 8 (PG 49:770–71; trans., Harkins, *Incomprehensible*, 218). In most cases, John compared the widow of Sidon directly to the widow

such as Isaiah, Jeremiah, and Ezekiel directly to Moses and David, classifying their work as an emulation of the virtue of such patriarchs.[16] The most commonly used passage concerning almsgiving from the Old Testament comes from the book of Daniel. Daniel admonishes King Nebuchadnezzar by saying, "Therefore, O king, may my advice be pleasing to you: break away now from your sins by doing righteousness and from your iniquities by showing mercy (ἐλεημοσύνην) to the poor, in case there may be a prolonging of your prosperity."[17] John referred to this verse on a number of occasions, especially regarding the idea of redemptive almsgiving, which will be discussed further in chapter 7.[18]

John also used the apocryphal writings of the LXX throughout his homilies, in every case treating them as scriptures. He alluded to the Maccabean martyrs and the books of the Maccabees, most often referring to the virtue of the martyrs and the Maccabean teaching that the poor were a sacramental altar on which one might present his or her sacrifices to God.[19] John's references to the Maccabees are unique because for years he clashed with the Maccabean cult in Antioch that was operating under a Judeo-Christian banner.[20] He also referred to the books of Tobit and Sirach, on occasion, most often concerning the practice of almsgiving and

---

who gave two copper mites in Luke 21:1–4. Both were continual examples of those who gave alms despite their poverty.

16. *In Matt. hom.* 2.3 (PG 57:27; NPNF 1.10:24); 55.6 (PG 58:548; NPNF 1.10:466).

17. Daniel 4:27 (NASB). It is important to note that, in the Masoretic text, this verse appears as 4:24. For uses by other early Christian authors, see Garrison, *Redemptive Almsgiving*, 46–70.

18. *In Rom. hom.* 25.6 (PG 60:635; NPNF 1.11:705); *In 1 Cor. hom.* 23.4 (PG 61:194; NPNF 1.12, 187); *In Tit. hom.* 6.2 (PG 62.698; NPNF 1.13:727). See also Garrison, *Redemptive Almsgiving*, 51. In more than one case, John compared Daniel's words to King Nebuchadnezzar with Jesus' words to the rich young man in Matthew 19.

19. 2 Maccabees 2:19, 8:8; Sirach 1:12, 14. All references to the Apocrypha are from Metzger, et. al, *The Apocrypha*. The idea of the poor as altar will be discussed later in this chapter and a "sacramental" interpretation will be offered in Chapter 8.

20. Joslyn-Siemiatkoski, *Christian Memories of the Maccabean Martyrs*, 42–50. At least three sermons on the Maccabean martyrs have survived [*De Macc.* 1 (PG 50:617–24; trans., Mayer and Neil, *Cult of the Saints*, 135–46); *De Macc.* 2 (PG 50:623–26; trans., Mayer and Neil, *Cult of the Saints*, 147–54); *De Eleaz.* (PG 63:523–30; trans., Mayer and Neil, *Cult of the Saints*, 119–34)], each preached from a Christological perspective that refused to limit the martyrs' commitment only to the Torah. It is important to note that Siemiatkoski argues John misinterpreted much of the Maccabean story, intentionally skewing applications to support his condemnation of Judaizing in Antioch.

its soteriological implications.[21] During the reign of Constantine I, the Mishnah emerged as a key Hebrew text, used by both Jews and Christians.[22] As mentioned in chapter 2, John's view and practice of almsgiving were influenced by the Mishnaic tradition of the Judeo-Christian Roman world.

HOMILIES ON MATTHEW—
COUNTER-CULTURAL GENEROSITY

The largest part of John Chrysostom's theological exposition on the practice of almsgiving comes from his commentaries and sermons on the Gospels of Matthew, Luke, and John. While the majority of argumentation throughout these texts is meant for expositional reading, there are a number of practical elements referenced. John's homilies on Luke are nearly all concerning the Parable of the Rich Man and Lazarus (Luke 16:19–31), which will be discussed in the next chapter, and the continual use of Luke 11:41, which uses the word ἐλεημοσύνη in reference to purification needed among the Pharisees. In John's homilies on the Gospel of John, nearly every reference to almsgiving is regarding soteriology, which will be discussed in chapter 7. Of that which has survived, John Chrysostom's most comprehensive biblical teaching on almsgiving came from his homilies on the Gospel of Matthew.

John's homilies on Matthew were delivered in Antioch, most likely near the end of his tenure as pastor. These sermons represent some of his most important instructions concerning the poor and the proper treatment thereof. His ecclesiology in these homilies may be considered counter-cultural in that he teaches a more inclusive approach to the makeup of the church, particularly with regard to societal categories. This inclusiveness emphasized the idea that the poor, through what Leyerle aptly identifies

21. Specifically Tobit 4:7–11; Sirach 3:30, 29:7–13. For examples of usage of Tobit in John's homilies, see *De Stat. hom.* 6.7 (PG 49:92; NPNF 1.09:432); *In Phil. hom.* 4.5 (PG 62:212; NPNF 1.13:277–78); *In Heb. hom.* 9.4 (PG 63:81; NPNF 1.14:594). For Sirach, see *In Matt. hom.* 51.5 (PG 58:517; NPNF 1.10:437); *In Gen hom.* 31 (PG 53:282–92; Hill, trans., *Hom. on Gen*, 2:253–54); *In Heb. hom.* 9.4 (PG 63:81; NPNF 1.14:594). See also De Wet, "John Chrysostom's Use of the Book of Sirach," 1–10.

22. Neusner, *Judaism and Christianity*, 130; Neusner, *Torah*. See also Simon, *Verus Israel*, 115–17. Simon argues that the Mishnah did not enjoy such a favorable position with Christians just after this period. He cites the example of Jerome, who later in life joined other Christians who considered the Mishnah to be nothing more than a human commentary on the Hebrew Scriptures.

as a process of "mutuality" and exchange, have assets of value to offer the wealthy and middle class.[23] He also spent a great deal of time dealing with the extremes and abuses of wealth among Christians who were part of the churches in Antioch. One will find nearly every recurrent theological and ecclesiological theme of John's lifelong expositions included within these homilies.

The Sermon on the Mount and Unity through Diversity

According to Rhee, churches of the second and third centuries experienced a certain degree of demographic diversity within their ranks as the wealthy and the poor worshiped together.[24] In his commentaries regarding the Sermon on the Mount, John pointed out that Jesus' audiences were made up of all kinds of people, regardless of social distinction. In this way, Jesus addressed his main message toward every type of person so that all might receive the command to participate in the kingdom of God together.[25] Almsgiving is mentioned throughout John's discussions on Matthew 5–7. Two passages in particular, 6:1–4 and 6:19–21, contain the greater part of the content on the subject. In the first passage, Jesus implores his audience to avoid doing good works for the praise of others. He exhorts each person to strive toward giving generously while attracting as little attention as possible. This passage represents the only non-Lukan use of the word ἐλεημοσύνη in the New Testament.

John equated the good works or acts of mercy of which Jesus spoke with almsgiving. He preached that Jesus' teaching was more about the condition of one's heart and intentions as opposed to a legalistic view that required practicing almsgiving in secret. "For," according to John, "it is not on every occasion altogether possible to do it secretly. For this reason, setting you free from this restraint, He defines both the penalty and the reward not by the result of the action but by the intention of the doer."[26] He contrasted the concept of almsgiving with prayer and fasting, arguing that it is possible

23. Leyerle, "John Chrysostom on Almsgiving," 42–43.

24. Rhee, *Loving the Poor*, 59.

25. *In Matt. hom.*, 15.1 (PG 57:223; NPNF 1.10:130–31); Maxwell, *Christianization and Communication*, 73.

26. *In Matt. hom.* 19.1 (PG 57:274; NPNF 1.10:184).

to do the latter two in secret while the former must sometimes take place in view of others.[27]

Giving to the poor to gain attention and glory for oneself was more than a spiritual issue for John. The manner in which this was being done had grievous implications for the poor in Antioch. Apparently, some were giving alms sparingly to the poor and in such a way that the person's poverty would see no end. John believed this was done so that the rich could continue to receive praise and respect for their aid of the poor by purposely perpetuating poverty and the need for assistance. He quantified this type of giving as the true definition of the word hypocrite according to Jesus, "for [their] mask was of mercy, but [their] spirit was of cruelty and inhumanity. For they do it, not because they pity their neighbors, but that they themselves may enjoy credit."[28]

In the second passage, Matthew 6:19–21, John interpreted Jesus' discussion on the differences between treasures on earth and heaven to be directly related to spending. Using one's resources for the purposes of almsgiving for the poor was an investment, "so they will not be spent; and what is more, so far from being spent, they will actually receive a greater increase." By this, John meant two things. First, that which is spent on the poor will bring about good results for life on earth, both for the giver and receiver. Second, more will be "added unto" that which is given once heaven is reached. He interpreted Jesus' meaning by adding, "For [Jesus] said not only, 'If you give alms, it is preserved': but He threatened also the opposite thing, that if you do not give, it perishes."[29]

John saw the demographic inclusiveness of his congregations as a reflection of Jesus' audiences. John mentions this idea in his comments regarding the Parable of the Sower in Matthew 13: "Now these things He said, manifesting that He discoursed to all without grudging. For as the sower makes no distinction in the land submitted to him, but simply and indifferently casts his seed; so He Himself too makes no distinction of rich and poor, of wise and unwise, of slothful or diligent, of brave or cowardly; but He discourses unto all . . ."[30] If Jesus, who was Lord of all, did not show

27. Ibid., 20.1 (57:287; 1.10:198).

28. Ibid., 19.1 (57:274–75; 1.10:185).

29. Ibid., 20.2 (57:288; 1.10:200); See also Leyerle, "John Chrysostom on Almsgiving," 38.

30. *In Matt. hom.* 45.3 (PG 57:467; NPNF 1.10:387)

partiality toward those who sought to receive his message, neither should exclusivity dominate the Antiochene congregations.

In his homily on Matthew 18 concerning causing "little ones" to stumble, John addressed the congregation regarding the πένητες in Antioch and their inclusion in the churches. He instructed his congregations to treat blacksmiths, shoemakers, and plowmen with respect because of their hard work. He also reminded the workers that they were valuable to society by way of contribution and the encouragement of moderate lifestyles.[31] He empathized with the πένητες and the difficulties they encountered in their dealings with the Antiochene elites. His venerations of those who worked hard for a living were intended to encourage laborers while admonishing the elite to show respect and treat "social inferiors as religious equals."[32] John also helped to create situations where the wealthy and middle class members of his congregations were forced to interact with those of the lower classes. For example, the working poor were not only welcome in the churches, but many were actually put into service around the properties of the churches at times when they could not find employment.[33]

Some scholars have argued that John advocated aggressive evangelistic almsgiving in order to develop a primarily Christian worldview in Antioch, which would result in a commonality of faith that surpassed all Greco-Roman social distinctions.[34] Missiologists have compared the idea of worldview to a pair of glasses, or a lens, through which people view themselves, the world, and everything else as they relate to each other.[35] In John's view, if the churches were successful in the missionary effort to build unity and solidarity among believers while meeting the needs of the poor, the Antiochene worldview would forever be shaped by the gospel. Christian faith would eventually be the main topic of conversation among

---

31. Ibid., 59.4 (58:579;1.10:495).

32. Maxwell, *Christianization and Communication*, 72.

33. Brown, *Poverty and Leadership*, 63. Brown classifies many of the poor who worked in and around the churches as former slaves, who were skilled in various trades or labor activities.

34. Maxwell, *Christianization and Communication*, 144–47; Leyerle, "John Chrysostom on Almsgiving," 47; Sandwell, *Religious Identity*, 206, 212. Sandwell considers John's ministry a failure in terms of bringing about such unity because of the fact that social divisions continued in the increasingly Christianized Eastern Empire into the Middle Ages.

35. Geisler, "Philosophical Perspectives," 241–58; Hesselgrave, *Communicating Christ Cross-Culturally*, 196–99; Hesselgrave, "Fitting Third-World Believers," 215–22.

every person in Antioch, "at home, and at the market, at table, and at night, and . . . even in [one's] dreams."[36] John's teaching on diversity and a Christian worldview need not preclude social equality, however.[37] On the contrary, John maintained the importance of Christian relationships above any other, so that the unity of the church would be a priority over social advancement.[38]

Matthew 25 and God's Role in Almsgiving

In John's view, there were perhaps no greater words concerning the command to practice almsgiving than those of Jesus in the parables and instructions found in Matthew 25. John called the chapter "This Sweetest Passage," and used it throughout his homilies and commentaries on scriptures concerning almsgiving.[39] He began by combining the parables contained within the chapter with that of the faithful servant in Matthew 24:44–51. John taught that each of the four parables was arguing the same point in different ways: that one cannot be saved unless he is willing to demonstrate "diligence in almsgiving, and about helping our neighbor by all means which we are able to use . . . spend[ing] abundantly his goods upon the needy."[40] The faithful servants, prepared virgins, and sheep were proven worthy not only by their faith, but by their actions. For John, these parables could only be understood in light of the verses that followed, about which John had much to say throughout his ministry career.

To this day, Matthew 25:31–46 remains the key Christian text concerning almsgiving. According to Brändle, "Matt. 25:31–46 is the integrative force behind the central thoughts of John's theology."[41] Within this famous text, Jesus offers six key principles of caring for "the least of these," from which the most traditional New Testament categories of alms have been taken. They are: 1) Feeding the hungry, 2) Offering drink to the thirsty, 3) Showing hospitality to strangers, 4) Providing clothes for those who

---

36. *In Matt. hom.* 88.3 (PG 58:779; NPNF 1.10:703).

37. Holman, *God Knows*, 14.

38. *In Matt. hom.* 59.5 (PG 58:581; NPNF 1.10:496–97).

39. Ibid., 79.1 (58:718; 1.10:639); Brändle, "This Sweetest Passage," 127; Kelly, *Golden Mouth*, 98.

40. *In Matt. hom.* 78.1 (PG 58:711; NPNF 1.10:634).

41. Brändle, "This Sweetest Passage," 136.

need them,[42] 5) Looking after those who are sick, and 6) Visiting those who are in prison. While the interpretive crux of the recipients, "the least of these brothers of mine," is heavily debated, God's concern for the physical provision of every basic human need is clear.[43]

For John, this passage was at the same time practical, ecclesiological, and eschatological. From a practical standpoint, John asserted the relative ease of the actions which Jesus venerates. Jesus did not ask to be set free from prison or healed from sickness. He only asked that someone might visit him. Jesus did not demand an expensive table with a lavish meal, only necessary food such as bread. He did not ask for expensive clothing, but maintained willingness to be clothed only with supplication.[44] John's point was that almsgiving, according to "This Sweetest Passage," is not something that is meant to put unnecessary burden on the giver. Almsgiving is measureable in the sense that virtually anyone can do it by providing for the basic necessities of their fellow man. Doing so is to provide vicariously for Jesus.

From an ecclesiological point of view, John used this text to illustrate further the idea that the systems of the church, while initiated by God, are useless if they fail those in need. It is senseless, he argued, to honor Christ's body in the church, or at the Lord's Table, if one ignores His body represented by the living poor. To bring "silken garments" to the altar while forgoing Jesus' command to clothe the poor was fruitless. He used the Apostle Peter as an example on account of his willingness to honor Christ in nearly every way except allowing his feet to be washed. According to John, if one is truly to honor Christ he must do so in the ways that Christ himself commanded. This was done best through almsgiving and care for the poor. He offers yet another analogy of the Lord's Table:

> Since God has no need at all of golden [cups], but of golden souls. And these things I say, not forbidding such offerings to be provided; but requiring you, together with them, and before them, to give alms. For He accepts indeed the former, but much more the latter. For in the one the giver alone is profited, but in the other the receiver also. Here the act seems to be a ground even of ostentation; but there, all is mercifulness and love to man. For what is

42. Blomberg, *Matthew*, 377. Blomberg points out that the Greek word γυμνός (*gymnos*), which is sometimes translated "naked," is best understood as meaning "ill-clad," or often one who is wearing only an undergarment.

43. Ibid.; Hagner, *Matthew* 14–28, 744.

44. *In Matt. hom.* 79.1 (PG 58:718; NPNF 1.10:639–40).

the profit, when His table indeed is full of golden cups, but He perishes with hunger? First fill Him, since He is hungry, and then abundantly deck out His table also. Do you make Him a cup of gold, while you do not give Him a cup of cold water? And what is the profit? Do you furnish His table with cloths bespangled with gold, while to Him you do not afford even the necessary covering? And what good comes of it?[45]

For John, "This Sweetest Passage" was also eschatological. The poor represented an investment that would, above any other, bring about eternal results.[46] According to Brown,

For a later Roman preacher, such as Chrysostom, this passage amounted to a statement of "continued redemption" offered by Christ, first, as the historical Jesus, on the Cross, and now, in the present, through the poor. To approach the poor with mercy was to receive mercy from Christ, who lingered among them. John repeatedly urged this theme upon his hearers.[47]

John closed his main homily on this passage by reminding his audience that almsgiving is redemptive (Luke 11:41),[48] more pleasing to God than sacrifices (Hos 6:6), and a doorway to heaven (Acts 10:4).[49] The blessings applied to both giver and receiver, therefore, had unseen ramifications that only God could accomplish.

45. Ibid., 50.4 (PG 50:508–9; NPNF 1.10:428–29).

46. Leyerle, "John Chrysostom on Almsgiving," 38.

47. Brown, *Poverty and Leadership*, 95.

48. The idea of redemption through the mercy toward was a key tenet of the Social Gospel movement. This mentality oversimplifies Jesus' teaching in Matthew 25, failing to take into account the wider context of New Testament soteriology. See Dorrien, *Social Ethics in the Making*, 1, 89, 103–4, 319. Dorrien argues that leaders of the Social Gospel movement, such as Rauschenbusch, taught consistently that God intended salvation to be as social as it was personal. See also Rauschenbusch, *Christianizing the Social Order*, 464–65. Rauschenbusch argued that salvation could be realized on earth through a realization of "the Kingdom of God, the perfect life of the race . . . the moral forces of progress . . . [and} social solidarity." He goes on to say, "To concentrate our efforts of personal salvation, as orthodoxy has done, or on soul culture, as liberalism has done, comes close to refined selfishness." Several other aspects of "redemptive almsgiving" will be discussed in chapter 7.

49. *In Matt. hom.* 50.4 (PG 58:510; NPNF 1.10:430); Brändle, "This Sweetest Passage," 135; Brown, *Poverty and Leadership*, 95. Both Brändle and Brown point out that John referred to Matthew 25 as the major reference for his homily on almsgiving found in *In Rom. hom.* 16 (PG 60:547–48; NPNF 1.11:625–27).

Matthew 25 was also foundational for John's teaching concerning God's inception of and participation in the missionary work of the church through the practice of almsgiving. Almsgiving is not only a command because of its scriptural underpinnings, but also because God has chosen to be involved in the practice. John described God's active role in almsgiving as twofold. God is the creator and initiator of almsgiving and He is the ultimate recipient of almsgiving. As the author of almsgiving, God was clearly the most generous and skilled in the practice. John compared God to a master gardener, fisherman, or wrestling coach. "If," he said, "one is learning to be a wrestler, to whom does one look. . . . For tell me, who has the skill of almsgiving? Plainly, it is God, who has made known the thing, who knows it best of all, and practices it without limit."[50] John, therefore, joined other patristic voices whose ethical teachings concerning almsgiving were based on a divine model of φιλανθρόπια.[51] As Rhee notes, "Ultimately, charity is a fundamental marker for Christian identity because it is an imitation of God's character—generosity and φιλανθρόπια."[52]

As the recipient of almsgiving, God shares His own dignity with the poor who are meant to be seen in His likeness. As the Gospel writers and the Apostle Paul had written, God descended and became flesh so that He might engage and be engaged by humanity. In this sense, the poor lived in the same state as God had lived in the flesh of Jesus Christ. When a believer practices almsgiving to meet the needs of a person who is poor, as described in Matthew 25, he or she is in fact giving and blessing God as if providing for Christ Himself.[53]

The Language of Mutuality and Exchange

John's teaching and practices concerning almsgiving were contrary to a number of theological and cultural presuppositions concerning charity. Despite his emphasis on the desperate plight of the poor and their physical circumstances, John reminded his congregations that even the helpless had valuable gifts to return to the almsgiver. Much like his counterpart in the Western Empire, Augustine, John saw almsgiving as a transaction between

50. *In Matt. hom.* 71 (PG 58:665; NPNF 1.10:586).

51. Constantelos, "The Hellenic Background," 198.

52. Rhee, *Loving the Poor*, 178.

53. *In Matt. hom.*79 (PG 58:718; NPNF 1.10:639–40); *In 2 Tim. hom.* 6.3 (PG 62:633; NPNF 1.13:667–68).

the rich and the poor which took place materially and spiritually.[54] John argued the wealthy needed the poor as much as the reverse was true. He advocated a "new Christian community based on mutuality," that included a system of "gift and countergift."[55] The countergift, in this case, would be a reward to be granted in this life or the next.

Ecclesiastical and philosophical teaching that preceded John defined the directional nature of almsgiving in such a way that the giver was not to expect anything in return from the recipients.[56] The exception to this perspective would be relationships of patronage, as discussed in the chapter 3.[57] Consider this statement from Lactantius, "We must therefore by all means keep in mind, that the hope of receiving in return must be altogether absent from the duty of showing mercy; for the reward of this work and duty must be expected from God alone."[58]

The unilateral understanding of almsgiving was compounded by the economic argument that giving to the poor was a waste of resources on depreciating objects that would produce no returns on one's investment.[59] John anticipated these types of objections from his congregations and addressed them in selected homilies. First, he encouraged his audience to give responsibly by acknowledging that some had become destitute because they gave to widows out of their own poverty and lost the ability to produce their own income.[60] Second, John confronted those who argued alms were wasted on the uneducated poor and argued the poor were devoid of ability to improve their social standing. He reminded them that the Apostles were described in similar ways; as unschooled and rhetorically untrained men.

54. Augustine, *Ench.* 19.72–73 (CCSL 46:49–114; trans., Harbert, *Enchiridion*, 315–17); Cardman, "Poverty and Wealth as Theater," 171. Augustine, who also supplemented many of the biblical categories of those who receive alms, listed matters of the heart as the greatest giving of alms. Examples included forgiveness and love for enemies. Almsgiving was in fact an external representation of an ongoing, internal transformation. This idea, however, goes as far back as Shepherd of Hermas, where the language of both material and spiritual exchange is present. See Osiek, *Shepherd of Hermas*, 161–64.

55. Leyerle, "John Chrysostom on Almsgiving," 42–43.

56. Rhee, *Loving the Poor*, 150; Heim, "Almsgiving," 267–69. Heim cites the philosophical tradition of Seneca, who also described charity as "unilateral" when performed at its best. See Seneca, *De Benef.* 4.29.1 (*Dial. Lib.* 2:1ff; trans., Griffin and Inwood, *On Benefits*, 104).

57. See Rhee, *Loving the Poor*, 14, 179–82.

58. Lactantius, *Divin. Instit.*, 6.12 (PL 6:676; ANF 7:264).

59. Leyerle, "John Chrysostom on Almsgiving," 40.

60. *De Stat. hom.* 1.10 (PG 49:30; NPNF 1.09:369).

Nevertheless, Jesus was willing to place his church into their hands.[61] Jesus had already rendered his decision on the eternal value of the economically and socially challenged.

Mayer argues that John emphasized the benefits received by the alms-giver because his typical audience equated gifts to the poor with "a one-way street that results in deficit."[62] The archetypal Hellenistic attitude among the wealthy toward the poor was one of rank. The poor remained a local version of the βάρβαροι (*barbaroi*), or those who were not truly participants in Greco-Roman culture.[63] In essence, even the resident poor were considered to be of the same standing as boorish foreigners. For the wealthy who made up the churches in Antioch, it was difficult to filter their learned, shared class behavior through their identity in Christ. As an integral part of the churches' mission in Antioch, the practice of almsgiving ran the risk of becoming "a movement from the superior to the inferior."[64] For this reason, John's view of almsgiving was based on "lateral relationships," as opposed to unilateral dependency, that were to exist inside and outside of the Christian community.[65] The kingdom of God includes those of all social strata, each with something to offer others, regardless of means. If the churches were able to build relationships through this type of giving, the Christian mission would be one step closer to achieving unity in diversity through mutual giving and receiving.[66]

According to John, those who give alms are giving directly to Christ to the praise and glory of the Father. Alms are to be given according to Jesus' instructions concerning prayer and offerings, which at times means first being reconciled to a brother or sister in Christ (Matt 5:23–24). Therefore,

---

61. *In 1 Cor. hom.* 3.4 (PG 61:27–28; NPNF 1.12: 23–24); Leyerle, "John Chrysostom on Almsgiving," 42.

62. Mayer, "Poverty and Generosity," 154–58. Mayer argues that many Christians were more apt to support ascetics and others who had chosen the way of voluntary poverty because they seemed more capable of making a reciprocal contribution to the good of society. The upstanding citizens of Antioch viewed voluntary poverty as morally praiseworthy, while conjunctural and structural poverty were "socially destabilizing and negative."

63. BGAD, 166; Bosch, *Transforming Mission*, 193.

64. Bosch, *Transforming Mission*, 193.

65. Holman, *God Knows*, 43, 130. Holman argues that John, along with the Cappadocian fathers and Cyprian, emphasized giving outside of Christian contexts idea in order to counter the esoteric nature of giving within the church. She classifies the idea that Christians were only asked to give alms within Christian circles to be fallacious.

66. Leyerle, "John Chrysostom on Almsgiving," 42; Sitzler, "Identity," 475–76; Cardman, "Poverty and Wealth as Theater," 170.

when alms are placed into the hands of the poor, an exchange takes place which can result in reconciliation between God and man, wealthy and poor, grantor and debtor.[67] As long as the poor exist within reach of the local church, the body of Christ will have the opportunity to experience God's blessings through almsgiving; in this life and in the life to come.[68] John argued this very thing during his sermon *De Eleem.*: "Likewise, God appointed almsgiving not only for the needy to be nourished but also for the providers to receive benefit, and much more so for the latter than for the former."[69] Reward was understood from an eschatological standpoint, but could also be temporal in the form of joy, friendship, and community.[70]

The ideas of mutuality and exchange are also emphasized in John's insistence that the poor were also expected to give alms. Because some had "used poverty as an excuse," he turned once again to the poor widow of Sidon and the widow who gave two mites in Luke 21:1–4 as examples of such giving:

> "I do not say this only to the rich," he says, "but also to the poor; not only to the free but also to slaves; not only to men but also to women." Let no one remain unaccomplished in this ministration. Let no one refrain from sharing in the gain; rather, let everyone contribute. Certainly, do not even permit poverty to become a hindrance to this contribution. And even if you are ten thousand times poor, you are not poorer than that widow who emptied herself of all her property.[71]

The poor might feel ashamed to give alms because their gifts are of little value, but John asserted that even the smallest gift of alms has value. In his teaching, everyone was required to give alms, without regard for personal worth or property ownership. The only requirement was "to give

---

67. *In Matt. hom.* 15.5 (PG 57:228–30; NPNF 1.10:136–38), 16.9 (57:251–52; 1.10:160–61); Cardman, "Poverty and Wealth as Theater," 171; Sitzler, "Identity," 475–76. Sitzler describes the vocabulary of these homilies as a spiritual usage of the language of "lending and banking."

68. *De Stat. hom.* 2.6 (PG 49:43; NPNF 1.09:382).

69. *De Eleem.* 4 (PG 51:266; trans., Christo, *ORA*, 141).

70. Leyerle, "John Chrysostom on Almsgiving," 37–38.

71. *De Eleem.* 3 (PG 51:265–66; trans., Christo, *ORA*, 139). See also *Eleem. et Dec. Vir.* 2 (PG 49:294; trans., Christo, *ORA*, 33); *Quod Ne.* 6 (PG 52:466; NPNF 1.09:297); *In 1 Tim. hom.* 14.1 (PG 62:572; NPNF 1.13:607). In the latter sermon from 1 Timothy, John exhorts each person associated with the church—from the bishop, to the widows, to the poor, to participate in almsgiving through various acts of charity and hospitality.

with joy and to believe that you receive more than you give."[72] If all believers participated in the practice of almsgiving, the Christian community would never have to worry about its level of respect throughout the rest of the empire.[73]

Excess

The hollowness of vanity was a major topic of John's preaching, for which he chastised both the elite and the middle class citizens of Antioch. The issue of excess, which John often describes as κενοδοξία (*kenodoxia*), or "vainglory," is seen throughout his homilies on the New Testament scriptures and in one of his lesser known works, *De Inan.*, which is often titled in English *On Vain Glory and How Parents Should Bring Up Children*, which will be discussed briefly in the later discussion on the book of Acts.[74] John's discourses on excess are found mostly in his homilies on Matthew, although this theme is also present in his homilies *De Laz.*, his homilies and commentaries on the Gospel of John, and in selected teachings on Pauline letters.

On more than one occasion, John used clothing as a visible example of overindulgence throughout the cities in which he preached. The typical clothing ensemble in the later Roman Empire consisted of a tunic, a mantle or coat, a belt, coverings, and some type of shoe or sandal.[75] John addressed some women in his congregation specifically about their obsessions with fancy clothing that was laden with gold and precious stones. Gaudy sandals, of a style that John described as "ornamented and glittering," had become popular for both women and men.[76] He denounced such vanity as being without profit, and exhorted them, "clothe yourselves instead with almsgiving."[77] Maxwell argues these exhortations concerning the vanity of apparel, which called the audience to empathize with the destitute who watched the wealthy gallivant in front of them, were attempts to motivate through guilt.[78] This must not necessarily be the case, however, as one will

---

72. *De Eleem.* 4 (PG 51:266–67; trans., Christo, *ORA*, 142).

73. Finn, *Almsgiving*, 214.

74. Kelly, *Golden Mouth*, 86–87; *De Inan.* (SC 188:64–196). For a modern English translation, see Laistner, *On Vainglory*, 75–122.

75. Hamel, *Poverty and Charity in Roman Palestine*, 58.

76. *In Matt. hom.* 49.4 (PG 58:501; NPNF 1.10:421).

77. Ibid., 89.3 (58:783; 1.10:709).

78. Maxwell, *Christianization and Communication*, 71.

see that John used such imagery in order to help his congregations to see the poor, who were so often ignored, so that some would be motivated to appropriate their surplus for the purpose of almsgiving.

Greed also preyed on the youth in the city, many of whom John accused of becoming servants to the rich in order to gain benefits from their wealth. Many of the youth were also into glamour, as John described the use of gold in the "decking out of their shoes, on their trailing garments, on the dressing of their hair."[79] Conversely, the lack of footwear by the beggars was a clear evidence of their low standing in society, as footwear was itself a sign of status.[80] For this reason, John saw the needless accentuation of one's shoes as tantamount to a slap in the face of those who had nothing to wear on their feet.

John also considered the disproportionate luxury of many Antiochene homes, some of which were owned by his congregants, to be a form of κενοδοξία. If the wealthy were giving "in proportion to their substance," they would not be so eager to "build houses of two and three stories."[81] John believed this type of residential investment was fruitless in terms of Christian living. John sought to demonstrate that almsgiving, in its nature, practice, and results, had the potential to be a better representation of earthly life in its fullness than any other human expression. The beauty of almsgiving surpassed all degrees of aestheticism associated with the carnal desires of κενοδοξία:

> . . . let us show how almsgiving is an art, and better than all arts. For if the peculiarity of art is to issue in something useful, and nothing is more useful than almsgiving, very evidently this is both an art, and better than all arts. For it does not make shoes for us, nor does it weave garments, nor build houses that are of clay; but it procures life everlasting, and snatches us from the hands of death, and in either life shows us glorious, and builds the mansions that are in Heaven, and those eternal tabernacles.[82]

For John, the best biblical example concerning the meaninglessness of κενοδοξία, and the dignity of those who were truly classified as the πτωχοί, was the Parable of the Rich Man and Lazarus.

---

79. *In Matt. hom.* 49.7 (PG 58:503; NPNF 1.10:423).

80. Hamel, *Poverty and Charity in Roman Palestine*, 75.

81. *In Matt. hom.* 52.3 (PG 58:522; NPNF 1.10:443.)

82. Ibid., 52.4 (58:523–24; 1.10:444).

6

Engagement and Cooperation

But there was a disciple in Joppa named Tabitha . . . she was full of many good works and acts of almsgiving.

—Acts 9:36

HOMILIES ON LUKE/ACTS

Since the bulk of New Testament teaching concerning ἐλεημοσύνη comes from Lukan writings, it is no surprise that many of John Chrysostom's most important sermons on almsgiving come from Luke-Acts. As has already been demonstrated, John referred to Luke 11:41 on a number of occasions. However, his most important homilies preached directly from the book of Luke are all concerning the Parable of the Rich Man and Lazarus (Luke 16:19–31). In these homilies, John presented the practice of almsgiving as an activity wrought by God in order to provide a context for Christian living, reward, and punishment.[1] No other passage of Scripture more explicitly illustrates John's teachings on the wealthy, the poor, and the role almsgiving played between the two groups than Luke 16:19-31. The basis for John's argument throughout these homilies is summarized in one of his final sermons on the parable: "Nothing tends so much to disturb and scandalize the majority of people as the fact that rich people living in wickedness enjoy great good fortune while righteous people living with virtue

1. Cardman, "Poverty and Wealth as Theater," 171.

are driven to extreme poverty and endure a multitude of other troubles even worse than poverty."[2]

HOMILIES ON THE RICH MAN AND LAZARUS— ENGAGEMENT

John's seven sermons on The Rich Man and Lazarus were preached in Antioch, most likely during the years of 388 and 389 CE. Because of the parable's significance for the churches in Antioch and the fact that they seemed unaltered by its impact, John preached on this passage several times over the period of more than a year.[3] The sermons are highly theological in their content, dealing much more with attitudes of the heart as opposed to practice. The practical aspects of the sermons are clearly implicit, however, as John reviled the rich man most often for his lack of action toward the suffering Lazarus, which revealed the rich man's hardened heart. This portrayal of the rich man was meant to exemplify the attitudes and lack of almsgiving John saw within his own congregations. González argues that while Christian monasticism aligned itself with the poor in the Eastern Empire, the churches had by and large ignored biblical teaching on faith and wealth.[4]

John addressed the middle class and the poor in the homilies, but it was the wealthiest congregants who received the most direct addresses. He confronted their dishonesty concerning almsgiving and their willingness to take advantage of the poor. Despite the overwhelming majority of the middle class in the urbanized empire, the wealthy elite maintained control of the effective power structures leaving the rest of the population at a disadvantage. In Antioch in particular, John noted that some wealthy Christians had been advocating a more stringent and structured system of almsgiving that would require the poor to demonstrate their "worthiness" in order to be eligible to receive alms.[5] Many people within the churches, who depended on their share of alms in seasons of economic distress,

2. *De Laz. hom.* 4.2 (PG 48:1008; trans., Roth, *OWP*, 82).

3. Roth, *OWP*, 10. See also Kalantzis, "Crumbs from the Table," 156–68; Mayer, "John Chrysostom's Use of the Parable of Lazarus and the Rich Man," 45–59.

4. González, *Faith and Wealth*, 166.

5. *De Laz. hom.* 2.6 (PG 48:990; trans., Roth, *OWP*, 53); Cardman, "Poverty and Wealth as Theater," 172.

would be in danger of falling into shallow poverty if their circumstances declined for an extended period of time.[6]

The middle class members were also targets of his reprimands, however. Not only were they the greatest in number within the churches of Antioch, but some had joined the rich in taking advantage of the poorest citizens for their own personal gain. Mayer argues one of the more difficult issues John dealt with in Antioch was members of his congregation who embellished their poverty by comparing themselves to the wealthy, when in fact they did not truly live in shallow or deep poverty. This was not difficult to accomplish when comparing oneself to the wealthier Christians in the churches.[7]

John described the parable in terms of its dual-setting: this life and the afterlife. From the beginning of the first sermon, John made his intentions to present a "condemnation of luxurious living" abundantly clear.[8] From his perspective, the poor were in danger of dying physically, while the wealthy were in danger of dying spiritually.[9]

The Rich Man (πλούσιος [*plousios*])

John provided vivid descriptions of the two main characters in the story. For both characters, the conditions they experienced in the afterlife were direct results of the conditions of this life. The Roman Empire, even late into the fourth century, resembled Jesus' day in many ways. For this reason, John saw this parable as Jesus had intended, with accurate descriptions of imperial life. The lifestyle of the rich man in the parable matches the description of a typical, wealthy, Jewish landowner of the first century.[10] Many of these landowners were known for being among the εὐεργετές who practiced φιλανθρόπια in very public ways.[11] Brown refers to the existence

---

6. Brown, *Poverty and Leadership*, 48–49.

7. Mayer, "John Chrysostom: Extraordinary Preacher, Ordinary Audience," 123.

8. *De Laz. hom.* 1.5 (PG 48:970; trans., Roth, *OWP*, 20).

9. González, *Faith and Wealth*, 209.

10. Hamel, *Poverty and Charity in Roman Palestine*, 9–23.

11. Brown, *Poverty and Leadership*, 4. See also Mark 12:41–44. This is a parallel passage to the aforementioned passage in Luke 21:1–4, in which Jesus praises a poor widow for giving two copper mites of little value into the temple treasury. In the Markan passage, it is noted that the rich were putting in large amounts in what seemed to be a demonstrative fashion.

of several documented gravestones from John's day that extol the departed for being a devoted almsgiver.[12] Nevertheless, John's portrayal of the rich man was intended to reveal that the practice of charity among many of the wealthy and middle class in the churches was nearly indistinguishable from the larger cultural spectrum.

John's characterization of the rich man is one of tranquility and self-centeredness in this life. The rich man had few unpleasant surprises and his daily routine was one of ease. For this reason, the pitiful scene of Lazarus, or any other suffering, left him unaffected.

> For if he did not give alms to this man who was continually pros-trate at his gate, lying before his eyes, whom he had to see every day once or twice or many times as he went in and out, for the man was not lying in the street nor in a hidden or narrow place, but where the rich man whenever he made his entrance or exit was forced unwillingly to see him, if (I say) he did not give alms to this man, who lay in such grievous suffering, and lived in such destitu-tion, or rather for his whole life was troubled by chronic illness of the most serious kind, whom of those he encountered would he ever have been moved to the pity?[13]

Perhaps the most scathing indictment of the rich man is that he knew Lazarus' name, which is clear in Luke 16:24. According to John, the rich man's acknowledgement of Lazarus' existence was a clear indication of his deliberate failure to provide assistance, even from his excess, in order to im-prove Lazarus' quality of life. The lack of noticing the miserable state of the destitute was an inherent problem among the wealthy in the empire. The affluent members of John's congregations were no exception. As a result, John joined the voices of other church leaders who "strove to render these unfortunate fully visible."[14]

According John, the rich man was more than just oblivious concern-ing Lazarus and the needs of the destitute. It was not the case that the rich man merely failed to see Lazarus. On the contrary, he had chosen not to see Lazarus despite the fact that the beggar lay outside his gate every day. The rich man deliberately passed by Lazarus unmoved, "like a stone, shamelessly and mercilessly."[15] John compared the rich man to a cruel beast on a careless

---

12. Ibid., 1.

13. *De Laz. hom.* 1.6 (PG 48:970–71; trans., Roth, *OWP*, 21).

14. Finn, "Portraying the Poor," 144; De Vinne, "The Advocacy of Empty Bellies," iv.

15. *De Laz. hom.* 1.10 (PG 48:976; trans., Roth, *OWP*, 30); Cardman, "Poverty and Wealth as Theater," 163.

path toward destruction: "The rich man had his ship full of merchandise, and it sailed before the wind. But do not be surprised: he was hastening to shipwreck, since he refused to unload his cargo with discretion."[16]

Lazarus

John believed that Jesus' description of Lazarus, for whom Luke uses the word πτωχός, was also meant to be an authentic representation of the poorest in the empire. Libanius described the πτωχοί in Antioch in similar terms. Finn, referring to Libanius, describes the destitute as "the naked and half-naked beggars, some crippled, sitting and standing in the cold in Antioch, probably near the entrance to the baths, who cry out for alms in the hope of receiving a piece of bread or an obol from the passers-by."[17] Finn includes a number of beggars among these groups who came in large numbers to major cities like Antioch, and found their way by one means or another to the most public areas.[18] In the parable itself, Luke used the passive voice to describe Lazarus' placement at the rich man's gate, which would seem to indicate that someone had relocated Lazarus to that spot because of circumstances beyond the beggar's control. Finn describes this scenario as it often played out in real life: "You expect beggars to be found on thoroughfares, at crossroads, because they will search out or be left in places where the large number of people who encounter them increases how much they are likely to receive alms."[19]

The interactions between the rich man and Lazarus in this life were also representative of relations in Antioch as John saw them. For the rich, late antiquity was a time when the lives of beggars did not affect the lives of the rich in significant ways. Most of time, according to Parkin, the servants of the rich kept beggars at a safe distance, which may have contributed to the ignorance of the destitute by the wealthy, even those who were Christians.[20] As mentioned in chapter 5, it is likely that John often struggled

16. *De Laz. hom.* 1.7 (PG 48:972; trans., Roth, *OWP*, 23).

17. Finn, "Portraying the Poor," 141; Libanius, *Orat.* 7. See also Knight, "Luke 16:19–31," 279. Knight argues that the description of Lazarus as a πτωχός might have been intended to convey a dual meaning—one who is both a beggar and one who is in such a state of poverty as to be dependent on others for the rest of his or her life.

18. Finn, *Almsgiving*, 12.

19. Finn, "Portraying the Poor," 141. See also Finn, *Almsgiving*, 19.

20. Parkin, "You Do Him No Service," 68.

against learned class behavior among the Christian elite which would have been an obstacle to their responsibilities of faith. The severed relationship between the two groups inevitably led to mocking the poor, whether explicitly or implicitly.

John described nine chastisements faced by Lazarus, which he believed were also felt by most of the destitute in Antioch.[21] The first three—poverty, illness, and loneliness—were interconnected and resulted in damage to Lazarus' physical and emotional health. The fourth concerned location, as his position at the city gate made him feel ignored, despite the fact that many passed by. Fifth, Lazarus was constantly forced to see others who experienced good fortune.[22] Sixth, Lazarus was close to what he desired, the provision afforded to the rich man, and yet he could not obtain it. Seventh, he could find no other person with whom to compare his misery.[23] Eighth, his confidence in resurrection was waning because his present situation seemed hopeless and final. Finally, like the majority of the poorest citizens in the empire, what was left of Lazarus' reputation was constantly being maligned by others.[24]

The Story—The Eternal Quality of Missional Almsgiving

John's presentation of the parable was in keeping with its intrinsic rhetoric of storytelling, using common images of the Antiochene theater and celebrations to draw the audience into its content.[25] John's ultimate purpose for using this type of imagery was that his congregations might move from

21. *De Laz. hom.* 1.9–11 (PG 48:974–80; trans., Roth, *OWP*, 29–35).

22. Ibid., 1.10 (48:976; 30). According to John, "We all naturally perceive our own misfortunes more acutely by comparison with others' prosperity."

23. Ibid. About this, John commented, "Finding companions in our sufferings either in fact or in story brings a great consolation to those in anguish."

24. Ibid., 1.10, 11(48:977, 979–80; 31–32, 35). John described this type of slander, "For most people, when they see someone in hunger, chronic illness, and the extremes of misfortune, do not even allow him a good reputation, but judge his life by his troubles, and think that he is surely in such misery because of his wickedness." John believed that Lazarus had originally had a very good reputation. According to his interpretation of Hebrews 12:6, John argued that Lazarus' suffering might have been the direct result of his faithfulness to God, who disciplines those whom He loves.

25. Leyerle, *Theatrical Shows*, 12; Cardman, "Poverty and Wealth as Theater," 160–61. Cardman suggests an ulterior motive on behalf of John, which was to discourage his congregation from "frequenting" immoral shows. If they desired to please their senses with the rhetoric of the theater, they could simply attend his sermons, which were free.

an examination of the external distinctions of the characters to the condition of their hearts.[26] Brown argues John taught the parable in such a way that the relationship between rich and poor would be analogous to that of God and the believer. According to Brown, "It was an analogy of brutal simplicity. God was to the believer as the rich man was to the poor. For the poor looked up to the rich man as to a minor 'god' on earth."[27] Every believer's quantity of possessions, whether large or small, originated from God. This made the practice of almsgiving an issue of stewardship. Since each person's goods actually belonged to God they were the property of all, especially the poor.[28]

The parallel relationships between rich and poor, and God and the believer, gave momentum to the eschatological nature of John's homilies on the parable. He argued the suffering of Lazarus improved the quality of his soul, providing a better inheritance in the afterlife. The rich man, on the contrary, failed to take advantage of the opportunity to sacrifice his own well being in order to "reduce the burden of sin" regarding the life to come.[29] John went on to say that it is impossible for a person who habitually indulges the sinful life, lives in utter selfishness, and makes no attempt to control evil desires, to receive honor in the age to come. Therefore, the idea that the wealthy expected the poor to prove that they deserved alms was absurd. The poor were proven worthy by the nature of their suffering on earth. For this reason, the afterlife is the setting in which reward and punishment are reversed.[30] Each person, regardless of economic status, will

26. *De Laz. hom.* 1.12 (PG 48:980; trans., Roth, *OWP*, 37).

27. Brown, *Poverty and Leadership*, 87. Brown notes this type of "social asymmetry" continued into the Middle Ages, as the Eastern Empire assimilated with many parts of Slavic culture. This was true even in language, as the Bulgarian word *bogat*, meaning "wealthy," derived from the root *Bog*, which was their word for God. See also *In 1 Cor. hom.* 30.5 (PG 61:255–56; NPNF 1.12:248–49). In this homily, John noted this very parallel between the rich and the poor and the fact that, even though God had been faithful in His dealings with believers, the rich Christians were failing in their benevolence toward the poor.

28. *De Laz. hom.* 2.4 (PG 48:988; trans., Roth, *OWP*, 50).

29. Ibid., 3.8–10 (48:1002–1006; 67–73).

30. Cardman, "Poverty and Wealth as Theater," 161–72; *In John hom.* 77.4 (PG 59:419; trans., Goggin, *Commentary on St. John*, 2:333–36; NPNF 1.14:427). In this homily on John 15–16, John revisited the Parable of the Rich Man and Lazarus in order to remind his audience of Jesus' words concerning almsgiving and respect for the poor. He linked the parable directly with Matthew 25:31–46, as a reminder of his interpretation that in the age to come the righteous will be separated from the unrighteous in terms of their almsgiving.

be forced to answer for his or her sins in the life to come. The destitute, like Lazarus, will receive a "lighter punishment" on account of their suffering on earth. The rich can also experience a similar degree of forgiveness if their actions toward others are proven virtuous.[31]

Contextual Application—From Encounter to Engagement

Despite the theological primacy within his homilies on the parable, John intended them to be interpreted as a call to action. The first context for action involved "seeing" the poor with one's eyes and heart. According to Cardman, "Chrysostom's preaching on the rich man and Lazarus is strikingly visual, setting scenes, bringing characters before the eyes of his congregation, and drawing the congregation into the story by asking them to *see* it."[32] In his second homily on the parable, he alternated the words ὁράω (*horaō*), "to see or notice," and βλέπω (*blepō*), "to see or perceive," in order to express the difference between observing the poor and discerning their state of need.[33]

For John, the need to recognize the conditions of the poor was valid from both a physical and eternal standpoint, with the difference being the state of each character from this life to the next:

> You saw (εἴδετε) him then at the gate of the rich man; see (βλέπετε) him today in the bosom of Abraham. You saw him licked by dogs; see him carried in triumph by the angels. You saw him in poverty then; see him in luxury now. You saw him in hunger; see him in great abundance. You saw him striving in contest; see him crowned with victory. You saw his sufferings; see his recompense, but you who are rich and you who are poor: the rich to keep you from thinking that wealth is worth anything without virtue; the poor, to keep you from thinking that poverty is evil.[34]

31. *De Laz. hom.* 3.4 (PG 48:997; trans., Roth, *OWP*, 63). See also Gordon, *The Economic Problem*, 121. Gordon argues Augustine and some later monastic movements used this same type of economic language concerning eschatological reward and punishment concerning almsgiving.

32. Cardman, "Poverty and Wealth as Theater," 161–62. See also Brown, *Power and Persuasion*, 71–117; De Vinne, "The Advocacy of Empty Bellies," 88–91. Both Brown and De Vinne discuss this emphasis in John's homilies in the sense that he sought to make "the invisible visible."

33. Cardman, "Poverty and Wealth as Theater," 161–62. For lexical definitions of the verbs referenced, see BDAG, 178–79, 719.

34. *De Laz. hom.* 2.1 (PG 48:981; trans., Roth, *OWP*, 39).

Some scholars are critical of John on this point, arguing he presented the poor more as objects than individuals. In this sense, the poor unwittingly play a dual role as spectacle and means. The former served to benefit the preacher, which was John in this case; the latter to benefit the wealthy, whose desire was to use the poor to improve their status.[35]

John did not, however, only address these homilies to the wealthy and middle class. On the contrary, he used the parable to encourage the poor concerning the merit of their lifestyle and the lack thereof among the wealthy elite. To the rich, John communicated that wealth without virtue is useless and of no value. To the poor, he emphasized their virtue by nature of their poverty.[36] Concerning the disparity between lifestyles, John preached:

> Rather, if we are to tell the truth, the rich man is not the one who has collected many possessions but the one who needs few possessions; and the poor man is not the one who has no possessions but the one who has many desires. We ought to consider this the definition of poverty and wealth. So if you see someone greedy for many things, you should consider him the poorest of all, even if he has acquired everyone's money. If, on the other hand, you see someone with few needs, you should count him the richest of all, even if he has acquired nothing. For we are accustomed to judge poverty and affluence by the disposition of the mind, not by the measure of one's substance. Just as we would not call a person healthy who was always thirsty, even if he enjoyed abundance, even if he lived by rivers and springs (for what use is the luxuriance of water, when the thirst remains unquenchable?), let us do the same in the case of wealthy people, . . . let us not think that they enjoy any abundance. For if one cannot control his own greed, even if he has appropriated everyone's property, how can he ever be affluent? For whoever has no need of others' property but is happy to be self-sufficient is the most affluent of all.[37]

John believed the vile character bred by wealth was worse than any condition of destitution. He reminded the poor that their misfortunes afforded them the privilege of lacking the despicable qualities that defined the character of the wealthy.[38]

---

35. Cardman, "Poverty and Wealth as Theater," 174; Sitzler, "Identity," 477.

36. *De Laz. hom.* 2.1 (PG 48:981; trans., Roth, *OWP*, 39).

37. Ibid., (48:982–83; 40).

38. Hartney, *John Chrysostom and the Transformation of the City*, 167.

He further abated the senseless argument that the poor had something to prove in terms of almsgiving by stating: "Charity is so called because we give it even to the unworthy."[39] He applied this concept with a maritime example which serves as the title of this book:

> The almsgiver is a harbor for those in necessity: a harbor receives all who have encountered shipwreck, and frees from danger; whether they are bad or good or whatever they are who are in danger, it escorts them into its own shelter. So you likewise, when you see on earth the man who has encountered the shipwreck of poverty, do not judge him, do not seek an account of his life, but free him from misfortune.[40]

John considered "seeing" to be the first step in the application of the parable to the situation in fourth century Antioch. Once his congregations learned to see the poor, they were then to engage them through acts of relieving and protecting. John's methods of engagement led to a process of cooperation and evaluation, in order to streamline the practice of almsgiving in the churches for optimal effectiveness.

HOMILIES ON THE BOOK OF ACTS—COOPERATION

John taught that almsgiving had been a priority practice of the earliest churches, beginning in Jerusalem immediately following the ascension of Jesus. Acts 2:46–47 records significant growth in the Jerusalem church that was accompanied by "favor with all the people." This favor, according to John, could only be the result of the church's generosity in almsgiving.[41] Likewise, the success of the Antiochene churches' mission to the poor would rise and fall on the willingness of the believers within to work together.

John classified the ministry activity of the disciples as including the practice of almsgiving, using the example of Acts 3:1–9. In this passage, the apostles Peter and John gave to a crippled beggar who had asked them specifically for ἐλεημοσύνην, even though they had no money to offer. The most important part of this exchange, according to John Chrysostom, was that the Apostles were compelled to act, offering spiritual as opposed to

---

39. *De Laz. hom.* 2.5 (PG 48:989; trans., Roth, *OWP*, 52).

40. Ibid.

41. *In Acts hom.* 7.2 (PG 60:66; NPNF 1.11:71).

physical care.[42] As the church continued to grow and develop new leadership (Acts 6:1–7), John attributed its successes directly to "the virtue of alms and good order."[43] Above any other content in his homilies and commentaries on Acts, however, John used three primary examples of cooperation through almsgiving in the early churches, each of which was already mentioned in the discussion on the New Testament use of almsgiving in chapter 2 and will be discussed further below.

The Collection—Cooperative Giving

The first example is that of the collection taken on behalf of the church in Judea, and specifically that which is mentioned as having come from Antioch (Acts 11:27–30). The collection, which was carried by Paul and Barnabas, was for John a clear example of almsgiving. The purpose of the prophets from Jerusalem having come to Antioch was that the cities and their churches, one the receiver and the other the giver, would benefit from the "fruit of alms."[44] According to Acts 11:29a, "The disciples, as each one was able, decided to provide help." John pointed out that not all were able to give money in large amounts and some could give none. Nevertheless, alms could be given in many forms, including acts of service, physical or emotional support, defending the victims of injustice, and offering one's skills freely as an act of charity.[45] In his sermon *De Eleem.*, John used the same example to ask that a similar collection be taken for the poor in and around Antioch.[46]

John differentiated between resources distributed within the churches and those that went outside of church doors. Those distributed to widows, orphans, and virgins within the church he called διακονία (*diakonia*), or "ministrations," while those given to the poor in the community he called ἐλεημοσύνη.[47] In both cases, John encouraged his congregations to cooperate by giving alms or offering services as needs presented themselves in

42. Ibid., 8.1 (60:69–70; 1.11:77).

43. Ibid., 14.1 (60:113; 1.11:130).

44. Ibid., 25.1 (60:192; 1.11:230).

45. Ibid., 25.4 (60:196–97; 1.11:235).

46. *De Eleem.* 1 (PG 51:261–62; trans., Christo, *ORA*, 132–33). He referred to the work of the church in Antioch (Acts 11), the ministry of Paul and Barnabas among the Gentiles (Gal 2:9–10), and collections taken among churches (1 Cor 16:1–2).

47. *In Acts hom.* 14.1 (PG 60:113; NPNF 1.11:129).

the church or during its outreach. Finn lists a number different forms that
ἐλεημοσύνη might have taken in fourth-century Antioch including coins,
oil, wine, bread, clothing, medical care, and hospitality.[48] John mentioned
clothing, medical, and emotional care as a part of his description of the collection. He asked his members to help clothe the naked, while beseeching
physicians and counselors in his congregations to offer their skills to the
needy as an act of almsgiving.[49]

Providing education was also a form of almsgiving. Libanius, in a letter to the Cappadocian father Basil of Caesarea, mentioned the fact that
most of the poor in Antioch were highly uneducated.[50] As a result, John
used education as a means of evangelism and improvement among the uneducated masses.[51] Augustine also mentioned a number of alternate forms
of almsgiving including food, drink, clothing, hospitality, shelter, visiting
the sick and imprisoned, freeing captives, assisting the weak, leading the
blind, comforting the grieving, healing the sick, directing the wandered,
giving advice to the confused, and supplying the needy. He listed matters of
the heart, such as forgiveness and love for enemies, as some of the greatest
and most important forms of almsgiving.[52]

Tabitha—Meeting the Needs within the Church and the Family

The second example is Tabitha, about whom Luke says, she "was full of
many good works and acts of almsgiving."[53] According to John, Tabitha
lived a life of virtue that was pleasing to God because of her obedience in
almsgiving, even though she was poor. Her Greek name, Δορκάς (*Dorkas*),
of which Holder attributes John's definition "antelope," was befitting of her

48. Finn, *Almsgiving*, 78–81, 132. Finn refers to the discovery of jars which are believed to have stored oil, wine, and bread discovered in Alexandria. He also mentions
a fourth century inventory from an African Donatist church's "clothing closet" which
lists, "82 women's tunics, 38 capes, 16 men's tunics, 13 pairs of men's shoes, 47 pairs of
women's shoes, 19 peasant clasps." For a copy of the inventory, see Maier, *Le Dossier*, i,
219.

49. *In Acts hom.* 25.4 (PG 60:196–97; NPNF 1.1:235).

50. Libanius, "Libanius Basilio," in Basil, *Epist.* 338 (PG 32:1084; NPNF 2.08:605).

51. Maxwell, *Christianization and Communication*, 91. See also Halton, "Saint John
Chrysostom on Education," 163–75.

52. Augustine, *Ench.* 19.72–73 (CCSL 46:49–114; trans., Harbert, *Enchiridion*,
315–17).

53. Acts 9:36, translation mine. η διερμνευομενη . . . αυτη ην πληρης εργων αγαθων
και ελεημοσυνων ων εποιει.

character, for her almsgiving was not just occasional in this circumstance.[54] On the contrary, the qualities of attentiveness, hospitality, and generosity were a part of Tabitha's character and lifestyle.[55] Tabitha, like the widow of Sidon and the poor widow in Luke 21:1–4, was a woman who gave alms generously even at the expensive of her own needs.[56]

Tabitha, and later Cornelius, served as examples for John of those who gave alms faithfully but were careful to look after the needs within the church and their households first.[57] According to Hartney, John believed the family was the "foundation of society,"[58] which was his reason for instructing the congregations in Antioch to put the needs of the family ahead of any other pursuit. John demonstrates this belief in his commentary on Paul's instructions for the Christian home in Ephesians 6:

> How is it not absurd to send children out to trades, and to school, and to do all you can for these objects, and yet, not to "bring them up in the discipline and admonition of the Lord"? And for this reason truly we are the first to reap the fruits, because we bring up our children to be insolent and profligate, disobedient, and mere vulgar fellows. Let us not then do this; no, let us listen to this blessed Apostle's admonition: "Let us bring them up in the discipline and admonition of the Lord." Let us give them a pattern. Let us make them from the earliest age apply themselves to the reading of the Scriptures.[59]

54. *In Acts hom.* 21.3 (PG 60:167–68; NPNF. 1.11:194).

55. Ibid., 21.3–4 (PG 60:167–72; NPNF 1.11:194–200).

56. See also *In Acts hom.* 25.4 (PG 60:197–98; NPNF 1.11:236). John used Thecla as a fourth example of such generosity in a woman. Thecla is mentioned in the New Testament apocryphal work known as *The Acts of Paul*. In this story, a poor woman named Thecla gave her remaining gold and a silver mirror to a jailer in order to gain access to Paul in prison. During the visit, Thecla reportedly sat at Paul's feet in order to receive instruction in Christian living and to afford the imprisoned Apostle the chance to do further ministry through her. For a good modern translation of the *Acts of Paul*, see Bremmer, *The Apocyphal Acts of Paul and Thecla*.

57. *In Acts hom.* 22.1 (PG 60:171–72; NPNF 1.11:201). In the case of Tabitha, the main examples were the Apostles and her family members. Cornelius, who was faithful in almsgiving, was also concerned for the needs of his household and his soldiers.

58. Hartney, *John Chrysostom and the Transformation of the City*, 192.

59. *In Eph. hom.* 21.2 (PG 62:150–51; NPNF 1.13:220); See also *In Matt. hom.* 37.7 (PG 57:427–28; NPNF 1.10:345). In the latter homily, John explains an old adage by saying: "nothing is sweeter than children and wife, if one is willing to live honestly."

Tabitha's faithfulness in almsgiving was not just of succor to the πτωχοί. Her commitment to charity in and outside the home also benefited the Christian community through building up the family unit, meeting the needs of others, and the overall encouragement of unity.[60] Augustine also asserted the importance of taking alms for one's own household first, because alms are provided for one's own well-being "through the mercy of a pitying God." For Augustine, this meant the giving of alms must not always mean self-deprivation.[61]

In John's view, neither almsgiving nor any other offering ought to be detrimental to one's family. Because some had fallen into poverty as a result of giving to the church's widows,[62] the churches developed separate resources to be used to care for the needy who were housed within.[63] In a later homily, John used Isaiah 58 and 1 Timothy 2:15 to restate the command to care for one's family:

> For if a man deserts those who are united by ties of kindred and affinity, how shall he be affectionate toward others? Will it not have the appearance of vainglory (κενοδοξίαν), when benefiting others he slights his own relations, and does not provide for them? And what will be said, if instructing others, he neglects his own, though he has greater facilities; and a higher obligation to benefit them? Will it not be said, These Christians are affectionate indeed, who neglect their own relatives? "He is worse than an infidel."[64]

In John's teaching, the home emerges as the third most important training ground for righteousness outside of churches and monasteries. Kelly refers to John's treatise *De Inan.* regarding this matter. In this composition, John stated that even some of the poorest parents were known to buy precious jewelry, fine clothing, or even hire a servant for their children in order to maintain the appearance of status in the unhealthy pursuit of κενοδοξία. He encouraged parents to protect their young boys from the temptations of sex and their young girls from the temptation of "pretty clothes and expensive jewelry."[65] He mentioned a number of mothers who

---

60. Brown, *Poverty and Leadership*, 96.

61. Augustine, *Ench.* 23.90 (CCSL 46:49–114; trans., Harbert, *Enchiridion*, 325)

62. *De Stat. hom.* 1.10 (PG 49:30; NPNF 1.09:369).

63. *In Matt. hom.* 66.3 (PG 58:630; NPNF 1.10:548–49); Finn, *Almsgiving*, 88–89.

64. *In 1 Tim. hom.* 14.1 (PG 62:571; NPNF 1.13:606).

65. Kelly, *Golden Mouth*, 85–86. Here Kelly is referring to *De Inan.* 90 (SC 188:196, trans., Laistner, *On Vainglory*, 122). In Laistner's translation, this passage is rendered:

taught their children to give alms from a young age. This included some children who were also the recipients of alms. Some children who did not give alms had alms given on their behalf by their parents. This, John believed, was a means of redemption by proxy for such children.[66] In ideal situations, John encouraged parents to provide their children with a Christian education.[67]

John's twentieth commentary/homily on Ephesians, which describes his interpretation of Paul's view of the family found in Ephesians 5:22–24, is cited by some scholars as misogynistic.[68] The content within, however, speaks clearly about John's view on the importance of family health in the Christian community. According to John, "when they are in harmony, the children are well brought up, and the domestics are in good order, and neighbors, and friends, and relations enjoy the fragrance. But if it be otherwise, all is turned upside down, and thrown into confusion."[69] John did not only put the burden on wives and mothers to maintain such accord. He exhorted husbands to be leaders and to manage their money wisely. He instructed families to pray, discuss God's Word, attend church, and participate in the Eucharist together. As Roth has interpreted John's teaching, "If parents expect their children to be obedient, they must train the children in virtue. Above all, they should read the Bible together, to provide good examples which may counteract the bad examples offered by worldly entertainments."[70]

"Let his mother learn to train her daughter . . . to guide her away from extravagance and personal adornment and all other such vanities . . . and guide the youth and the maiden away from luxury and drunkenness. . . . Young men are troubled by desire, women by love of finery and excitement. Let us therefore repress all these tendencies. Thus we shall be able to please God by rearing such athletes for Him, that we and our children may light on the blessings that are promised to them that love Him (cf. 1 Cor 2:9), by the grace and mercy of our Lord Jesus Christ, to Whom with the Father and the Holy Spirit be ascribed glory, power, and honor, now and forevermore. Amen." See also Repp, "John Chrysostom on the Christian Home," 937–48.

66. *In Acts hom.* 21.3 (PG 60:169; NPNF 1.11:198). More will be discussed on this issue in the final section of this chapter concerning John's homilies on the Gospel of John.

67. Ameringer, *Second Sophistic*, 21.

68. *In Eph. hom.* 20 (PG 62:135–49; NPNF 1.13: 205–218); Hartney, *John Chrysostom and the Transformation of the City*, 6; Kelly, *Golden Mouth*, 50–51; Bloch, "Medieval Misogyny," 15.

69. *In Eph. hom.* 20.1 (PG 62:136; NPNF 1.13:206).

70. Roth and Anderson, *On Marriage and Family Life*, 19.

If they should teeter on the line of shallow poverty, John admonished them to follow the examples of Peter and Paul in the book of Acts who experienced poverty, hunger, thirst, and imprisonment regularly and yet remained faithful to God.[71]

Cornelius—The Gospel Extends Outward

The final example from Acts is that of Cornelius, who John argued was chosen to be the "man of peace" among the Gentiles specifically because he was "proved to be worthy by his works," and specifically his almsgiving.[72] Despite his "disadvantage" of having been Gentile, Cornelius understood the command to give alms. He took care of those in his household and the soldiers under his command. Despite his Gentile understanding of God, John argued, "Both his doctrines and his life were right."[73] Like Tabitha, Cornelius' willingness to invite Peter and his companions into his home was evidence of his virtuous character and lifestyle.

John also believed almsgiving was a crucial component of God's miraculous extension of the gospel into Cornelius' household in multiple ways. First, Cornelius' faithfulness in almsgiving added to the virtuosity of

71. Ibid., 20.8 (62:146–47; 1.13:216–17); Brown, *Poverty and Leadership*, 97; Maxwell, *Christianization and Communication*, 163. Regarding husbands, John mentioned some who spent their income recklessly and wasted the dowries they had received at their time of marriage. He also encouraged couples to avoid giving lavish dinner parties with immodest entertainments. They were to use their homes to bless the poor, through whom God will bless their homes. See also *In Matt. hom.* 5.1 (PG 57:55; NPNF 1.10:51), 77.6 (58:709–10; 1.10:632). In these passages, John encouraged husbands and wives to take communion together followed by spending time in the Scriptures once they arrived at home. In this way, the family could apply the truths learned during the church service at home, and not waste the "refreshment" of interacting with God like rushing off to the marketplace just after bathing.

72. *In Acts hom.* 22.2 (PG 60:173–74; NPNF 1.11:205); *In Heb. hom.* 11.3 (PG 63:93–94; NPNF 1.14:606–7). On the idea of the "man of peace," see Luke 10:5–6, where Jesus says, "Whatever house you enter, first say, 'Peace be to this house.' If a man of peace is there, your peace will rest on him; but if not, it will return to you." This concept has been used by missionaries for decades as a strategy to establish relationships with individuals within a group which can result in easier access into closed communities. For a contemporary example of this strategy, see Breen, "Man of Peace," 1–3. See also Larkin, "Mission in Luke," 166, 169. Larkin argues that Jesus told the seventy-two to find a person of peace because they did not have time to waste with those who were highly unreceptive. He says, "What Luke emphasizes about the mission is its urgency (Luke 10:4) and its personal eschatological significance for those who receive or reject the messenger."

73. *In Acts hom.* 22.1–2 (PG 60:171–74; NPNF 1.11:201–5).

his character. Second, almsgiving provided a platform for Peter and later Cornelius to preach good news to the Gentiles. Third, the nature of Cornelius' almsgiving on behalf of the poor made his good deeds effective for God's kingdom, even before he became aware of his inclusion in it.[74]

As will be demonstrated in the next chapter, Cornelius played a major role in fourth-century teaching concerning almsgiving as it related to eternal salvation. John saw both Tabitha and Cornelius' stories as having included salvation as a result of almsgiving: "See how great the virtue of alms, both in the former discourse, and here! There, it delivered from death temporal; here, from death eternal; and opened the gates of heaven."[75] In *Eleem. et Dec. Vir.*, John reiterated this idea by asserting that almsgiving functioned as an advocate on behalf of Cornelius' sins, paying the debt he owed to God.[76]

74. Ibid., 28.3 (60:213–14; 1.11:255).

75. Ibid., 22.3 (60:175; 1.11:207).

76. *Eleem. et Dec. Vir.* 1 (PG 49:292–93; trans., Christo, *ORA*, 30–31).

7

Communicating the Good News

Do not turn your face away from anyone who is poor, and the face of God will not be turned away from you.

—Tobit 4:7b

As has been demonstrated, John Chrysostom understood the importance of rhetoric, contextualization, and clear communication. He went to great lengths to communicate the gospel in ways that were relevant, memorable, and applicable. His preaching on almsgiving was no exception. There are certain aspects of his teaching on almsgiving, however, which are problematic for interpretation. In particular are numerous correlations between almsgiving and salvation. John's homilies on the Gospel of John contain more references to this correlation than any other.

THE JUDEO-CHRISTIAN BACKGROUND OF ALMSGIVING AND SOTERIOLOGY

The question of redemptive almsgiving does not begin or end with John Chrysostom. On the contrary, the connection between almsgiving and salvation can be found throughout the literature of Judaism and both pre- and post-Nicene Christianity. The Christian idea of redemptive almsgiving has its roots in Hebrew writings and traditions.[1] Both the Old Testament and

---

1. Anderson, "Redeem Your Sins by the Giving of Alms," 39–70; Rhee, *Loving the Poor*, 75–77; Ferguson, "Spiritual Sacrifice in Early Christianity," 1161–62.

its Apocrypha contain passages that were used as proof texts of sort for redemptive almsgiving by early Christian writers.[2] Roman Garrison, whose scholarship on the topic of redemptive almsgiving is noteworthy, traces the first soteriological implications of almsgiving to the Prophets. He argues that the Torah, which gives specific instructions regarding the collection and dispensation of alms, gives no indication that alms are redemptive or have any power to earn the forgiveness of sin.[3] The most obvious Hebrew origin for the idea comes from the aforementioned instructions from Daniel to King Nebuchadnezzar, "Therefore, O king, may my advice be pleasing to you: break away now from your sins by doing righteousness and from your iniquities by showing mercy (ἐλεημοσύνη) to the poor, in case there may be a prolonging of your prosperity."[4]

According to Garrison, many Jews believed God, through Daniel, promised forgiveness to the king if he would give alms to the poor. Garrison argues this was especially true among Jews schooled in the Talmudic tradition.[5] Most who interpret Daniel 4:27 in this way, however, do so from a reading of the Septuagint as opposed to the Masoretic text; and John Chrysostom was no exception.[6] Many fail to take into account that, in the Septuagint, the word ἐλεημοσύνη is used interchangeably to mean both "practicing mercy" and "practicing righteousness." More than one scholar has argued this synonymy was also found in similar Aramaic passages, making a somewhat formidable argument for the idea that almsgiving was a form of practicing faith as opposed to replacing faith. In this case, almsgiving becomes a way that God provides an earthly provision of salvation to the poor through an outpouring of compassion and resources.[7]

The Old Testament Apocrypha contains a number of references that are much more tantamount to redemptive almsgiving. Polycarp referred directly to the apocryphal work Tobit by saying, "When you are able to do good, do not put it off, because mercy (ἐλεημοσύνη) delivers one from

2. For a comparative list and description of the passages listed below, see Rhee, *Loving the Poor*, 76-n.

3. Garrison, *Redemptive Almsgiving*, 47.

4. Daniel 4:27 (NASB).

5. Garrison, *Redemptive Almsgiving*, 59.

6. Anderson, "Redeem Your Sins by the Giving of Alms," 54; Talbert, *Reading the Sermon on the Mount*, 104–5; Hays, "Beyond Mint and Rue," 387–402.

7. Garrison, *Redemptive Almsgiving*, 51–52; Rad, *Old Testament Theology*, 1:383.

death."[8] The pseudonymous author of Tobit mentioned almsgiving in advice to his son:

> Give alms from your possessions, and do not let your eye begrudge the gift when you make it. Do not turn your face away from anyone who is poor, and the face of God will not be turned away from you. If you have many possessions, make your gift from them in proportion; if few, do not be afraid to give according to the little you have. So you will be laying up a good treasure for yourself against the day of necessity. For almsgiving delivers from death and keeps you from going into the Darkness. Indeed, almsgiving, for all who practice it, is an excellent offering in the presence of the Most High.[9]

The author concluded by arguing almsgiving is better for obtaining righteousness than both prayer and fasting because almsgiving "saves from death and purges away every sin."[10]

Another apocryphal work, Sirach, described the intrinsic power of almsgiving to protect and save the practitioner:

> Many refuse to [give], not because of meanness, but from fear of being defrauded needlessly. Nevertheless, be patient with someone in humble circumstances, and do not keep him waiting for your alms. Help the poor for the commandment's sake, and in their need do not send them away empty-handed. Lose your silver for the sake of a brother or a friend, and do not let it rust under a stone and be lost. Lay up your treasure according to the commandments of the Most High, and it will profit you more than gold. Store up almsgiving in your treasury, and it will rescue you from every disaster; better than a stout shield and a sturdy spear, it will fight for you against the enemy.[11]

If this passage were not clear enough concerning redemption from sin, the author of Sirach added, "As water extinguishes a blazing fire, so almsgiving atones for sin."[12] John quoted this verse as Scripture in a number of his homilies.[13]

8. Polycarp, *Ep. Phil.* 10.2 (PG 5:1015; trans., Holmes, *Letter to the Philippians*, 291).

9. Tobit 4:7–11.

10. Tobit 12:8–9.

11. Sirach 29:7–13.

12. Sirach 3:30.

13. *In Gen hom.* 31 (PG 53:282–92; trans., Hill, *Homilies on Genesis*, 2:253); *In John*

The aforementioned Lukan passages have also been interpreted from a soteriological standpoint. Both Origen and Cyprian, like John, cited Luke 11:41 as a foundational scripture referencing the redemption of sin through almsgiving.[14] Origen listed almsgiving as one of the practices through which a person can receive the remission of sins.[15] Clement of Alexandria clarified the redemptive role of almsgiving even further: "You buy incorruption with money."[16] The Cappadocian father Basil of Caesarea compared almsgiving in this passage to "a green olive tree in the house of God," which will remain eternally green in righteousness just as almsgiving makes everything clean.[17] Augustine also cited Luke 11:41 in his teaching on almsgiving. Augustine, however, made a clear distinction between redemptive and sacramental almsgiving. Augustine perpetually maintained that no one could truly be made clean without being born again. His admonitions concerning alms and forgiveness were specifically for believers.[18] Finn notes that Augustine seemed to avoid using texts within his homilies or written works that might "emphasize redemptive almsgiving in atonement for sin."[19]

Following the death of Augustine (430 CE) and the "fall" of Rome (476 CE), the practice of almsgiving diminished in many parts of the increasingly Christianized world. According to Garrison, the early church understanding of material wealth and its hindrances to the kingdom of God was replaced with the later patristic understanding of redemptive almsgiving. As a result, almsgiving developed into an alternative to rebirth in terms

---

hom. 73.3 (PG 59:398; trans., Goggin, *Commentary on St. John*, 2:288; NPNF 1.14:405); *In Heb. hom.* 9.4 (PG 63:81; NPNF 1.14:594).

14. Origen, *In Lev. hom.* 2.4 (PG 12:416–17; trans., Barkley, *Homilies on Leviticus*, 47); Cyprian, *De Opera et Eleem.* 2 (PL 4:604; ANF 5:782). In Luke 11:37–45, Jesus was pronouncing woe to the Pharisees because they were impure on the inside. He compared them to a cup or dish that is clean on the outside but full of evil on the inside. His command to them in vs. 41 is, "Give alms on behalf of those things that are within you, and then all things will be clean for you." (Translation mine) πλην τα ενοντα δοτε ελεημοσυνην και ιδου παντα καθαρα υμιν εστιν.

15. Origen, *In Lev. hom.* 2.4 (PG 12:416–17; trans., Barkley, *Homilies on Leviticus*, 47). According to Origen, the remission of sins can come through baptism, martyrdom, forgiving others, converting a sinner, the abundance of love for others, penance, or through the giving of alms.

16. Clement of Alexandria, *Quis Dives Salv.* 32 (PG 9:637–38; text and trans., Butterworth, LCL 92:337–39).

17. Basil, *Hex. hom.*5.5 (PG 29:110; NPNF 2.08:220).

18. Augustine, *Ench.* 20.75 (CCSL 46:49–114; trans., Harbert, *Enchiridion*, 317–18).

19. Finn, "Portraying the Poor," 139.

of salvation and forgiveness in the formalized Roman Catholic Church.[20] According to the most recent Vatican II version of Catholic catechisms, almsgiving and the practice of charity are included in the various ways that penance may be applied, and are deeds "which cover a multitude of sins."[21] Holman argues this development actually began in the third century, as the focus of many church leaders shifted from the dangers of wealth to its usefulness as "redemptive transfer by the rich for the sake of their own souls."[22] As a result, the poor were viewed as a form of collateral and a point of theological reference rather than the favored recipients of charity and almsgiving according to biblical command.[23]

As mentioned in chapter 6, both Tabitha and Cornelius also served as examples of redemptive almsgiving in early Christian teaching. Cyprian argued Tabitha was raised from the dead in Acts 9:36–42 as a direct result and reward for her almsgiving.[24] A basic study of Greek syntax, however, reveals that Luke most likely meant to identify almsgiving as the primary content of Tabitha's good works. In the phrase, both nouns appear in the genitive case, functioning in simple apposition to one another, and joined together by the word καὶ (kai).[25] The fact that Tabitha was known for giving alms was a direct result of her righteousness, but not the cause of it. John Chrysostom described Peter's healing of Tabitha not as a result of almsgiving but as a form of evangelism through miracle for the benefit of Tabitha and those surrounding her.[26]

John believed there was perhaps no better New Testament example for exposition on almsgiving and soteriology than Cornelius.[27] The fact that

20. Garrison, *Redemptive Almsgiving*, 10, 75. Garrison concludes appropriately that the view of redemptive almsgiving and "the salvific power of charity is in conflict with the view of Jesus' death as the unique and sufficient means of atonement."

21. Vatican, "Article 1434: The Many Forms of Penance in Christian Life," 322; See also McCarthy, *Talking with Catholic Friends and Family*, 24, 64.

22. Holman, *The Hungry are Dying*, 12–20, 61.

23. Ibid., 12.

24. Cyprian, *De Opera et Eleem.* 6 (PL 4:607; ANF 5:784).

25. For a basic description of genitive apposition, see Wallace, *The Basics of New Testament Syntax*, 52–53. According to Wallace, "Simple apposition requires that both nouns be in the same case. . . . It is frequently used when the head noun is ambiguous or metaphorical. . . . To do this, insert 'which is,' 'namely,' or 'who is' between the head noun and the genitive noun. If this makes sense, an appositional genitive is likely. See also Young, *Intermediate New Testament Greek*, 39–41.

26. *In Acts hom.* 21.3 (PG 60:167–68; NPNF 1.11:196).

27. John was not the only patristic preacher who used the story of Cornelius in this way. See also Cyprian, *De Orat. Dom.* 32 (PL 4:540; ANF 5:750).

Cornelius received a supernatural revelation from God is attributed directly to the angel's proclamation that his ἐλεημοσύναι had "ascended before God" (Acts 10:4, 31). John preached, "'Before God' means that even if you have many sins, you should not be afraid if you possess almsgiving as your advocate. For no higher power opposes it. She pays the debt demanded by sin. . . . Therefore, regardless of how many other sins you have; your almsgiving counterbalances all of them."[28] This statement represents one of many John used as method of communicating the eternal significance of almsgiving.

REDEMPTIVE ALMSGIVING IN HOMILIES ON THE GOSPEL OF JOHN

Throughout his homilies on the Gospel of John, John Chrysostom used soteriological language to describe the eternal results of almsgiving for those who participate in the practice. The idea of "theological syncretism," described by Bruce J. Nicholls as a synthesis between popular worldview and biblical theology, is perhaps the best description of John's preaching in this area.[29] In an attempt to communicate the significance of the practice, John combined some of the theological and cultural traditions mentioned above concerning redemptive almsgiving with his own unique views on the matter. It will be demonstrated that his teaching concerning almsgiving and soteriology was inconsistent in certain areas. On a few occasions, he seemed to overstate the postmortem and eschatological implications of the practice, which has led some to interpret his teaching as incorporating a works-based theology.

Most of John's homilies on the Gospel of John which include a redemptive view of almsgiving are based on non-Johannine scriptures. On more than one occasion, John used Jesus' parable concerning the ten virgins and their lamps (Matt 25:1–13) to offer interpretation on the practice of almsgiving. John argued the best way to collect oil for one's lamp and prepare for the arrival of the Bridegroom was by giving alms to the poor. The oil God requires to produce pure light cannot be bought after death; it is only

---

28. *Eleem. et Dec. Vir.* 1 (PG 49:293; trans., Christo, *ORA*, 30–31). Both Clement of Rome and Cyprian also represent examples of this interpretation and use nearly verbatim language to that of John Chrysostom. See Clement of Rome, *Ep. II ad Cor.* 16.1-4 (*AF*, 158–59); Cyprian, *De Lapsis* 35 (PL 4:492; ANF 5:733). For more on Clement and Cyprian's eschatological interpretations regarding almsgiving, see Rhee, *Loving the Poor*, 61–64.

29. Nicholls, *Contextualization*, 8–9, 30–31, 34.

available from the hands of the poor. He went on to say, "It is impossible, I repeat, even if we perform countless good works, to enter the portals of the kingdom without almsgiving."[30] In another homily on this parable, John asserted, "Give to the poor, so that even if you keep silent (and thousands upon thousands of mouths defend you), almsgiving will take your side and plead on your behalf. Almsgiving is the salvation of the soul."[31]

Concerning the latter half of Matthew 25, almsgiving connects the believer to "promised blessings" in this life and the next. John used the example of a heavenly robe, which is better than the most expensive grave clothes. As the almsgiver lives in obedience to the principles of caring for the needy (Matt 25:31–46), so God is faithful to the promise to clothe him or her with righteousness.[32] At times, however, it is difficult to discern John's interpretation of such a reward. On the one hand, he was adamant that salvation is a provision of God's grace, through faith in Jesus Christ, offered to the believer by the Holy Spirit.[33] Each of John's homilies on the Gospel of John ended similarly:

> If we are careful so to conduct ourselves, we will be able to obtain by the grace of God mercy and pity and pardon in abundance for the sins which we have committed during all this long time, and escape the river of fire. May it be that all of us, being delivered from that [penalty], may go up to the kingdom of heaven by the grace and mercy of our Lord Jesus Christ, through whom and with whom glory be to the Father, together with the Holy Spirit, now and always and forever and ever. Amen.[34]

On the other hand, in numerous homilies John taught that almsgiving can, by its own nature, earn God's forgiveness. In the same way, the failure to give alms can send a person to hell, such as in the case of the rich man who ignored Lazarus (Luke 16:19–31).[35] Krupp described John's view of

30. *In John hom.* 23.3 (PG 59:142–43; trans., Goggin, *Commentary on St. John*, 1:231; NPNF 1.14:128). For more on John Chrysostom's use of the parable concerning the ten virgins and their lamps, see Broc-Schmezer, *Les figures féminines . . . de Jean Chrysostome.*

31. *Eleem. et Dec. Vir.* 2 (PG 49:294; trans., Christo, ORA, 32–33).

32. *In John hom.* 66.3, 85.5 (PG 59:370, 466; trans., Goggin, *Commentary on St. John*, 2:226, 442–43; NPNF 1.14:372, 481).

33. *In Heb. hom.* 7.1 (PG 63:60–61; NPNF 1.14:573–74).

34. *In John hom.* 13.4 (PG 59:92, trans., Goggin, *Commentary on St. John*, 1:129–30; NPNF 1.14:75).

35. *De Laz. hom.* 2.6 (PG 48:990–91; trans., Roth, *OWP*, 54–55); Cardman, "Poverty and Wealth as Theater," 161; Leyerle, "John Chrysostom on Almsgiving," 38. See also *In*

regeneration as "synergism," the idea that a person joins God in the process of salvation through confession, faith, and commitment.[36] It is therefore difficult to ascertain whether or not John considered almsgiving to be a requirement for salvation or a necessary demonstration of salvation. In either case, for John, selfish wealth was a clear indication of spiritual depravity while virtuous poverty, generosity, and contentment were evidences of the work of salvation in the life of the believer. According to Neusner, the issue of genuine salvation was the key issue that drove John's discourses against the Jews and those Christians who had committed apostasy under the influence of Judaizers in the various churches in which he taught.[37]

Almsgiving was also a necessary part of repentance and training in righteousness. John compared almsgiving to a salve that one applies to a wound. If the wound is caused by coveting, almsgiving relieves the desire for accumulation. In the same way, one should apply the remedy of chastity to sexual immorality and kindness to a vicious tongue. Almsgiving, according to John, is the greatest remedy of all. It surpasses asceticism and fasting. When one practices almsgiving, vices such as pride, jealousy, and anger will evaporate and be replaced by a sober mind. Just as a physician contemplates the fragility of life while tending to a dying person, so the almsgiver is humbled and made wise by interactions with the poor. The almsgiver will develop a new sense of thankfulness when considering his or her own situation. He or she will also gain a greater understanding of the pointless nature of avarice, and a growing desire for eternal blessings.[38]

John, like many early Christian writers, referred to poor widows in the church and poor beggars in the public sphere as "altars" on which gifts of sacrifice and praise might be given back to God by his people.[39] In a lesser known set of homilies concerning Satan, demons, and temptation, John listed five ways a person may display repentance: 1) the condemnation of sins, 2) forgiving the sins of others, 3) repentant prayer, 4) almsgiving, 5)

---

1 Tim. hom. 14.2 (PG 62:573; NPNF 1.13:608); *In 2 Tim. hom.* 6.3 (PG 62:633; NPNF 1.13, 667).

36. Krupp, *Shepherding the Flock*, 85.

37. Neusner, *Judaism and Christianity in the Age of Constantine*, 61.

38. *In John hom.* 81.3 (PG 59:441–42; trans., Goggin, *Commentary on St. John*, 2:385–86; NPNF 1.14:451–52); *In Matt. hom.* 78.3 (PG 58:714–15; NPNF 1.10:637).

39. *In John hom.* 13.4, 73.3 (PG 59:92, 398; trans., Goggin, *Commentary on St. John*, 1:129, 2:288; NPNF 1.14:74, 405); Holman, *God Knows*, 21; Finn, *Almsgiving*, 181; Osiek, "The Widow as Altar," 159–69. See also *In Matt. hom.* 47.3 (PG 58:485; NPNF 1.10:406), 66.3 (58:630; 1.10:548).

humility.[40] In terms of repentance and forgiveness of sins, almsgiving is like a purifying fire, such as is needed to rid one's crops of thorns, leaf-eating animals, snakes, and scorpions who destroy one's produce in hiding. For John's congregations, almsgiving was needed to purify their passion for wealth.[41]

John's inconsistency on these matters is also evident in his understanding of the ability of almsgiving to wash away one's sins. On some occasions John preached, based on the traditional interpretation of Daniel 4:27 (LXX) and Sirach 3:30, that the practice of almsgiving had the ability to cleanse any sin a believer could commit.[42] On other occasions, John taught almsgiving only had the power to cleanse a person from some sins as opposed to all sins. He lists fornication and adultery as sins that no good deed can replace. Above any other sin, he classified pride as the most egregious. Pride was comparable if not equal to the unpardonable sin, because it represented an absolute refusal to acknowledge God. It was pride that caused the devil to become evil; pride which destroyed his soul. It seems clear, therefore, that John understood almsgiving as having power over sin only when it was used by the believer to replace unhealthy behavior in certain areas. For such sins as pride and sexual immorality, a more intense, internal cleansing was necessary.[43] In each of these cases, John taught almsgiving was effective only when it accompanied repentance and healing which displayed internal and external congruence.

In other homilies on the Gospel of John, John Chrysostom argued almsgiving is ineffective from God's perspective if it is inauthentic or done for selfish reasons. John believed the major teaching of Scripture, from

40. *De Diab. Tent. hom.* 2.6 (PG 49:263–64; NPNF 1.09:206). See also *De Laz. hom.* 4.7 (PG 48:1016; trans., Roth, *OWP*, 96). In this fourth homily concerning the rich man and Lazarus, John added tears, confession, fasting, and self-control to this list of repentant acts.

41. *In John hom.* 24.3 (PG 59:148; trans., Goggin, *Commentary on St. John*, 1:240–41; NPNF 1.14:133).

42. Ibid., 7.2 (59:65–66; 1:79–80; 1.14:48); *In Acts hom.* 25.4 (PG 60:196–97; NPNF 1.1:235). In this homily on Acts, John used medicinal language to illustrate cleansing: "there is no sin, which alms cannot cleanse, which alms cannot quench, all sin is beneath this." He used the example of Zaccheus, for who is a sinner if not a tax-collector?

43. *In John hom.* 16.4 (PG 59:106–8; trans., Goggin, *Commentary on St. John*, 1:158–61; NPNF 1.14:90–91); *In Matt. hom.* 32.11 (PG 57:388; NPNF 1.10:303); *In Heb. hom.* 7.1 (PG 63:60–61; NPNF 1.14:573–74); *De Laz. hom.* 3.4 (PG 48:997; trans., Roth, *OWP*, 62). In the latter two homilies John used Proverbs 20:9: "For who will boast he has a pure heart? Or who will say confidently he is free from sin?"

Moses, to Jesus, to the Apostles, was intended to lead the believer to a state of "lowliness of mind," so that in humility, modesty, and simplicity, one might be pleasing to God.[44] He went on to say that prayer, almsgiving, fasting, and simplicity are of no use to anyone if the believer's life is more often characterized by pride, greed, gaudiness, violence, and the love of money in any form.[45]

Adding to this inconsistency, John taught a form of almsgiving by proxy on more than one occasion. In other words, alms could be given on behalf of the sins of others, even if they did not choose to make such offerings by their own volition. When commenting on the death of Lazarus in John 11, John Chrysostom implied alms could be given on behalf of the dead. He argued weeping was of no value to Lazarus, but generous almsgiving by his loved ones might have helped "to procure some comfort for him."[46] John also presented this idea regarding one's spouse or children.[47]

Alternate Views

More than one scholar has challenged the idea that John Chrysostom believed in the redemptive power of almsgiving. The reformer Chemnitz answered this interpretation by arguing, simply, that early Judeo-Christian writers like John used hyperbole or overstatement in order to emphasize the importance of almsgiving. According to Chemnitz, "Indeed, when some of the older fathers of the churches saw the love of their parishioners growing cold, they went a little overboard in ensuring that their exhortations struck home with their audience."[48] Maxwell, similarly, suggests that perhaps John thought too highly of his own opinions which resulted in a somewhat overzealous degree of adamancy concerning almsgiving, redemption, and eschatology.[49] She goes on to say he seemed to have underestimated the authenticity of his congregations' faith, as a result of their apparent lack of faithfulness, which represented a difference in worldview and communication rather than conversion. This, she argues, is evidenced by the fact he mentioned rumors that

---

44. *In John hom.* 33.3 (PG 59:192; trans., Goggin, *Commentary on St. John*, 1:329–31; NPNF 1.14:180).

45. Ibid., 40.4 (59:233–34; 1.14:222–23).

46. Ibid., 62.5 (59:347–48; 1.14:346–47).

47. *In Acts hom.* 21.3 (PG 60:169; NPNF 1.11:198).

48. Chemnitz, *On Almsgiving*, 20.

49. Maxwell, *Christianization and Communication*, 122, 143.

many had grown tiresome of his preaching on these matters and some had even encouraged him to stop.[50] John, of course, did not acquiesce to such petitions.[51]

It is also plausible to argue John connected almsgiving with soteriology not only as a result of early Christian cultural and theological influences, but as a way of demonstrating the work of salvation in the life of the believer. In *De Eleem.*, John defined almsgiving as a "work [resulting from] grace," not as a source of grace.[52] In one of his final homilies on the Gospel of John, he argued almsgiving only has the power to make things clean when it has already been freed from sin and injustice.[53] In this sense, he advocated almsgiving as a work of righteousness as opposed to a source of righteousness. Nevertheless, his teaching concerning redemptive almsgiving is problematic on account of rhetorical and biblical inconsistency.

Communication remains the most important aspect of John's teaching concerning almsgiving and soteriology. In nearly every case, fourth-century preachers like John addressed groups of professed believers. Such preachers realized the Constantinian style of evangelism, which was "conversion under pressure," was unlikely to have genuine and sustainable results.[54] Rather than using the growing political arm of the church in the Eastern Empire as momentum for his teaching on almsgiving, John chose to use the theological and cultural language of redemptive almsgiving as symbols that were recognizable by his audiences. If lasting results are considered an essential mark of effective communication, then John's teaching concerning redemption in Christ appears to have been transmitted successfully. Consider this medieval Byzantine liturgy, developed from an Antiochene Eucharistic service led by John Chrysostom:

50. Ibid., 143–44, 162.

51. *In 1 Cor. hom.* 12.5 (PG 61:103; NPNF 1.12:97). According to John, "nevertheless, I will not cease repeating these things: for there is, there is surely a chance, that although not all, yet some few will receive our saying . . ."

52. *De Eleem.* 5 (PG 51:268; trans., Christo, *ORA*, 144).

53. *In John hom.* 81.3 (PG 59:441–42; trans., Goggin, *Commentary on St. John*, 2:385–86; NPNF 1.14:451–52). It may be worth noting that John likely preached the sermon *De Eleem.* in 387 CE during the early part of his ministry while his homilies on John may have been delivered closer to his departure from Antioch which occurred in 398 CE. As has been mentioned, John was highly disappointed with the lack of response among many in his congregations and it is likely that his approaches toward almsgiving became more forceful in the latter days of his tenure in Antioch.

54. Macmullen, *Christianity and Paganism*, 153, 168.

With these blessed powers, Lord and Lover of mankind, we too cry out and say: holy and all-holy are you. You have so loved your world that you gave your only-begotten Son in order that whoever believes in him may not perish but have life eternal. After he had come and accomplished for us all that was appointed, on the night that he was betrayed or rather gave himself up for the life of the world, he took bread into his holy, all-pure, and blameless hands, and when he had given thanks and blessed it, sanctified and broken it, he gave it to his holy disciples and apostles, saying: "Take, eat, this is my body which is broken for you for the remission of sins."[55]

SUMMARY OF ALMSGIVING IN THE HOMILIES ON THE GOSPELS

For John Chrysostom, almsgiving was a central tenet of God's missionary concern for the empire. God had called every believer, regardless of economic status, to participate in this practice according to the command of Scripture. Almsgiving was initiated by God in the book of Genesis, perfected by Jesus as recorded in the Gospels, and meant to continue until the return of Christ. The inclusion of the Gentiles, like Cornelius, displays God's desire for diversity in His kingdom. John sought to develop his churches according to such diversity so they would be a temporal picture of an eternal reality.

The implications of the practice of almsgiving are meant to reach far beyond the exchange of goods. For John, almsgiving was eschatological and its results would not be fully realized until the next life. John went to great lengths to communicate the essentiality of almsgiving as a part of God's good news for the poor. The good news was not only for the economically poor, but also for the spiritually poor. As he preached concerning the book of Acts, the Christian church would only be successful in accomplishing its mission in the world through the cooperative obedience of God's people. In his homilies on the Pauline epistles, John merged the command for individuals to give alms with a practical, ecclesiastical structure for almsgiving in the churches.

---

55. Kucharek, *The Byzantine-Slav Liturgy of St. John Chrysostom*, 588. For similar language in John's homilies, see *De Laz. hom.* 3.10 (PG 48:1006; trans., Roth, *OWP*, 78); *In Heb. hom.* 7.2 (PG 63:63; NPNF 1.14:576). On the topic of correctly associating liturgies like those of John Chrysostom with ancient antecedents, see Taft, "The Authenticity of the Chrysostom Anaphora Revisited," 5–51.

8

Strategic Ecclesiology and the Christian Life

When then you see a poor believer, think that you are beholding an altar.

—JOHN CHRYSOSTOM

HOMILIES ON THE PAULINE EPISTLES

In John Chrysostom's view, the epistles of the Apostle Paul represented the most important early Christian literature concerning the practice of almsgiving in the churches. Paul believed the ultimate fulfillment of the biblical command to practice almsgiving would be realized only within the context of Christian community. Paul envisioned that the practice of almsgiving, as it pertained to God's missionary advancement among the economic and spiritual poor, would evolve from personal, to ecclesiastical, to a personal ecclesiology of compassion and generosity. In many of John's letters from exile, which will be discussed in this chapter, a Pauline understanding of "missionary activities" and "networks" is demonstrated.[1] John believed that missional living started in Christian homes, which made up the Christian community, which had the power to influence the Roman masses by meeting the needs of humanity.[2]

1. Mayer and Allen, *John Chrysostom*, 45.
2. Brown, *Poverty and Leadership*, 19.

Margaret Mary Mitchell's work is exceptional vis-à-vis John's interpretation of Pauline literature. According to Mitchell, Paul was the perfect example for John among the Antiochene churches for a number of reasons. First, Paul was a legendary hero to fourth-century Christians in Antioch; for they believed Paul to be primarily responsible for the spiritual development of the first Christians in Antioch.[3] Second, John felt a somewhat mystical connection with Paul because they dealt with many of the same religious, cultural, and ethical issues.[4] Third, Paul had chosen to forsake a life of wealth and status in favor of a ministry to the poor and specifically to the previously excluded Gentiles. Paul's ministry was one of hard-work and voluntary poverty, which afforded him a "true spiritual richness" also seen in the poor of fourth century Antioch.[5]

ALMSGIVING AND ECCLESIOLOGY

For John, Paul's letters were the key texts concerning ecclesiology and the social implications of the gospel message. For this reason, most of John's exposition on Pauline literature was delivered with a moral or social interpretation.[6] According to Brown, Paul's ideal message "was that of a 'loving' community made up of benevolent and generous householders. It was an ideal eminently suited to the distinctive social composition of an early Christian urban community."[7] In the same way, John sought to lead the churches in which he preached to produce individuals, households, and faith communities that were actively engaged in the practice of almsgiving as the social mission of the gospel. Besides Jesus, Paul served as John's most prolific example of evangelism and transformational mission.

---

3. *In Acts hom.* 25.1 (PG 60:191–93; NPNF 1.11: 230–31); M. Mitchell, *The Heavenly Trumpet*, 44, 67. Mitchell argues John's reference in his thirtieth homily on Romans to "the table at which the saint ate, and a seat on which he sat, and the couch on which he lay," referred to what is known as "The Grotto of St. Paul," which is located on Mount Tauris outside of Antioch. This spot was supposedly the location of one or more of Paul's sermons. See *In Rom. hom.* 30.4 (PG 60:665; NPNF 1.11:736). See also Downey, *A History of Antioch*, 284; Baur, *John Chrysostom and His Time*, 1:33.

4. M. Mitchell, *The Heavenly Trumpet*, 68. She lists "inner-church conflict, Judaizing Christians, immoral behavior in the congregation, and thorny issues in the relationship between Christians and the larger social order."

5. Ibid., 360. See also Blomberg, *Neither Poverty nor Riches*, 177–78.

6. Kelly, *Golden Mouth*, 96.

7. Brown, *Poverty and Leadership*, 19.

John used Paul's writings to remind his congregations that the negative connotations with which many viewed the poor did not weaken the command to practice almsgiving and prioritize the needy. John worked ardently to reshape the presuppositions held by many throughout Antioch, Constantinople, and the empire as a whole, concerning the poor. The ascetics and πένητες, as has been demonstrated, were often denigrated on account of their low status.[8] John denounced such slander and deemed their hard work commendable. This was especially true when their lifestyles were compared to those who, by means of inherited wealth, were idle and did not work for a living. Many who were heirs in this sense lived in perpetual lethargy with a multitude of servants. From a practical standpoint, the πένητες had clearer minds and consciences because they were not idle. They had developed skills and crafts that were useful for their own good, the good of their families, and the good of others. Their bodies were healthier and they remained focused on pursuits of greater benefit to themselves and their communities. Just as Paul had written in 1 Corinthians 1:26–27, the rich lived according to the wisdom of the world, while the "foolishness" of the πένητες was being used by God for noble purposes.[9]

8. Downey, *A History of Antioch*, 419–33. This tension climaxed with the "Riot of the Statues" in Antioch (387 CE). A combination of famine, economic downturn, animosity between the elites and the poor, and new forms of taxation that had emerged just prior to and during the reign of Theodosius I, caused the city of Antioch to erupt in chaos. During the riots, the statues of Theodosius and the empress Flacilla were torn down and dragged throughout the city. Because of harsh punishments that had been levied on other cities in similar situations, John preached his sermons *De Stat.* in order to encourage those who feared retribution, to implore the mercy the imperial seat, and to challenge his congregations to improve their virtue and eradicate their vices. See preface by Stephens in *De Stat.* (NPNF 1.09:342–47); Libanius, *Orat.* 19–20; Heayn, "Urban Violence in Fifth Century Antioch," 16–17.

9. *In 1 Cor. hom.* 5.6 (PG 61:47–48; NPNF 1.12:42); Maxwell, *Christianization and Communication*, 72–73. Along with his complimentary language among the wealthy and the middle classes concerning the working poor, John also addressed those who worked in hard labor fields about the struggles of interacting with the elite. He exhorted those of all demographics to treat each other with respect and to do their best to disregard social and economic divisions. See also *In Matt. hom.* 59.4 (PG 58:579; NPNF 1.10:495). This passage, which was mentioned in chapter 5, venerated the working poor in various categories. Regarding John's emphasis on the useful attributes of the poor, see *De Anna hom.* 5 (PG 54:669–76).

Sacramental Almsgiving

John used Paul's writings to uphold the value of the destitute by reminding his congregations of their biblical responsibility to care for them. As of the late fourth century, many churches in the Eastern Empire had developed a rudimentary sacramental system based upon the teachings of Cyril of Jerusalem (315–386 CE). The large number of Christians who still took pilgrimage to Jerusalem for the purpose of worship allowed Cyril's teachings to permeate the empire at a faster rate.[10] Baptism and the Eucharist were celebrated and expected above any other ordinance in the churches, as they had been celebrated since the New Testament.[11] According to Brown, by the end of the fourth century the majority of the population had been baptized and participated in the Eucharist regularly, if not weekly.[12] In his lectures, Cyril of Jerusalem mentioned a number of other sacramental practices that followed baptism including an early form of confirmation called "chrismation," or "chrism," which he also refers to as a "Seal". Cyril also mentioned catachumens, Eucharistic liturgy, and other ecclesiological liturgies.[13] John Chrysostom was responsible for teaching and administering each of the sacraments in Antioch and Constantinople, especially on occasions surrounding Lent and Easter.[14] John used sacramental language to describe the poor in order to emphasize their representation of the body of Christ. In the same way that Christ's presence in the Eucharist served to

10. Cross, *St. Cyril of Jerusalem's Lectures*, xix. For original source and translation, see Cyril of Jerusalem, *Catecheses* (PG 33:331–1180; NPNF 2.07:2–278).

11. Conzelmann, *History of Primitive Christianity*, 76–77.

12. Brown, *Poverty and Leadership*, 95–96. The Eucharist was observed by nearly everyone on Easter, whether or not they attended the churches regularly during the rest of the year.

13. Cyril of Jerusalem, *Catecheses* 1.2-3 (PG 33:372–73; NPNF 2.07:79), 21.1–7 [*Catec. Myst. 3*] (33:1085–94; 2.07:285–88). See also Dragas, *The Holy Sacraments*; Cross, *St. Cyril of Jerusalem's Lectures*, xx–xxiv. The practice of exorcisms, especially around the time of Easter during the catechumenal addresses, was also a part of Cyril's lectures concerning sacramental practices. For more on early Christian exorcisms see Kalleres, "Exorcising the Devil." For catechumens and creeds used as a part of liturgy, see. Kelly, *Early Christian Creeds*, 296–331.

14. Kelly, *Golden Mouth*, 88–89; *In 1 Cor. hom.* 35.3, 44.2 (PG 61:300, 376; NPNF 1.12, 290, 364). In these passages from his homilies on 1 Corinthians, John mentioned the language and practice of the Eucharistic liturgy and catechumens.

protect the believer against evil, so also his presence indwelt the poor to offer forgiveness through almsgiving.[15]

John viewed baptism and the Eucharist as the only sacraments of greater importance than almsgiving. In a homily on 2 Timothy, John compared almsgiving to two common practices by which Christians were identified: ritual washing and the frequent use of the hand motion known as The Sign of the Cross. He described many who practiced both so frequently they had become akin to involuntary habits. According to John, these practices were good for setting Christians apart from others in the empire, but giving alms according to the same routine would be even better.[16] In his homlies *De Stat.*, John mentioned prayer, oathtaking, honesty, and patience as good works that were a necessary part of the churches' internal practices and external influence. Even these, however, were of a lesser value than almsgiving.[17] In his homily on Jesus' prayer for the world in John 17, John Chrysostom added fasting and asceticism to the growing list of sacramental practices.[18]

John's common illustration of the poor as an altar on which the believer can place an offering is also relevant in terms of the sacramental nature of almsgiving. He presented this illustration in such a way that the πτωχοί were an altar on which the almsgiver offers gifts and sacrifices directly to God.[19] In a homily concerning God's provision as recorded in 2 Corinthians 9, John preached:

> This altar may you see lying everywhere, both in lanes and in market places, and you may sacrifice upon it every hour; for on this too is sacrifice performed. And as the priest stands invoking the Spirit, so you too invoke the Spirit, not by speech, but by deeds. For nothing so sustains and kindles the fire of the Spirit, as this oil largely poured out. . . . When then you see a poor believer, think that you are beholding an altar: when you see one who is a beggar, not only insult him not, but even reverence him, and if you see another insulting him, prevent and repel it.[20]

15. Brown, *Poverty and Leadership*, 95–96.

16. *In 2 Tim. hom.* 6.4 (PG 62.634–35; NPNF 1.13:668–69).

17. *De Stat. hom.* 16.6 (PG 49:169–70; NPNF 1.09:515).

18. *In John hom.* 81.3 (PG 59:441–42; trans., Goggin, *Commentary on St. John*, 2:385–86; NPNF 1.14:452).

19. Finn, *Almsgiving*, 181; Osiek, "The Widow as Altar," 159–69; Broc-Schmezer, "De l'aumône faite . . . Jean Chrysostome," 131–48.

20. *In 2 Cor. hom.* 20.3 (PG 61:540; NPNF 1.12:514–15). See also *In Matt. hom.* 47.3

John believed the command to give alms, according to the Apostle Paul, was about more than giving one's money. Believers were to treat the πτωχοί with respect, and they were to promote such an attitude among others.

Almsgiving and the Clergy

By the end of the fourth century, the churches of the Eastern Empire served as the central location for the collection and distribution of alms in every major city. As the amounts received through almsgiving increased from one city to the next, suspicions grew concerning the accountability of such a system. According to Finn, churches with gifted preachers like John Chrysostom often accrued larger amounts of alms because of their reputations and dynamic preaching. As a result, many people became apprehensive about the honesty of those involved and in some cases charges of corruption and misuse were levied against church leadership.[21]

Issues regarding the clergy and almsgiving were further complicated by the fact that many church leaders claimed a large portion, if not all of their financial support, from that which was given in the churches.[22] At the same time many cities, including Antioch and Constantinople, were frequented by itinerant bishops, ascetics, and pagan orators who took up residence temporarily and entreated the public for financial support.[23] As the number of individuals who received income for their religious duties increased, so did the amount of those who entered the "enterprise of religion."[24] As a

---

(PG 58:485; NPNF 1.10:406). In this homily on Jesus' words "Blessed are the poor" in Matthew 5, John refers to the poor as "a golden altar and a spiritual place of sacrifice." This is a direct reference to the aforementioned apocryphal traditions found in 2 Maccabees 2:19, 8:8 and Sirach 1:12, 14.

21. Finn, *Almsgiving*, 37; Leyerle, "John Chrysostom on Almsgiving," 33.

22. Brown, *Poverty and Leadership*, 20.

23. Mayer and Allen, *John Chrysostom*, 4; Johnson, *The Fear of Beggars*, 16; Little, *Religious Poverty*, 77, 82. Throughout the patristic era, there were an increasing number of itinerant apostles, evangelists, and prophets. According to the apostolic tradition of the New Testament (2 Cor. 9:1–8; Gal. 6:6), many of these traveling ministries were supported in one way or another by the generosity of local believers. These types of itinerant preachers were a precursor to the mendicant, or begging orders that would emerge in the twelfth and thirteenth centuries. According to the aforementioned traditions of the Torah, the priests and other clergy distributed alms among the poor and also among themselves depending upon setting and need.

24. Brown, *Poverty and Leadership*, 20–31. Brown argues persons of the lower and middle classes attempted to participate in professional religion in larger numbers so that

result of these impediments, John was compelled on occasion to defend the role of the clergy in the churches. In his homily on unity and the offices of the churches in Ephesians 4, John reminded his audience that it is the work of the Lord to consecrate the clergy for service as he has done since the time of Aaron and his sons (Exod 29). For this reason, the clergy of the fourth century were no less entitled to their share of almsgiving than were the Levites.[25]

According to Paul's own view of his calling as recorded in Titus 1, John described the role of the clergy as one of leadership and accountability. Each, according to his virtue, will be accountable to God.[26] John was grieved on account of many in his congregation who were quick to be suspicious of the clergy. He encouraged them to become more faithful in their own almsgiving and service to the poor so that they might gain a greater appreciation for the role of ministers.[27] On more than one occasion, he reminded his congregations that those who serve in the ministry are held to a higher standard of accountability by God because of their responsibility to distribute resources as the Spirit directs.[28] Many preachers, according to John, were highly skilled in their trade. Nevertheless, it was a job which required significant time and labor in study, service, and nurturing. John reminded his congregations that there was never a season when members of the clergy were given a reprieve from fulfilling these arduous tasks.[29]

Clergy Impropriety

John did, however, deem the activity of many clergy members less than perfect in the area of almsgiving. He compared members of the clergy who had become corrupt to a ship captain guilty of a careless shipwreck.[30] He

they might be connected to the support system of the ecclesiastical body.

25. *In Eph. hom.* 11.5 (PG 62:86; NPNF 1.13:154–55).

26. *In Tit. hom.* 1 (PG 62:663–70; NPNF 1.13:696–701).

27. *In 1 Cor. hom.* 21.6–7 (Field, *Sancti Patris*, 256; trans., Mayer and Allen, *John Chrysostom*, 174; PG 61:179; NPNF 1.12:172).

28. *De Laz. hom.* 2.4 (PG 48:988; trans., Roth, *OWP*, 50); *De Sac.* 6.7 (PG 48.683; trans., Neville, *OP*, 145–46; NPNF 1.09:86–87).

29. *De Sac.* 5.5 (PG 48:672; trans., Neville, *OP*, 131–32; NPNF 1.09:79–80). See also Davis, "St. John Chrysostom on Ministry," 411–12. Davis' article uses a number of passages from *De Sac.* to discuss contemporary applications of John's views on the calling and activity of ministry.

30. *De Sac.* 3.15 (PG 48:652; trans., Neville, *OP*, 92–93; NPNF 1.09:59).

was also compelled to reprove members of the clergy who were shirking their ministerial responsibilities to the needy in favor of managing the "business of the church."[31] In one of his final homilies on the Gospel of Matthew, John exhorted the clergy to leave such matters to "innkeepers, and tax-gatherers, and accountants, and stewards."[32] Instead, they were to be obedient to their calling to interact with the poor in full view of the public through the churches.[33] According to *De Sac.*,

> Our present inquiry is not about dealings in wheat and barley, or oxen and sheep, or anything else of the kind. It concerns the very Body of Jesus. For the Church of Christ is Christ's own Body, according to St. Paul, and the man who is entrusted with it must train it to perfect health and incredible beauty, by unremitting vigilance to prevent the slightest spot or wrinkle or other blemish of that sort from marring its grace and loveliness. In short, he must make it worthy, as far as lies within human power, of that pure and blessed Head to which it is subjected.[34]

John also discussed more serious issues plaguing the churches throughout the Eastern Empire during the fourth century. From his viewpoint, a reckless changing of leadership was occurring in the churches that had not been perpetrated by the proper authorities. Such precariousness was causing division in the church and damaging the reputation of Christianity among the pagans. According to John, many outside the church were jeering Christians for having major councils and disagreements about beliefs and practices that were essentially the same.[35] There were also serious issues regarding fraudulence in managing finances in certain parishes. While in Constantinople, John mentioned bishoprics that were

31. Walsh, "Wealthy and Impoverished Widows," 184.

32. *In Matt. hom.* 85.4 (PG 58:762; NPNF 1.10:685–86).

33. Finn, *Almsgiving*, 14.

34. *De Sac.* 4.2 (PG 48:663; trans., Neville, *OP*, 114; NPNF 1.09:70). John's reference to the Apostle Paul in this selection is cited from Colossians 1:24b: "for the sake of his body, which is the church."

35. *In Eph. hom.* 11.4–6 (PG 62:84–88; NPNF 1.13:155–57). See also Mayer, *Provenance*, where she argues this homily may have been delivered in Constantinople as opposed to Antioch. In either case, both Antioch and Constantinople were popular fourth-century locations for ecumenical councils held for the purpose of discussing issues of church polity and relationships. See also Sozomen, *Hist. Eccl.* 1.2–9.17 (PG 67:848–1630; NPNF 2.02:342–613). Sozomen listed the details of a number of these meetings and councils throughout his historical records.

up for sale and some who bought their way out of criminal punishment.[36] Basil of Caesarea mentioned similar issues in a few Cappadocian churches. Both preachers asserted that such dishonesty among the clergy was severe enough to be punishable by hell.[37]

Questions Concerning John Chrysostom

To this day, some suggest John's emphasis on almsgiving might have been motivated, at least partially, by a desire for personal gain. First, like most clergy of his day, John relied on congregational giving for his livelihood.[38] As a result, he would have many personal reasons to emphasize faithfulness in giving. According to the fifth-century historian Palladius, John became heavily involved in directing and correcting the financial affairs of the churches under his care. Upon arriving in Constantinople, for example, he immediately transferred a significant portion of the church funds, which he felt were used for "extravagance," to hospitals throughout the city.[39] As a part of the trumped up charges brought against him near the end of his tenure in Constantinople, John was accused of selling decorative church property for the benefit of the poor. Because many priests acquired sustenance from that which was given to the church through almsgiving, some of John's contemporaries suggested he benefited personally from the sale of the items.[40]

The second allegation has developed from modern critical scholarship. It is, nevertheless, related to the first. The argument is based on the idea that John intentionally used his position and sermons to elevate the reputation of the elite. According to Sitzler, the demographic disparities John described were "designed in order to distinguish rich and poor and strengthen the identity of the wealthy within the community."[41] The argument concludes, therefore, that the purpose of John's emphasis on almsgiv-

36. *In Eph. hom.* 6.4 (PG 62:48; NPNF 1.13:116). See also Kelly, *Golden Mouth*, 101; González, *Faith and Wealth*, 154. According to González, John felt like the priesthood was "up for sale" in many different venues throughout the empire.

37. *In Eph. hom.* 6.4 (PG 62:48; NPNF 1.13:116); Basil, *Epist.* 53 (PG 32:396–400; NPNF 2.08:335–36).

38. Leyerle, "John Chrysostom on Almsgiving," 44–45.

39. Palladius, *Dial. de Vita. Chrys.* 5 (PG 47:20; trans., Meyer, *Dialogue*, 39). Meyer bases his translation on Coleman-Norton, *Palladii Dialogus de Chrysostomi*.

40. Allen, Neil, and Mayer, *Preaching Poverty in Late Antiquity*, 57.

41. Sitzler, "Identity," 478.

ing was to reinforce the role the wealthy played within the churches which would in effect strengthen the churches and benefit John personally.[42] If this were the case, it was certainly not evident from the language of John's sermons. As has been demonstrated, perhaps no other fourth-century preacher took such a "sharply critical view" of wealth.[43]

Third, as Brown has noted, churches and clergy members received significant tax exemptions that were based loosely on their effectiveness. Brown suggests that John, along with other fourth-century preachers, might have exaggerated the magnitude of poverty in the empire in order to influence imperial giving. He also argues the "urgency" with which preachers like John preached on giving to the poor was in many ways meant to maintain their churches' innocence in terms of using resources for anything other than it was supposed to in the eyes of the state.[44] John would likely argue, however, that poverty is best understood not by a majority opinion but by those who experience it. For this reason, he often described himself as an ambassador, patron, or intermediary to the wealthy on behalf of the poor.[45]

Issues Concerning Church and State

As the number of individuals who began new religious movements escalated, the Roman state increased its watchfulness on the churches and their leaders. In some cases, this backfired by causing more dependency on the part of religious leaders who had less time to practice their original profession. The state began to control certain aspects of almsgiving and charity which led to misuse on a political level. The knowledge that the state was

42. Ibid. This, according to Sitzler, was the reason John went to such lengths to describe almsgiving using soteriological language and as chief among virtues. As has been demonstrated, however, John was not the only preacher to use such language thus weakening the argument that his language was initiated primarily in response to the Antiochene context.

43. Kelly, *Golden Mouth*, 98.

44. Brown, *Poverty and Leadership*, 29–30, 32, 48. Brown challenges the long held opinion that the later Roman Empire continued to see an increase in those below the poverty line. He argues that most people throughout the empire had enough means to own property and live fairly well. See also Heayn, "Urban Violence in Fifth Century Antioch," 14. Heayn argues that John functioned as somewhat of a political rhetorician at times, which helped Christianity to continue its dominance at the imperial level.

45. *De Eleem.* 4 (PG 51:266–67; trans., Christo, *ORA*, 141). See also Brändle, "This Sweetest Passage," 127.

watching church practices closely in the cities caused many urban churches to adjust their practices of almsgiving accordingly. According to Sozomen, the Emperor had a temporary home in Antioch during the middle of the fourth century. When in the city, he had active involvement with the churches, their leadership, and their dealings.[46] As a result, the charity of the church and the philanthropy of the state became interconnected. The Emperor and the bishops, as the most prominent figures involved in the distribution of resources among the needy, emerged as the primary source of social welfare and its administration in Antioch.[47] Finn suggests the church and state benefited from each other, with the poor receiving supplemental resources from both entities.[48]

John discussed issues of church and state in a few of his Pauline homilies. He challenged his congregations first and foremost to pray for their political leaders and other elected officials.[49] In Constantinople, he affirmed the privilege and responsibility that accompanied the political aspects of his position,[50] yet he reminded his members that the relationship between earthly powers and subjugants was only temporary. In many ways, it was analagous to the relationship between masters and slaves.[51]

Some scholars argue John sought to maintain the social order of his day which included the economic separation between classes.[52] Others argue he longed for a "Christian governance" that would be heard above the mounting Jewish voices in society and the waning influence of paganism.[53] If the government of the empire was going to continue responding to religious sway, Christianity would need to have the strongest presence. In the Western Empire, Augustine wrote about such issues in *De Civitate Dei*, in

---

46. Sozomen, *Hist. Eccl.* 3.20 (PG 67:1100-1; NPNF 2.02:426–27).

47. Mayer, "Patronage," 60.

48. Finn, *Almsgiving*, 56–58. Finn mentions the possibility of taxes on certain business that were put directly into welfare based programs for the poor, and specifically the πτωχοί.

49. *In 2 Cor. hom.* 2 (PG 61:391–404; NPNF 1.12:379–91). See also the Byzantine liturgy attributed to John in Kucharek, *The Byzantine-Slav Liturgy of St. John Chrysostom*, 346.

50. *In Col. hom.* 3.5 (PG 62:324; NPNF 1.13:374–75).

51. *In Eph. hom.* 22.1–2 (PG 62:155–57; NPNF 1.13:224–27).

52. Holman, *God Knows*, 14; Mayer, "Poverty and Generosity," 141.

53. Neusner, *Judaism and Christianity*, 61; Krupp, *Shepherding the Flock*, 7.

which he discussed the tension between God's principles of government and those of earthly authorities.[54]

A COMMAND FOR ALL

Paul's emphasis on ecclesiastical almsgiving did not soften the command to practice personal almsgiving. In John's view, effective and efficient almsgiving through the churches only served to enhance almsgiving by the people. Personal almsgiving was not only expected of the voluntary poor, who were known for their almsgiving, but of every believer.[55] Despite the primarily wealthy and middle class makeup of his congregations, John made clear his belief that almsgiving was a biblical command for all regardless of rank. Being poor should not "disable" the believer from practicing almsgiving. On the contrary, to give out of one's poverty, through meager resources or care, was to give with abundant generosity in the tradition of the aforementioned women of Scripture—the widow of Sidon, the poor widow in Luke 21:1–4, Tabitha, and Thecla.[56] The result of this teaching in Antioch, according to Finn, was that almsgiving was practiced by lay people, both men and women, which resulted in a higher level of respect for others within the Christian community.[57] John described new forms of unity in the church that resulted from "doing good to one another."[58] The practice of almsgiving by all believers was a process of mutuality and exchange, whereby the wealthy, middle class, and poor helped initiate spiritual growth in one another through a shared social mission.[59]

54. Augustine, *De Civ.* 14 (CCSL 48; trans., Bettenson, *City of God,* 547–94). Augustine, whose background prior to Christianity was heavily influenced by Neoplatonist dualism and Manichaeism, contrasted two different cities in which the Christian must reside. The earthly is based on the human love of self, which leads ultimately to contempt for God. The heavenly city is based on love for God, which leads ultimately to contempt for self. In the latter city, godliness has erased the need for human wisdom. See also Matthews, *The Development of St. Augustine.*

55. *In* 1 *Cor. hom.* 21.6–7 (Field, *Sancti Patris,* 255–58; trans., Mayer and Allen, *John Chrysostom,* 173–76; PG 61:179–80; NPNF 1.12:172); Finn, *Almsgiving,* 101.

56. Along with the above references, see *Quod Ne.* 6 (PG 52:466; NPNF 1.09:297); *De Stat. hom.* 1.10 (PG 49:30; NPNF 1.09:369); *In* 1 *Tim. hom.* 14.1 (PG 62:572; NPNF 1.13:607).

57. Finn, *Almsgiving,* 214.

58. *In 1 Tim. hom.* 14.1 (PG 62:571; NPNF 1.13:606).

59. González, *Faith and Wealth,* 211. Brown, *Power and Persuasion,* 152. According to Brown, the process of mutuality and exchange that developed in Antioch during John's

The failure among believers to teach and practice almsgiving was "devoid of all good." The command to practice almsgiving was clear in every part of Scripture. It was evident from God's benevolent act of creating "Heaven, and earth, and the sea," and "far more so that He became a servant."[60] The biblical foundation for almsgiving was of utmost importance, but John was also compelled to deal with the practice from an ethical standpoint. Because of the contextual aspects of care for the poor in the Eastern Empire, John sought to incorporate the mores of social philosophy and a Greco-Roman understanding of virtue as an impetus to encourage more fervent activity in Christian generosity.[61]

Almsgiving and Christian Living

John was convinced that, as a result of his churches' increasing mission to the poor, many Christians had forsaken individual acts of almsgiving in favor of giving money to the church. In one homily/commentary on the Book of Acts, John referenced 1 Timothy 5:16, where Paul says, "If any woman who is a believer has widows in her care, she should continue to help them and not let the church be burdened with them, so that the church can help those widows who are really in need." John commented,

> "Why, does the Church not have means" you will say? She has: but what is that to you? That they should be fed from the common funds of the Church, can that benefit you? If another man prays, does it follow that you are not bound to pray? Wherefore do you not say, "Do not the priests pray? Then why should I pray?" "But I," you will say, "give to him who cannot be received there." Give, as though it is to that one: for what we are anxious for is this, that you should give at any rate. . . . "The Church," you say, "has lands, has money, and revenues." Does she not also have? I ask; and does she not have expenditure? "No doubt," you will say. Why then do you not lend aid to her moderate means? I am ashamed indeed to

---

ministry continued toward the end of Late Antiquity and the beginning of the Middle Ages. "Solidarity" developed between numerous people of different classes, based upon a shared sense of citizenship and the "common bond of human flesh."

60. *In 2 Tim. hom.* 6.3 (PG 62:634; NPNF 1.13:667).

61. Greco-Roman virtue language used by John Chrysostom will be discussed later in this chapter.

say these things: however, I compel no man, if any one imagines what I am saying is for gain.[62]

Brown sees this particular selection as indicative of John's beliefs about the long-term effects of generosity. According to Brown, "If individual Christians were more generous, [John Chrysostom] argued, the clergy would not be burdened with the time-consuming business of poor relief."[63]

John also used language of theological significance to call attention to the separation between ecclesiastical and personal almsgiving. Concerning the collection in 1 Corinthians 16, John emphasized the personal responsibility of dispersing God's resources: "Become a guardian of sacred wealth, a self-ordained steward of the poor. Your benevolent mind assigns to you this priesthood."[64] In other words, the priesthood of the believer comes with priestly responsibilities. Almsgiving was of equal importance to any activity of the Jewish priestly traditions as well, as it had the power to cleanse a person's soul even more effectively than rites of purification.[65]

The Right Christian Attitude toward the Poor

According to John, Paul taught believers of all social strata to treat the poor as they would their own loved ones, just as Jesus had said in his discourses on the second great commandment and in the Sermon on the Mount. In a homily on these very ideas as seen in 2 Thessalonians 3:3–5, John instructed his congregations to venerate the poor while practicing almsgiving; always doing so with the utmost respect. If their almsgiving needed to be accompanied by any rebuke of indiscretions in the life of the receiver, John implored them to do so as "he who admonishes his brother, [who] does it not publicly."[66] By so doing, almsgiving can be accompanied by pleasure. The giver, as well as the receiver, will reap the benefits of generosity and encouragement in righteousness as part of their spiritual growth.[67]

In John's view, there was no better demonstration of God's missionary concern for the world than the consistent practice of almsgiving by

---

62. *In Acts hom.* 45.4 (PG 60:319; NPNF 1.11:382–83).

63. Brown, *Poverty and Leadership*, 65–66.

64. *In 1 Cor. hom.* 43.1 (PG 61:368–69; NPNF 1.12:356).

65. *In 2 Tim. hom.* 6.4 (PG 62:634–35; NPNF 1.13:668–69).

66. *In 2 Thess. hom.* 5.3 (PG 62:495–96; NPNF 1.13:535).

67. Ibid. (62:496; 1.13:536).

believers who demonstrated a gracious and benevolent attitude. As Paul had written to Timothy (2 Tim 2:20–21), the most effective religious symbols were the bodies of believers put into service. Just as God had willingly lowered Himself as an act of service to mankind, so the believer can fulfill God's missionary purpose for His people with the same willingness through almsgiving. In this way, almsgiving was the clearest expression of righteous living above any religious rite performed within the churches or in the world.[68] The attitude of the believer, which was to represent the attitude of Christ, was best demonstrated as submission to God through submission to others.

John also attributed Pauline authorship to the book of Hebrews, as many previous church leaders had done. In his homily concerning repentance in Hebrews 6:1–3, John compared almsgiving to the medicinal herbs used by physicians of his day. Almsgiving, according to John, "is the essential herb," which allows repentance to bring healing to the transgressor.[69] John implored his congregation to develop friendships with the needy, as did the Shrewd Manager in Jesus' parable (Luke 16:9), for the purpose of receiving salvation through relationships. He further instructed them to use these relationships as an opportunity to practice almsgiving. By sharing one's possessions with others, one might gain "everlasting habitations." This type of behavior was expected of the rich, the middle class, and the poor.[70] In the same way, almsgiving was a necessary component of repentance. This is perhaps an early understanding of what modern Catholics deem acceptable responses of penance following "acts of contrition."

As has been demonstrated, John encouraged every person in his congregations, regardless of their economic situation, to give alms through financial offerings or other acts of compassion. As Brändle has pointed out, "It may include the kind word just as much as material help."[71] John reminded those who could only give small amounts, whether to the church or directly to the poor, that God received their gifts with honor and considered them to be admirable. As such, the one who gives alms out of his or her poverty will receive the same reward as the one who gives out of abundance. This was especially the case when the giver was characterized

68. *In 2 Tim. hom.* 6.4 (PG 62:634–35; NPNF 1.13:668).

69. *In Heb. hom.* 9.4 (PG 63:81; NPNF 1.14:594). Here John again uses Luke 11:41, Tobit 4:11, and Sirach 3:30.

70. *In Heb. hom.* 1.4 (PG 63:19–20; NPNF 1.14:533–34).

71. Brändle, "This Sweetest Passage," 131.

by a good attitude and humility, for, "the greatness of the charity is not shown by the measure of what is given, but by the disposition of the giver."[72]

Discipleship

Some scholars have argued John was not personally involved in the actual execution of ministering to the poor in Antioch.[73] It is doubtful, however, that John could display such a detailed awareness of the situation of the poor without personal contact with individuals who were poverty-stricken. Many of his letters, most of which were written in his exile to the Black Sea, offer evidence of his investment into the lives of others for the purpose of discipleship. Some of these letters include statements regarding private counseling of individuals and pastoral encouragement to younger clergy.[74] Mayer and Allen cite as examples two letters to a young pastor named Constantius who was doing mission work in the East and needed some assistance. John referred to Constantius' work managing the mission effort, struggling against paganism and syncretism, planting churches, practicing discipleship, and caring for the needy.[75] In another letter, John assures presbyters and monks in Phoenicia that Constantius has secured funding for the purchase and delivery of clothing, including shoes and food, to support their work.[76]

Two other letters from exile record John's pleas for support of the expanding missionary movements to the poor throughout the Eastern Empire. John was likely involved in a number of these endeavors as a part of the archbishopric in Constantinople. In a letter to one Valentinus, John requested aid for a presbyter named Domitian whom he had placed in

---

72. *In Heb. hom.* 32.3 (PG 63:224; NPNF 1.14:744). See also *In Heb. hom.* 1.4 (PG 63:19–20; NPNF 1.14: 533).

73. Mayer and Allen, *John Chrysostom*, 46; Allen and Mayer, "Through a Bishop's Eyes," 345–97.

74. Mayer and Allen, *John Chrysostom*, 44–45.

75. *Epist.* 221, "Constantio" (PG 52:732–33); *Epist.* 225, "Constantio" (PG 52:735–36). For a recent discussion regarding John's letters from exile, see Mayer, "The Bishop as Crisis Manager," 159–71; See also Delmaire, "Les 'lettres d' exil' de Jean Chrysostome," 120–21. According to Delmaire, a man named Constantius was a well-known pastor in Antioch, and was likely the same Constantius mentioned in these letters from near the end of John's life.

76. *Epist.* 123, "Phoen. Presb. et Mon." (PG 52:676–78).

charge of ministry to widows and virgins somewhere near Constantinople.[77] In another letter to one Diogenes, John addressed a friend who had sent him money which was refused by one named Aphraates. John encouraged his friend to give the money instead to those planting churches in Phoenicia in the face of significant pagan opposition.[78]

ALMSGIVING AS PERSONAL AND SOCIAL VIRTUE

For John, the increase of knowledge within the churches regarding the biblical practice of almsgiving was significant, but it was far from sufficient. John joined other fourth and fifth-century preachers such as Ambrose, Jerome, and Augustine, who "grappled with the problems of harmonizing orthodox doctrine with the way Christians led their lives."[79] Almsgiving was more than a doctrinal or epistemological issue. Its theological and biblical implications would be rendered ineffective unless they were applied to personal and social morality.[80] John used the Greco-Roman language of virtue to discuss several aspects of Christian living. He described almsgiving above any other form of morality, however, as "the queen of virtues."[81]

Almsgiving was not the only social issue in Antioch and the Eastern Empire which John addressed. In his homilies on Romans, John condemned abortion, which he called "murder before the birth," and, "something even worse than murder . . . since it does not take off the thing born, but prevent its being born . . . mak[ing] the chamber of procreation a chamber for murder."[82] He also confronted gender inequalities in the churches. In a homily on 1 Thessalonians, John denounced the idea that women should be regarded with a greater degree of guilt than men in cases of adultery. Krupp argues John's perspective was unpopular. Nevertheless, he maintained treating a woman as if she had greater fault in an adulterous relationship of mutual consent was a matter of breaking God's law which

77. *Epist.* 217, "Valentino" (PG 52:730–31; trans., Mayer and Allen, *John Chrysostom,* 201–2).

78. *Epist.* 51, "Diogeni" (PG 52:636–37; trans., Mayer and Allen, *John Chrysostom,* 202–3). See also Smith and Wace, *A Dictionary of Christian Biography,* 1:840.

79. Brown, "Christianization and Religious Conflict," 661–63. See also Maxwell, *Christianization and Communication,* 145–46.

80. Kelly, *Golden Mouth,* 96.

81. *Eleem. et Dec. Vir.* 1 (PG 49:292; trans., Christo, *ORA,* 30).

82. *In Rom. hom.* 24.4 (PG 60:626–27; NPNF 1.11:695–96).

was above Roman law.[83] John also addressed the issues of spousal abuse, the mistreatment of slaves, and homosexuality.[84] Like many preachers of his day, John was often compelled to confront issues of virtue or the lack thereof in the empire at large.

The Secular Language of Virtue

Almsgiving, much like the issues of abortion and adultery, was not to be interpreted exclusively according to the Roman understanding of virtue. At the same time, John saw value in using the mechanism of Greco-Roman philosophy, as it related to ethics, to garner momentum for Christian action. John argued all virtuous action, though valuable, is fruitless if one fails to practice almsgiving. This included even the most important aspects of asceticism.[85] He intentionally separated uniquely Christian ideas from those of pagan philosophy, while communicating clearly those Greco-Roman ethical components that were of value to the believer. One example comes from a homily on the Gospel of John, where he pointed out the refusal by many of the wealthy to enter the marketplace, baths, and fields without their servants for fear of ridicule by fellow elites. He revealed the irony that, while the servant was free to go about without the master during his off time, the master seemed ceaselessly bound to the servant.[86] This idea was reminiscent of common Stoic philosophy, which often asked the satirical question, "Which one is truly the slave?"[87]

Some scholars have disagreed with the idea that John saw value in secular philosophy after the conclusion of his rhetorical training by Libanius. Eighteenth-century scholar and Roman historian Edward Gibbon argued John was "indifferent," or even "hostile" toward pagan literature concerning virtue.[88] Gibbon's opinion was considered by many to be defini-

---

83. *In 1 Thess. hom.* 5.2 (PG 62:425-26; NPNF 1.13:470–71); Krupp, *Shepherding the Flock*, 177.

84. *In Eph. hom.* 15.3 (PG 62:109–10; NPNF 1.13:178-79); Schroeder, "John Chrysostom's Critique of Spousal Violence," 413–42; *Adv. Opp. Vit. Mon.* 3.8 (PG 47:362; trans., Hunter, *A Comparison*, 141–43).

85. *In 2 Tim. hom.* 6.3 (PG 62:633–34; NPNF 1.13.667).

86. *In John hom.* 80.3 (PG 59:436–37; trans., Goggin, *Commentary on St. John*, 2:374–75; NPNF 1.14:446).

87. Leyerle, "John Chrysostom on Almsgiving," 35.

88. Gibbon, *History of the Decline and Fall of the Roman Empire*, 5:468.

tive for over a century, but was refuted convincingly by Ameringer's work in 1921. Ameringer argued John's hostility toward pagan philosophy was against strict adherents of Second Sophistic practices who, like Libanius, were ambivalent regarding true morality. The sophists were more focused on the virtue of their rhetoric and styles of delivery than the true virtue of righteous living as found in Scripture. Nevertheless, John believed the "profane rhetoric" of sophistic language was useful for exposition of Scripture, and valuable for maintaining the inertia of social action.[89]

Ameringer presented an exhaustive selection of linguistic examples and illustrations which demonstrate that John, while interested in the biblical foundation for virtue according to righteousness, was also skilled in the "virtuosity" of Second Sophistic rhetorical artistry.[90] Specifically, Ameringer examines John's use of the expositional form known as "Ecphrasis," which was used to create images from words in the mind of the receptor in order to form "a painting in words."[91] This technique was also used by the Cappadocian father Gregory Nazianzen, who "transformed the futile sophistic ecphrasis, which served only for display, into a means of edification and moral instruction . . . giving to its orators ideas of vital and absorbing interest in place of the frivolous and immoral themes of pagan mythology."[92]

Begging and Stewardship

Kelly S. Johnson has said it well: "Beggars stand in an untidy corner of ethics. The presence of beggars . . . raises questions that [Christianized] societies would sometimes prefer not to address."[93] Many people in John's

---

89. Ameringer, *Second Sophistic*, 20–25, 28. See also Anderson, *The Second Sophistic*; Viansino, "Aspetti dell'opera di Giovanni Crisostomo," 137–205; Bosinis, "Two Platonic Images in the Rhetoric of John Chrysostom," 433–38. Both Viansino and Bosinis discuss John's use of Platonic philosophical forms despite his sharp criticism of their content and value.

90. Ameringer, *Second Sophistic*, 45–47.

91. Ibid., 56–86. Ameringer cited dozens of examples of John's skillful use of metaphors and comparisons which are indicative of his training in the Second Sophistic style. Some of these include military imagery, the Olympic games and other athletic contests, the racetrack, the sea and navigation, the theaters, music and the arts, animals, and agriculture.

92. Ibid., 100.

93. Johnson, *The Fear of Beggars*, 4.

audiences viewed the disciplined lifestyles of the mendicant ascetics with great respect. Their opinions of common beggars, however, were much more diminished. As a result, John saw the use of moral philosophy as integral in terms of reshaping societal perspectives concerning beggars.[94] As he addressed the Great Church of Antioch following the destruction of the imperial statues, John used the example of Job as virtuous action in the midst of destitution. Job, who before his calamities was generous toward mankind, reached a new level of virtue through his suffering. Job was forced to embrace poverty and his disposition remained almost completely free of impetuousness in a way reminiscent of the Stoics in terms of emotion. The intensity of Job's suffering, which resulted in a new degree of simplicity, propelled him to an even higher level of wisdom.[95]

The persistence of beggars also raised questions concerning stewardship, particularly in the areas of property ownership and possessions. According to Johnson, it was not John's goal to abolish property ownership. On the contrary, he encouraged righteous ownership and virtuous stewardship.[96] In a sermon to the rich in his congregation concerning 1 Timothy 4:10, John discussed Paul's confession that laboring for God is based on the hope of salvation for all people. As a result, the claims of entitlement to property and possessions by the wealthy were without biblical merit. Because everything a person "owns" actually came from God, selfishness and hoarding have no place in the kingdom of God. John argued all wealth, whether earned or inherited, was the result of injustice toward another person. "Why?" one might ask.

> Because God in the beginning did not make one man rich, and another poor. Nor did He afterwards take and show to one treasures of gold, and deny to the other the right of searching for it: but He left the earth free to all alike . . . but is not this an evil, that you alone should have the Lord's property, that you alone should enjoy what is common? Is not "the earth God's, and everything

---

94. Maxwell, *Christianization and Communication*, 11.

95. *De Stat. hom.* 1.9–10 (PG 49:29; NPNF 1.09:368); Cardman, "Poverty and Wealth as Theater," 166–67. Cardman compares John's presentation of appearances regarding the wealthy and the poor to the Stoics, Epicureans, and Platonists. His interpretation of the reality of poverty, suffering, and their ethical advantages has more similarities to Stoic Ethics than any other. For an example of a Stoic parallel to John on the ethics of poverty, see Seneca, *Epist.* 110, "On True and False Riches" (trans., Gummere, *Ad Lucilium Epistulae Morales*, LCL 77:265–76).

96. Johnson, *The Fear of Beggars*, 4, 24.

in it"? If then our possessions belong to one common Lord, they belong also to our fellow-servants. The possessions of one Lord are all common.[97]

He concluded by comparing the world's wealth to common spaces in the cities, such as marketplaces and sidewalks, which each person was given the same right to utilize.[98]

In a conversation with his friend Basil, as recorded in *De Sac.*, John classified stewardship not as a quality some are given with greater measure, but rather as the result of cognoscente self-control. Stewardship is not based on wealth, poverty, or status. On the contrary, it is something every Christian ought to practice through obedience with a good attitude.[99] Brändle argues John's sotierological language concerning almsgiving was meant to be understood from the standpoint of ethics. If good works like almsgiving are indeed a part of sanctification, the believer should perform them on a regular basis. According to Brändle:

> Continual meditation on (Matt. 25:31–46) allowed John's conviction to grow that the Risen One was not only giving us a steady stream of impulses to help the poor but was also promising us his helping presence. For he who feeds the hungry, gives drink to the thirsty, clothes the naked, and visits the sick and imprisoned comes into contact with Christ the Redeemer. . . . He is hungry so that we do not need to starve. It is for our salvation that Christ goes naked.[100]

John affirmed this idea: "Yet He endures this very treatment for our sake. He gladly goes hungry that you may dine and remains naked that He may furnish for you the covering of the garment of immortality."[101]

---

97. *In 1 Tim. hom.* 12.4 (PG 62:563; NPNF 1.13:598–99).

98. Ibid., (62:563–64; 1.13:599).

99. *De Sac.* 3.16 (PG 48:654–55; trans., Neville, *OP*, 95–96; NPNF 1.09:60). John mentioned a group of widows in his churches who, despite their poverty, age, and supposed level of wisdom, complained often about possessions. John referred to such older women comically, as those who "use an unbridled freedom of speech—to call it no worse!"

100. Brändle, "This Sweetest Passage," 137.

101. *In John hom.* 27.3 (PG 59:161; trans., Goggin, *Commentary on St. John*, 1:266; NPNF 1.14:147).

STRATEGIC EVALUATION AND BENEVOLENCE

As almsgiving increased among individual believers in Antioch and its churches, John and other church leaders were tasked with implementing a system that furthered the practice while maximizing its efficiency. Several problematic issues often arise when any benevolent ministry experiences growth. John acknowledged some recipients were dishonest in their attempts to procure assistance, while others seemed to be ungrateful.[102] Church leaders had a difficult time maintaining a balance between sufficient evaluation and unnecessary investigation. John also recognized that almsgiving could be abused by those who refused to work, which was detrimental to the overall societal good. Thomas Malthus, a pastor and renowned economic theologian in eighteenth and nineteenth centuries England, encouraged his audiences to practice charity with caution, because benevolence "easily undermines the common good."[103] John's desire was not to control the practice of almsgiving, but to enable the churches to distribute alms with greater impact to the gospel mission in Antioch.

Case Management

Case management involves evaluating the specific needs of individuals and groups in order to offer the appropriate level of care and assistance. According to Brown, one of John's main goals was to decipher which needs were in fact legitimate among the clergy, widows, and orphans who were receiving aid. Throughout his ministry, John found there were many benefiting from the churches' distribution of alms "who were by no means poor."[104] He referred to some beggars as λώτάγας (*lōtagas*), or "strollers," who pretended to be poor in order take advantage of the benevolence of others.[105] The situation in Antioch was similar to that which is referred to by Ambrose in

---

102. *In Acts hom.* 45.4 (PG 60:319–20; NPNF 1.11:382–83).

103. Johnson, *The Fear of Beggars*, 123. Johnson paraphrases Malthus' discussion on benevolence which may be found in Malthus, *The Works of Thomas Robert Malthus*, 3:454.

104. Brown, *Poverty and Leadership*, 59.

105. *In Eph. hom.* 13.3 (PG 62:97; NPNF 1.13:166). Many of these individuals were known to be gamblers or professional conmen. According to a note by the translator, the word λώτάγας was rare and can also refer to soothsayers, traveling musicians, and professional tricksters.

Milan, which was discussed in chapter 3. Ambrose described the situation further by saying, "Never was the greed of beggars greater than it is now."[106]

Despite such dishonesty, John urged members of the clergy to be careful about taking their investigations too far. He instructed that they not inquire about a person's situation more than was necessary, and to err on the side of generosity when faced with a person who appeared destitute.[107] Otherwise, the continuation of overzealous examination might result in greater levels of dishonesty among patrons. According to John,

> I do not say these things haphazardly now, but rather because many are often overly investigative toward the needy; they examine their lineage, life, habits, pursuit, and the vigor of their body. They make complaints and demand immense public scrutiny of their health. For this precise reason, many of the poor simulate physical disabilities, so that by dramatizing their misfortunes they may deflect our cruelty and inhumanity.[108]

In the argument preceding his first homily on Romans, John described the principles of case management by offering a comparison to the professions of physician and teacher. The doctor does not handle each patient alike, but offers treatment that is consistent with their level of infirmity. In the same way, those who teach offer instruction on graded levels depending on the prior advancement of their students.[109] In the same way, the structure within which almsgiving operated in the churches was not to override the command to treat each person as an individual in need of God's grace.

Organized and Structured Distribution

Diligent case management led to new developments in the churches' regular distributions of alms. According to Cameron, a number of common practices concerning almsgiving throughout the Eastern Empire were developed during John's pastorate, while others were inherited from the previous systems.[110] John demanded that widows supported by the church were to be over the age of sixty, able to demonstrate good works, and provide

106. Ambrose, *De Off. Min.* 2.16.76–77 (PL 16:123; NPNF 2.10:104).

107. *De Laz. hom.* 2.6 (PG 48:990; trans., Roth, *OWP*, 53).

108. *De Eleem.* 6 (PG 51:269; trans., Christo, *ORA*, 146).

109. *In Rom. hom.* 1.2, arg. (PG 60:393–94; NPNF 1.11:457–58).

110. Cameron, *The Later Roman Empire*, 177.

evidence they had only been married once.[111] Such widows were entered into a register so that sufficient records could be kept concerning their assistance.[112] In *De Sac.*, John discussed the roles of priests and deacons who were in charge of such registers so that no widows or others seeking assistance might be granted access to regular church assistance without meeting requirements for eligibility.[113] According to Finn, the churches in Antioch scheduled specific times of the year to collect alms above the regular offerings, as well as allotting certain occasions to collect extra resources when the demand for alms was greater.[114]

As an expression of good biblical stewardship, John implored his congregations to give alms equitably to the poor as needs dictated. He advised his congregations to avoid giving alms personally to those who put on the grandest shows in the marketplace. He criticized those in his congregations who gave more to street performers than common beggars, for to do so was disgraceful and encouraged "making a fine show of other people's miseries."[115] This type of behavior was a form of favoritism, which is unacceptable in God's kingdom economy.[116]

Supplemental Income

John was quite aware of a problem faced by all benevolent ministries: giving things away can be a means to apathy on the part of recipients. Along with the criteria set for the widows supported by the church, John also instructed that alms not be given to those who were able to work. Some,

111. *In 1 Tim. hom.* 14.1 (PG 62:572; NPNF 1.13:607).

112. *In Matt. hom.* 66.3 (PG 58:630; NPNF 1.10:548).

113. *De Sac.* 3.16–17 (PG 48:654–59; trans., Neville, *OP*, 94–100; NPNF 1.09:60–65).

114. Finn, *Almsgiving*, 39, 46–56.

115. *In 1 Cor. hom.* 21.6 (Field, *Sancti Patris*, 253; trans., Mayer and Allen, *John Chrysostom*, 171; PG 61:176–77; NPNF 1.12:170).

116. The late Southern Baptist pioneer in the field of Christian ethics, T. B. Maston, argued that favoritism is a fatal flaw of liberation theology, as the poor are elevated above the rich and the criteria for poverty and resulting blessedness are ambivalent. He argued missions and ministry among the poor must be based upon the idea that God is impartial and "no respecter of persons." See Maston, *Biblical Ethics*, 260–61. Maston goes on to say the reason the poor man is dishonored in James 2 is that he is not treated the "same" as the rich man. The application, therefore, should not be drawn that the poor man should be treated better than the rich man. True Christian social ethics should never seek to treat one person or group above another for there is no favoritism in the kingdom of God.

especially among the πένητες, were unable to work for social, seasonal, or other reasons outside of their control. For the able-bodied who were in such situations, John advocated almsgiving in ways that would provide supplemental income until they were able to secure gainful employment.[117] He called those who were able to work and refused, "busybodies," and reminded his congregations that their responsibility in almsgiving, according to the Apostle Paul, was for the clergy and those "not able to support themselves by work of their own hands."[118] The destitute, on the other hand, would always need the support of the churches and their members in order to have any semblance of quality of life.[119]

John also saw the importance of giving alms during times when they were most needed. For example, alms in the form of supplemental income were needed more during the violent winters of Antioch than in warmer months. It has long been believed that John delivered his sermon *De Eleem.* after walking through the marketplace during the winter season of 387 CE. He described the specific need for almsgiving in many forms during such severe conditions as opposed to other times of the year:

> During the summer season the poor find great consolation. Even if they walk nude they are free from danger, the ray of the sun sufficing them in the place of clothing. Even if they simply lie down to sleep upon the ground and pass the night in the open air, they are safe. Neither are shoes necessary for them, nor drinking wine, nor eating plentifully; rather, to some, the streams of water are enough, to others the most paltry vegetables, to others a few dried seeds, as this season of the year supplies them with a makeshift table. They have even greater consolation yet, the availability of work; for those who build houses, till the earth, and sail upon the sea have most need of their assistance. And what fields and houses and the other sources of revenue are to the wealthy, this body is to the poor; all their income is from their hands and from nothing else. For this reason, they enjoy some sort of consolation during the summer; but during the season of winter, the battle against them is mighty from all quarters, and the siege is twice as great— the famine that devours the viscera from within and the frost that freezes and deadens the flesh from without. Therefore, they need more nourishment, a heavier garment, a shelter, a bed, shoes, and many other things. And, indeed, what is altogether grievous, they

117. *De Eleem.*1 (PG 51:261; trans., Christo, *ORA*, 132).

118. *In 2 Thess. hom.* 5.2 (PG 62.494–95; NPNF 1.13:534–35).

119. *De Laz. hom.* 2.5–6 (PG 48:989–90; trans., Roth, *OWP*, 52–53).

cannot find work easily, since the season of the year does not allow it. Therefore, their need of the bare necessities is much greater, and besides, work passes them by, because no one hires the wretched, or summons them to service.[120]

If almsgiving in the churches and among believers accomplished nothing else, it was to help sustain those in need during difficult times so that they, at some point in the future, might be ripe to receive the gospel message that was spreading throughout the empire.

In the Wake of Tragedy

John also emphasized action by the churches and believers in times of widespread fear and upheaval. The aforementioned riots of Antioch in 387, about which John preached his homilies *De Stat.*, were a primary example of unrest among the people. According to Stephens, who translated this work for NPNF, the events following the riots provided John with unprecedented opportunities to bring the gospel message to the masses.[121] Along with the struggles associated with seasonal work shortages, Antioch also faced sporadic droughts and economic difficulties as a result of occasional military inhabitation.[122]

John also used the earthquakes that occurred from time to time in Antioch as a platform for the gospel message. He believed the earthquakes brought out the best in people because they were faced with their own mortality. During an earthquake just before his homilies *De Laz.*, John cited an absence of pride, greed, theft, subjugation, oppression, and exploitation. Instead of filling the theater, racetrack, and marketplace, "everything was shattered, the city was full of shrieking, and everyone ran to the church."[123] This particular earthquake, according to John, was to be seen as a message of the same nature as that of Nineveh (Jonah 3:4), sent to warn the people of Antioch that what is done on Earth matters, and God desired improvement to result from them.[124] Disasters on a national scale were also a reminder of the value of the πένητες. John believed the working poor would fare better in such times because of their ability to provide for themselves using their

---

120. *De Eleem.* 1 (PG 51:261; trans., Christo, ORA, 131–32).

121. Stephens, in *De Stat.*, pref. (NPNF 1.09:342–43).

122. Downey, *A History of Antioch*, 382–84, 419–20.

123. *De Laz. hom.* 6.1 (PG 48:1027; trans., Roth, OWP, 97–98).

124. Ibid., 6.2 (48:1028–29; 99).

skills, trades, and crafts along with their propensity for hard work.[125] As a result, the increasingly diverse churches of Antioch were filled with people who offered valuable physical and spiritual support in the wake of tragedy.

SUMMARY

John Chrysostom's homilies on the Pauline letters contain his most practical content concerning the ethical and ecclesiological aspects of almsgiving. Almsgiving was most effective when practiced regularly, and in various forms, by individual believers who made up the larger Christian community. The clergy were responsible to lead in the practice of almsgiving with integrity, and they were also entitled to a personal share of the resources given to the church. The church functioned within the confines of the empire, which brought advantages and challenges.

Almsgiving, as an act of virtue, was one of the clearest expressions of the work of righteousness in the lives of believers. John sought to bring order to the practice within the churches, so that resources given to the Lord might be managed with the utmost efficiency according to sound principles of stewardship. At the same time, the developing structure concerning charity and the churches was not to prevent action in times when needs were the most desperate. Almsgiving, according to the Pauline model of ecclesiology, was confessional as an act of faith in Christ, ceremonial as an act of worship, and practical for the purpose of the churches' mission to people of all demographics in the Eastern Empire and beyond.

125. *In 1 Cor. hom.* 34.5 (PG 61:292–94; NPNF 1.12:283–84).

9

Conclusion—Almsgiving and Contemporary Evangelicalism

[The Fathers] lived in a world in which contrasts between the rich and the poor were staggering; we live in a world populated by a few who have millions and millions who have nothing.

—JUSTO GONZÁLEZ

The practice of almsgiving was the most common form of benevolent ministry to the poor among the ancient Hebrews, the pre-exilic and post-exilic people of Israel, and the multiplying Christian churches of the first four centuries CE. Almsgiving was demonstrated by the giving and sharing of resources, provision of surplus goods, offering emotional or spiritual care to those in need, and the application of spiritual disciplines that were of benefit to others. Christian almsgiving peaked in the Roman Empire of the late fourth century, as evidenced by numerous references concerning the practice from Jerusalem, Cappadocia, Alexandria, the writings of Augustine, and John Chrysostom in Antioch and Constantinople.

John's sermons and commentaries contain arguably the highest concentration of teaching on Christian almsgiving from any single contributor in recorded history. John reinforced the biblical practice of almsgiving by emphasizing its importance as obedience to God's command. For this reason, almsgiving was a vital element of virtuous living by the individual according to biblical and Roman standards. John also reminded his congregations that almsgiving was a requirement for biblical ecclesiology and was to be preached as doctrine in every church he influenced.

For John, the practice of almsgiving was essential to the Christian mission. Almsgiving was confessional as a material representation of the spiritual presence of Christ in the Christian mission, ceremonial in its essentiality for biblical ecclesiology, and practical in order to maximize effectiveness for each circumstance. In the Eastern Empire of the fourth century, Christian churches and their leadership had become some of the most influential voices in culture and society. The Christian mission among the poor gave advocacy to many who had previously been ignored. Through John's leadership in Antioch, and later in Constantinople, the responsibility to care for the needy became a top priority for Christian churches. The Christian mission to the poor was a thrust which enabled the working poor to gain the possibility of social progress while the destitute attained new levels of representation. In Antioch, almsgiving in the churches was identified as the most generous activity among the poor. Christian benevolence clearly demonstrated the commitment of the Christian mission to transmit the hope of the gospel among all people regardless of ethnic, demographic, or economic distinctions.

I believe the Evangelical Christian mission in the developed world of the twenty-first century has similar opportunities to that of the fourth century. Despite the use of terms such as "post-Christian" and "post-Christendom," many among the general population continue to look for church leadership to speak regarding suffering and injustice in the world. According to Sider, "For the first time in decades, the larger institutions of society are astonishingly ready to welcome the contribution of religion to solving our most desperate social problems."[1] As a result, evangelicals must lead the way in missionary endeavors among the needy. The biblical practice of almsgiving, which was successfully demonstrated by John and the churches in Antioch, will help Evangelicalism move from enthusiasm to effectiveness in the Christian mission to the poor.

When John was ordained to the pastorate in Antioch, he directed much of his preaching and leadership toward the Christian mission to the poor. As the late missiologist Eugene A. Nida argued, effective communication of the gospel message uses the process of indigenization, and not syncretism, in order to reach people according to their own social rules.[2]

1. Sider, *Just Generosity*, 26.
2. Nida, *Message and Mission*, 135.

This process is beneficial so long as the mores of the host culture are not irredeemably beyond the standards of the gospel.

One example of a cultural and moral and conflict between bearers of the gospel and the larger society of the developed world, particularly in North America, is the issue of abortion. There are at least three categories of opinions on abortion among evangelicals: 1) Pro-choice, moral relativism, 2) Pro-choice, moral objectivism, which is based on human rights, and 3) Pro-life, biblical understanding of human nature that values personhood in the embryonic stage.[3] John addressed the issue of abortion on more than one occasion, each time condemning the practice as morally reprehensible by attributing personhood to the unborn child.[4]

The late missionary and missiologist Lesslie Newbigin stressed the importance of decoding contextual details of one's culture that could potentially lead to successful strategies for imparting the gospel.[5] That which began as impassioned homiletical fervor developed into a progression of organized teaching and leadership which were intended to revitalize John's churches in their commitment to the practice of almsgiving. John began by deciphering the issues underlying the decline in commitment toward almsgiving and the Christian mission in Antioch, Constantinople, and beyond.

One of the greatest challenges John faced in Antioch was its pluralistic culture. Each of the three major religious traditions had developed certain unhealthy practices in their approaches to the poor. Jewish forms of charity were increasingly ethnocentric, secular forms of philanthropy were self-serving for benefactors, and some among the Christian clergy had been accused of abusing the churches' resources for their own benefit. The idea

---

3. For the first category, see Maguire, *Sacred Choices*, viii. According to Maguire, "historically, women have been the principal cherishers and caretakers of life. We can trust them with these decisions. . . . The world's religions urge us to do so." For the second category, see Pojman, "Abortion," 275–90. Pojman offers a moderate defense of the pro-choice position while arguing against moral relativism. For the third category, see Moreland and Rae, *Body and Soul*, 344. These authors conclude, "abortion is the killing of an innocent person, and both fetuses and embryos (the latter whether extracorporeal or not) are deserving of full moral status as persons with all the protections therein."

4. *In Rom. hom.* 24 (PG 60:626–27; NPNF vol. 1.11:695–96); *In Matt. hom.* 28.5 (PG 58:357; NPNF 1.10:269). John classified the actions of those who terminated a pregnancy before, during, or immediately after birth of having "maimed their nature." For John, abortion was neither morally neutral nor was it an issue to be ignored by the Christian community.

5. Newbigin, *Foolishness to the Greeks*, 41. See also Van Rheenen, "Contrasting Missional and Church Growth Perspectives." Van Rheenen credits McGavran for helping to develop successful strategies according to the same type of cultural evaluation.

that Christians had digressed to equivalency with paganism since the time of Julian was both surprising and distressing to John in his early ministry career.

In John's view, however, the most appalling aspect of Christianity, especially in Antioch, was that benevolence had become indifferent, and at times malevolent, toward the poor. That which missiologists describe as "cultural syncretism" had occurred regarding Christian almsgiving, causing the practice to be indiscernible from other forms of charity that existed in the empire.[6] John believed the biblical practice of almsgiving was the most successful way to enhance the reputation of the Christian mission, the churches, and the God whom they represented.

John also addressed many of the problems that existed concerning the treatment of the poor in Roman society. When recounting the Parable of the Rich Man and Lazarus, John enumerated several hardships the beggar endured which were indicative of many poor persons throughout the empire. In his view, the most painful aspects of such poverty resulted from loneliness and the comparison of one's indigence to the affluence of others.[7] In nearly every case, the working poor and the destitute felt helpless to improve their economic situation without significant assistance from outside sources.

The late missiologist and leader of the Church Growth Movement (CGM), Donald McGavran, attributed the same heartache to the poor in the developed world of the twentieth century: "Being poor and hopeless in a society where most are not produces a deep sense of alienation."[8] As has been demonstrated, the Christian mission of the fourth century helped the poor to gain prominence and their needs received a greater share of attention. This was certainly the case in Antioch as a result of the churches and John's leadership in the latter part of the century.

Viv Grigg, a missiologist and church planter from New Zealand, discusses various levels of poverty as they are experienced in different parts of the world today. Some are truly destitute and dependent on the help of others for their basic survival. Others experience physical, emotional, and

---

6. Nicholls, *Contextualization*, 31–34; Van Rheenen, "Modern and Postmodern Syncretism," 173; Carson, "Church and Mission," 219–20. See also Van Rheenen, *Contextualization and Syncretism*.

7. *De Laz. hom.* 1.9–10 (PG 48:975–77; trans., Roth, *OWP*, 29–32).

8. McGavran, *Understanding Church Growth*, 236.

social effects of poverty when compared with those around them. Grigg proposes two valuable delineations of poverty:

> *Absolute poverty* is a term used to describe poverty when people have an absolute insufficiency to meet their basic needs—food, clothing, housing. *Relative poverty* is found in the developed world and is measured by looking at a person's standard of living relative to others in the community or nation. It is often called secondary poverty. It is a measure of the extent to which people are on the margins of society.[9]

Like Lazarus, many people in the twenty-first-century experience both forms of poverty. In the majority world, relative poverty is primarily experienced through media. In the developed world, relative poverty is the norm among those who are most economically challenged. The poor in the United States, for example, experience a much higher standard of living according to the principles of absolute poverty.[10]

Economic distribution in the developed world of today is also not far removed from the fourth century. In the United States, household gains have remained among the wealthiest 20 percent despite the majority being from the middle class.[11] According to Sider, the wealthiest 5 percent see the most remarkable gains while the poorest 20 percent actually experience a decrease in average household income.[12] During the same period measured, Americans saw an unhealthy increase in caloric consumption resulting in more than 60 percent of the population being considered overweight. As a result, Sider compares developed countries to a medieval aristocracy that is monopolizing the largest portion of the world's resources, adding, "The richest one-fifth are incredibly wealthy and the poorest one-fifth are desperately poor."[13]

John believed the predicaments faced by Lazarus as described in Jesus' parable should urge Christians to engage the poor on a personal level. To do so, churches and individual believers had to practice counter-cultural generosity. The Christian practice of almsgiving was supposed to counteract popular forms of charity that perpetuated the poverty of certain individuals in order to maintain a relationship of dependence. John attributed the

9. Grigg, "Church of the Poor," 42.

10. Sachs, *The End of Poverty*, 20; Mandryk, *Operation World*, 1–82, 864–66.

11. Ibid., 861.

12. Sider, *Just Generosity*, 31.

13. Sider, *Rich Christians in an Age of Hunger*, 27–32.

primary responsibility of caring for the poor to the churches, and not the state, because the greatest need of those who were suffering was spiritual. Again, "The church has resources with which the state cannot compete . . ."[14] The churches' mission to the poor began with engagement by individual Christians.

If Christians were to engage the poor through almsgiving, they had to begin by *seeing* the poor. As Hesselgrave has noted, styles of communication that "reflect a true understanding of the plight of modern man and an empathy with his dilemmas" are of far more value in cultures that are permeated with materialism.[15] The failure to acknowledge the suffering of Lazarus on earth resulted directly in the condemnation of the rich man in the next life. John worked ardently to bring the needs of the poor before the churches so that believers would take notice as they encountered needs in their daily lives. John also believed awareness and generosity in almsgiving began in the homes of Christian people. If almsgiving was initiated in Christian homes, it would to spread to the Christian community and eventually to society as a whole.

Almsgiving was a shared practice among Christians, but it was also a matter of personal morality. Using the rhetoric of Greco-Roman virtue, John implored the educated within his congregations to practice personal almsgiving willingly and generously. Almsgiving was more than an issue of virtue, however. It was an issue of biblical stewardship. Each person's property and possessions belonged to God and were to be utilized according to His direction. Maston described the role of the church in similar terms. The church is set apart from the world in such a way that its uniqueness is obvious to those on the outside. At the same time, God has chosen to use the church in the world to represent Him in all of its dealings with mankind.[16] For John, responsible generosity through the organized practice of almsgiving was the clearest expression of good stewardship from the church toward the world.

Engagement by individual Christians was part of a larger picture in terms of the Christian mission to the poor. John's emphasis on personal almsgiving was followed by a swell of almsgiving in the churches. In order to continue progress in ecclesiastical almsgiving, John believed cooperation among believers and churches was imperative. Almsgiving, by its

14. Charry, "When Generosity is not Enough," 269.

15. Hesselgrave, *Communicating Christ Cross-Culturally*, 220.

16. Maston, *The Christian, the Church, and Contemporary Problems*, 55–56.

participatory nature, gave believers the opportunity to grow as individuals through submission to divine command and together through fellowship and discipleship.[17] Cooperation within and among the churches was crucial for the practice of almsgiving to have its most widespread impact as a part of the expansion of Christian faith.[18]

As Christianity became more prominent in the empire, churches were attended primarily by the middle and upper classes. The poor remained on the outside and were viewed as subjects instead of participants. By the time of John's return to the pastorate, the Antiochene churches were largely "homogenous."[19] For a sustainable unity to develop among the Christians in Antioch, John sought to increase the demographic diversity of his congregations. The Christian mission among the poor could not be effective if those of the lower classes felt unwelcome in the churches. The value of diversity remains intact for the Christian mission in urban areas of the developed world today. This trend is seen across denominational lines and is attracting unchurched people to the gospel and churches in new ways.[20]

17. This type of cooperation has been called "congruence," by which churches grow together and outwardly as a result of shared values and mission. See Britt, "From Homogeneity to Congruence," 138, 144.

18. To this day, the pattern of the early churches, John's churches in Antioch, and Augustine's ministry in the Western Empire remain influential. During the late nineteenth and early twentieth centuries, cooperation was at the heart of evangelical missions such as those the Southern Baptist Convention (SBC), its churches, its North American Mission Board (NAMB), and its International Mission Board (IMB). This cooperative approach to missions includes numerous ventures among the poor around the world. See Sutton, *A Matter of Conviction*, 78–79; Harper, *The Quality of Mercy*, 28; Compton, "Cooperation through Missions," 4–12.

19. McGavran, *Understanding Church Growth*, 85–87. In 1970, McGavran espoused what became known as the Homogenous Unit Principle (HUP). Mcgavran, a missionary to India and professor at Fuller Theological Seminary, described homogenous units as "a section of society in which all the members have some characteristic in common." According to McGavran, these units are comprised of political, geographical, cultural, and linguistic elements, with some room for elasticity depending upon the context. See also Wagner, *Your Church Can Grow*, 110. Wagner, another leader in the CGM and professor at Fuller Seminary adds, "a sign of a healthy, growing church is that its membership is composed of basically one kind of people." McGavran acknowledged at least one major limitation to the HUP which has been deemed "the urban exception." This exception seemed to be true in the case of Antioch, as it has also been demonstrated in urban centers of today.

20. A growing number of pastors and missionaries are finding success in urban settings through the encouragement of diversity. Urban churches that have a higher degree of cultural and ethnic integration are often more attractive to the unchurched and have greater success in identifying and meeting the needs of their communities. See Deyoung,

One of the ways John purposed to accomplish such tasks was to integrate the poor into the missionary activity of the churches. In order to combat many of the presuppositions with which those of means viewed the poor, John sought to demonstrate that the poor had much to contribute for the good of the Christian mission and society as a whole. Many of the working poor were given tasks within and around church properties, while others, such as widows, orphans, and virgins, participated in ecclesiastical duties. According to Hesselgrave, "the last word" in the process of communication comes from the recipients. The recipients "are not passive 'tablets' on whom the missionary communicator inscribes his message. Rather, they are active interpreters and 'responders' to his message."[21] By involving the poor in the regular activity of the church through the communication and practice of almsgiving, John introduced a new class of capable believers into the mission and ministry of the churches.

The building of unity through diversity did not come at the expense of sound church polity. On the contrary, John maintained the structure and offices of the churches according to principles which he discerned from Pauline literature. John taught his church leadership to handle the distribution of alms responsibly by examining each situation closely in order to provide the appropriate level of assistance. Such concern brought a new level of responsibility to the practice of almsgiving among the churches in Antioch as well as providing a foundation for helping people help themselves.

In a 2012 book concerning ministry among the poor entitled, *When Helping Hurts*, Steve Corbett and Brian Fikkert designate three levels of need: relief, rehabilitation, and development.[22] John saw the Antiochene

---

et. al., *United by Faith*, 132, 143. Yancey has also found the intentional pursuit of diversity in the church to be more successful in urban settings. He offers three exceptions to the proposed standard of a multi-racial, multi-ethnic congregation where it may not find as much success. The first is any location, usually in rural areas, where only one racial group resides. The second is a context that lacks a common language. The third are societies that struggle with the unique problems of first-generation immigrants and their challenges in crossing cultures. See also DeYmaz, *Building a Healthy Multi-Ethnic Church*; Schaller, ed., *Center City Churches*, 108. This chapter is written by William Stark and his predecessor Raymond H. Swartzback who saw a largely homogenous church become multi-cultural in Queens, NY in the late twentieth century. According to these pastors, multi-cultural congregations are successful as a result of shared representation in leadership, worship, education, fellowship, service, and outreach. This type of church will grow by from person to person as a result of the shared pursuit of faith.

21. Hesselgrave, *Communicating Christ Cross-Culturally*, 179.

22. Corbett and Fikkert, *When Helping Hurts*, 99–118. The authors argue that if relief is offered when it is not needed, damage can be done to the recipient. The goal,

situation from a similar point of view. His desire was that the practice of almsgiving not be done haphazardly, while at the same time avoiding unnecessary scrutiny toward recipients. Under his direction, the churches in Antioch developed a basic form of case management that was constantly refined. The distribution of alms was organized and structured in such a way that those with the most insurmountable needs took precedence. The disabled and destitute, for example, were able to receive alms on a more permanent basis. John encouraged his congregations to distribute alms to the neediest recipients with a good attitude, forsaking the negative presuppositions that many in the empire applied to them. Relief oriented almsgiving was also extended to those suffering from tragedy and disaster, such as resulted from military activity or the occasional earthquake. In many cases, the wake of tragedy affords Christians with fresh opportunities to participate in missionary endeavors in formerly closed situations.

For the working poor, John saw almsgiving as a form of temporary relief in times of seasonal work, so that provision of supplemental income might sustain those who would later be able to provide for themselves. Robert Lupton, founder of FCS Urban Ministries in Atlanta, GA and a recognized leader in the Christian Community Development Association, discusses the difficulty many churches have regarding the appropriate amount of benevolent assistance. Lupton draws a stark contrast between two missionary practices among the urban poor in the developed world: betterment and development. Most benevolence-type ministries of evangelical churches focus on betterment, which *"does for* others." Development, on the other hand, "enables others to *do for themselves.*"[23] He goes on to say that betterment often leads to unidirectional giving, which causes a church or organization's structure to develop policies based on an adversarial relationship with the recipients which involves moves and counter-moves.[24] As has been demonstrated, the practice of almsgiving, as modeled by John's churches in Antioch, encouraged reciprocity in giving among believers of all demographics. Almsgiving in the Antiochene churches was more than one-way benevolence. It was a shared practice because every believer had something to offer, and all were in need of its benefits.

---

therefore, should be to move people and communities from relief to development, which is, in effect, transitioning from receiver to giver. In some cases this will take a significant amount of time. In the end, however, it will be time well spent.

23. Lupton, *Compassion, Justice, and the Christian Life,* 38–39.

24. Ibid., 26–27, 100. For a more recent discussion by Lupton on development versus betterment, see Lupton, *Toxic Charity,* 165–85.

PARTING WORDS

Recent scholarship has posed questions regarding the application of patristic texts to contemporary settings.[25] While some have doubts regarding the validity of such pursuits, there are others who believe useful parallels exist, particularly in the areas of wealth, poverty, and social justice.[26] Part of my intention in this book has been to demonstrate several similarities between the Eastern Roman Empire of late antiquity and the developed world of today. Since I believe that to be the case, I also believe the missional practice of almsgiving at its apex in the fourth century, especially in the ministry of John Chrysostom, provides a useful model for effective ministry among the poor in urban areas. González offers valuable insight on the usefulness of later patristic thought like that of John Chrysostom:

> They lived in a world in which contrasts between the rich and the poor were staggering; we live in a world populated by a few who have millions and millions who have nothing. For them, these issues were indissolubly connected with the meaning of salvation. Has the world changed so much that what they had to say is no longer relevant? I believe not. Has our commitment waned to such an extent that we can no longer take seriously the questions they pose to our use of the world's resources? I hope not.[27]

John taught almsgiving as a command for every believer. It is clear, however, that he went too far in his communication of almsgiving and its relationship to salvation. One must be careful to not communicate Christian charity in such a way that it is understood to be a form of works-based

---

25. See Leemans, et al., *Reading Patristic Texts*.

26. González, *Faith and Wealth*, 233; Ramsey, "Almsgiving in the Latin Church," 259. Ramsey discusses the legitimacy of such interpretations in light of difficulties between Christology in late antiquity and today. According to Ramsey, "And when the Fathers exaggerated the Christological theme, their intention was, after all, not theoretical so much as practical: to provide for the feeding and clothing of the poor. Consideration of these alternatives may help us to appreciate more the somewhat imperfect understanding of almsgiving that the Latin Fathers seized upon and that we have, in part at least, inherited." See also Rhee, *Loving the Poor*, 219–21. Rhee affirms: "early Christian texts and practices concerning wealth and poverty still offer to us relevant, referential, and illuminating frameworks, principles, perspectives, and practices for our contemporary dealings with wealth and poverty and their attendant opportunities and challenges— enormous historical and sociocultural distance and 'otherness' notwithstanding."

27. González, *Faith and Wealth*, 233.

salvation. On the contrary, almsgiving is a clear evidence of the salvific work of Christ in the believer and among those in the Christian community.

Christian almsgiving is the act of conveying the gospel message from the hands of senders to receivers in the form of generous giving. A renewal of the biblical practice of almsgiving will bring about new opportunities to engage, evaluate, and evangelize the needy in urban settings. Alms are a visible expression of the good news of Jesus Christ which brings hope to even the most desperate situations. In this sense, the practice of almsgiving and mission among the poor are synonymous.

Epilogue

Almsgiving is a great thing. For this reason Solomon exclaimed, *"Man is great, and a merciful man precious"* (Prov. 20:6). Almsgiving's wings are great. She cleaves the air, surpasses the moon, and goes beyond the sun's rays. She rises up to the very vaults of the heavens. She does not stop there; rather, she surmounts heaven and overtakes the multitudes of angels, the choirs of archangels, and all the higher powers, and she stands next to the royal throne.[1]

1. John Chrysostom, *Eleem. et Dec. Vir.* 1 (PG 49:293; trans., Christo, *ORA*, 30).

The Life of John Chrysostom[1]

The dates of John Chrysostom's birth and life until 381 are highly disputed. Many of his writings can be traced only to a general period in his life; the dates given here are generally accepted. Not all of his writings could be listed here.

EARLY YEARS 349–371

349	Born in Antioch of Syria to Christian parents Secundus and Anthusa
363–367	Studies rhetoric and literature under pagan teacher Libanius
368	(Easter) Baptized at Antioch
368–371	Studies in a kind of monastic school; may have assisted bishop Meletius of Antioch
c. 368–371	Writes *Comparison between a King and a Monk* and several other works in favor of monastic life
c. 371	Ordained lector and serves the church of Antioch

LECTOR & DEACON 372–385

372–378	Lives in a semi-isolated state and then as a hermit until bad health forces him to give up this way of life
378–381	Lector (reads Scripture in worship) at Antioch
380 or 381	Ordained deacon (assists with sacraments); writes treatise of consolation to a young widow
381–385	Writes *On the Priesthood*
380 or 382	Two treatises condemning the cohabitation of clerics and virgins

1. This timeline is copied directly from Ettlinger, "John Chrysostom: Christian History Timeline," 22–23. While many of these dates are disputed by current scholarship, this timeline remains a useful tool as it represents more traditional views on the life of John Chrysostom.

PRIEST OF ANTIOCH 386–397

385 or 386	Ordained priest by Bishop Flavian of Antioch
386–387	Preaches homilies (sermons) I–X *On the Incomprehensible Nature of God* and *Against the Jews* (i.e., Christians who follow Jewish religious practices)
387	Antioch riots; John preaches sermons *On the Statues* and *On Almsgiving*
388 or 389	Eight instructions for baptismal candidates
390–397	Homilies on Genesis, Matthew, John, and six NT letters
397	Homilies on selected Psalms and on Isaiah

ARCHBISHOP OF CONSTANTINOPLE 398–403

398	Consecrated bishop of Constantinople. Takes steps to reform imperial court, clergy, and people; homilies XI–XII *On the Incomprehensible Nature of God*
398–402	Homilies on Philippians and Colossians
399	Gives Eutropius sanctuary and preaches two homilies on the vanity of human power
400	Homilies on the Book of Acts
402	Group of Egyptian monks (the "Tall Brothers") appeal to John for help
403	John tried at the Synod of the Oak; convicted, deposed, and exiled; immediately recalled
403–404	Homilies on Hebrews

EXILE 404–407

404	Deposed and exiled to Cucusus (in eastern Turkey)
404–407	Writes more than 200 letters to friends
407	Sent to Pityus on the Black Sea and dies en route, at Comana in Pontus (in northeast Turkey)

Bibliography

ANCIENT TEXT LIBRARIES

Austrian Academy of Sciences. *Corpus Scriptorum Ecclesiasticorum Latinorum* (CSEL). Vienna: Apud C. Geroldi Filium Bibliopolam Academiae, 1866–2006.

Dekkers, Dom Eligius. *Corpus Christianorum Series Latina* (CCSL). Turnhout, Belgium: Brepols, 1953–2010.

Field, Frederick. *Sancti Patris Nostri Ioannis Chrysostomi Archiepiscopi Constantinopolitani Interpretatio Omnium Epistolarum Palinarum per Homilias Facta.* Vol. 2. London: Oxford, 1847.

Loeb, James, et al. *Loeb Classical Library* (LCL). Cambridge: Harvard University Press, 1911–present.

Migne, J. -P, editor. *Patrologiae Cursus Completus: Series Graeca* (PG). Paris: Migne, 1857–66.

———, editor. *Patrologiae Cursus Completus: Series Latina* (PL). Paris: Migne, 1844–65.

Montfaucon, Bernard de. *Opera Saint Chrysostomi.* 13 vols. Edited and Translated by Bernard De Montfaucon. Paris: Caroli Robustel, et al., 1718–38. Reprint. London: Oxford University Press, 1862.

Roberts, Alexander, and James Donaldson, editors. *The Ante-Nicene Fathers* (ANF). Edinburgh, T. & T. Clark, 1867–73. The page numbers listed for ANF correspond to the digital editions of the 1994 version which are available in PDF format. In some volumes the original page numbers are in the margins of the PDF documents.

Schaff, Philip, editor. *A Select Library of the Nicene and Post Nicene Fathers* (NPNF). New York: Christian Literature Company, 1886–1900. The page numbers listed for NPNF series 1 and 2 correspond to the digital editions of the 1994 version which are available in PDF format. In some volumes the original page numbers are in the margins of the PDF documents.

ANCIENT SOURCES AND TRANSLATIONS

Ambrose. *De Officiis Ministrorum.* In PL 16:25–186. Translated by H. de Romestine, *On the Duties of the Clergy.* In NPNF 2.10:22–154.

Bibliography

Augustine. *De Civitate Dei.* In CCSL 47–48. Edited by B. Dombert and A. Kalb. Translated by Henry Bettenson, *Saint Augustine: City of God.* London: Penguin, 2003.

———. *Enchiridion ad Laurentium de Fide et Spes et Caritate.* In CCSL 46, edited by Ernest Evans, 49–114. Translated by Bruce Harbet, *The Enchiridion on Faith, Hope, and Charity.* In *Saint Augustine: On Christian Belief,* edited by Boniface Ramsey, 265–344. Hyde Park, NY: New City, 2005.

Basil. *Epistolae.* In PG 32:219–1114. Translated by Blomfield Jackson, *The Letters.* In NPNF 2.08:260–616.

———. *Homiliae in Hexaemeron.* In PG 29:3–208. Translated by Blomfield Jackson, *The Hexaemeron.* In NPNF 2.08:180–259.

Clement of Alexandria. *Liber Quis Dives Salvetur.* In PG 9:603–80. Text and Translation by George William Butterworth, *The Rich Man's Salvation.* In LCL 92:265–367.

Clement of Rome. *Epistola II ad Corinthios.* In PG 1:329–48. Text and Translation by Michael W. Holmes, *Second Clement.* In AF, 132–66.

Cyprian. *De Opera et Eleemosynis.* In PL 4:601–22. Translated by Robert Ernest Wallis, *On Works and Alms.* In ANF 5:781–95.

———. *De Oratione Dominica.* In PL 4:519–44. Translated by Robert Ernest Wallis, *On the Lord's Prayer.* In ANF 5:734–52.

———. *Liber De Lapsis.* In PL 4:463–94. Translated by Robert Ernest Wallis, *On the Lapsed.* In ANF 5:717–734.

Cyril of Jerusalem. *Catecheses.* In PG 33:331–1180. Translated by Edwin Hamilton Gifford, *The Catechetical Lectures of St. Cyril.* In NPNF 2.07:2–278.

Didache. Text and Translation by Michael W. Holmes, *Didache.* In AF, 334–80.

Eusebius. *Historia Ecclesiastica.* In PG 20:9–910. Translated by Paul L. Maier, *Eusebius: The Church History.* Grand Rapids: Kregel, 2007.

Lactantius. *Divinarum Institutionum.* In PL 6:111–822. Translated by William Fletcher, *The Divine Institutes.* In ANF 7:10–389.

Libanius. "Libanius Basilio." In PG 32:1084. Translated by Blomfield Jackson, "Letter 338: Libanius to Basil." In NPNF 2.08:605.

———. *Libanii Opera.* Edited by Richardus Foerster. 12 Vols. Leipzig: Teubneri, 1903.

Origen. *Homiliae in Leviticum.* In PG 12:395–572. Translated by Gary Wayne Barkley, *Homilies on Leviticus.* Washington: The Catholic University of America Press, 1990.

Palladius, Aspuna. *De Vita Sancti Joannis Chrysostomi.* In PG 47:5–277; P. R. Coleman-Norton. *Palladii Dialogus de Vita Sancti Joannis Chrysostomi.* Cambridge: Harvard University Press, 1928. Translated by Robert T. Meyer, *Palladius: Dialogue on the Life of St. John Chrysostom* New York: Newman, 1985.

Polycarp. *Epistola ad Philippenses.* In PG 5:1005–22. Text and Translated by Michael W. Holmes, *Epistle to the Philippians.* In AF, 272–97.

Salvian. *Ad Ecclesiam.* In CSEL 8. Translated by Jeremiah F. O'Sullivan, *The Writings of Salvian, the Presbyter.* New York: Catholic University of America Press, 2008.

Seneca. *De Beneficiis.* In *Lucius Annaei Senecae: Dialogorum Libri Duodecim,* edited by Herman Adolf Koch and Johannes Vahlen. Ulm, Germany: Wohler, 1884. Translated by Miriam Griffin and Brad Inwood, *Lucius Annaeus Seneca: On Benefits. Chicago:* University of Chicago Press, 2011.

———. *Epistolae.* Text and Translated by Richard M. Gummere, *Ad Lucilium Epistulae Morales.* In LCL 77. London: Heinemann, 1918.

Sozomen, Salaminius Hermias. *Historia Ecclesiastica.* In PG 67:843–1630. Translated by Chester D. Hartranft, *Ecclesiastical History of Sozomen: Comprising a History of the Church from AD 323 to AD 425.* In NPNF 2.02:282–613.

Tertullian. *Adversus Marcionem.* In PL 2:239–524. Translated by Peter Holmes, *The Five Books against Marcion.* In ANF 3:371–687.

———. *Apologeticus.* In PL 1:257–536. Translated by Sidney Thelwall, *The Apology.* In ANF 3:19–73.

Thomas Aquinas. *Summa Theologiae.* Vol. 34. Edited by R. J. Batten. Garden City, NY: Image, 1969.

JOHN CHRYSOSTOM PRIMARY SOURCES AND TRANSLATIONS

John Chrysostom. *Adversus Oppugnatores Vitae Monasticae.* In PG 47:319–87. Translated by David G. Hunter, *A Comparison between A King and A Monk/Against the Opponents of the Monastic Life. Two Treatises.* Lampeter, UK: Mellen, 1989.

———. *Commentarius In Galatians.* In PG 61:611–79. Translated by Gross Alexander, *Commentary on Paul's Epistle to the Galatians.* In NPNF 1.13:7–74.

———. *Conciones De Lazaro.* In PG 48:963–1054. Translated by Catherine P. Roth, *St. John Chrysostom: On Wealth and Poverty* (*OWP*). Yonkers, NY: St. Vladimir's Seminary Press, 1997.

———. *Contra Ludos et Theatra.* In PG 56:263–70. Translated by Wendy Mayer and Pauline Allen, "Against the Games and Theatres." In *John Chrysostom*, 118–25. London: Routledge, 2000.

———. *De Anna.* In PG 54:631–76. Translated by Robert Charles Hill, *St. John Chrysostom: Old Testament Homilies.* Vol. 1. Brookline, MA: Holy Cross Orthodox, 2003.

———. *De Diabolo Tentatore III.* In PG 49:243–76. Translated by T. P. Brandram, *Three Homilies Concerning the Power of Demons.* In NPNF 1.09:189–215.

———. *De Inani Gloria et de Educandis Liberis.* In SC 188:64–196 (*Sur la vaine gloire et l'éducation des enfants*). French translation by Anne Marie Malingrey. Paris: Cerf, 1972. Translated by Max L.W. Laistner, *An Address on Vainglory and the Right Way for Parents to Bring Up Their Children by John Chrysostom.* In *Christianity and Pagan Culture in the Later Roman Empire*, 75–122. 1951. Reprint. Ithaca, NY: Cornell University Press, 1967.

———. *De Sacerdotio.* In PG 48:623–93. Translated by Graham Neville, *St. John Chrysostom: Six Books On the Priesthood* (*OP*). Yonkers, NY: St. Vladimir's Seminary Press, 1996; W. R. W Stephens, *A Treatise Concerning the Priesthood.* In NPNF 1.09:28–94.

———. *Epistola LI—Diogeni.* In PG 52:636–37. Translated by Wendy Mayer and Pauline Allen, "Letter 51: To Diogenes." In *John Chrysostom*, 202–3. London: Routledge, 2000.

———. *Epistola CCXVII—Valentino.* In PG 52:730–31. Translated by Wendy Mayer and Pauline Allen, "Letter 217: To Valentinus." In *John Chrysostom*, 201–2. London: Routledge, 2000.

———. *Epistola CCXXI—Constantio.* In PG 52:732–33.

———. *Epistola CCXXV—Constantio.* In PG 52:735–36.

———. *Epistola CXXIII—Phoeniciae Presbyteris et Monachis.* In PG 52:676–78.

———. *Expositio In Psalms.* In PG 55:39–498. Translated by Robert Charles Hill, *St. John Chrysostom: Commentary on the Psalms.* 2 Vols. Brookline, MA: Holy Cross Orthodox, 2007.

———. *Homilia I De Maccabaeis.* In PG 50:617–24. Translated by Wendy Mayer and Bronwen Neil, *St. John Chrysostom: The Cult of the Saints,* 135–46. Yonkers, NY: St. Vladimir's Seminary Press, 2006.

———. *Homilia II De Maccabaeis.* In PG 50:623–26. Translated by Wendy Mayer and Bronwen Neil, *St. John Chrysostom: The Cult of the Saints,* 147–54. Yonkers, NY: St. Vladimir's Seminary Press, 2006.

———. *Homilia De Eleazar et Septem Pueris.* In PG 63:523–30. Translated by Wendy Mayer and Bronwen Neil, *St. John Chrysostom: The Cult of the Saints,* 119–34. Yonkers, NY: St. Vladimir's Seminary Press, 2006.

———. *Homilia De Eleemosuna et in Decem Virgines.* In PG 49:291–300. Translated by Gus George Christo, *On Repentance and Almsgiving,* 28–42. Washington, DC: The Catholic University of America Press, 1998.

———. *Homiliae De Incomprehensibili Dei Natura.* In PG 48:701–812. Translated by Paul W. Harkins, *Fathers of the Church: St. John Chrysostom On the Incomprehensible Nature of God.* Washington, DC: The Catholic University of America Press, 1999.

———. *Homiliae De Statuis ad Populum Antiochenum Habitae.* In PG 49:15–222. Translated by W. R. W. Stephens, *Homilies on the Statues to the People of Antioch.* In NPNF 1.09:342–565.

———. *Homiliae In Acts.* In PG 60:13–383. Translated by J. Walker, et al., *Homilies on the Acts of the Apostles.* In NPNF 1.11:11–451.

———. *Homiliae In Colossians.* In PG 62:299–392. Translated by John A. Broadus, *Homilies on Paul's Epistle to the Colossians.* In NPNF 1.13:350–438.

———. *Homiliae In Corinthians Primam.* In PG 61.9–380. Translated by Talbot W. Chambers, *Homilies on Paul's First Epistle to the Corinthians.* In NPNF 1.12:6–370; Wendy Mayer and Pauline Allen, "Homily 21 on 1 Corinthians." In *John Chrysostom,* 131–38. London: Routledge, 2000.

———. *Homiliae In Corinthians Secundam.* In PG 61.382–610. Translated by Talbot W. Chambers, *Homilies on Paul's Second Epistle to the Corinthians.* In NPNF 1.12:371–578.

———. *Homiliae In Ephesians.* In PG 62:9–176. Translated by Gross Alexander, *Homilies on Paul's Epistle to the Ephesians.* In NPNF 1.13:74–246.

———. *Homiliae In Genesis.* In PG 53:21—54:580. Translated by Robert Charles Hill, *St. John Chrysostom: Homilies on Genesis.* 2 Vols. Washington, DC: Catholic University of America Press, 2001.

———. *Homiliae In Hebrews.* In PG 63:89–235. Translated by Frederic Gardiner, *Homilies on the Epistle to the Hebrews.* In NPNF 1.14:501–757.

———. *Homiliae In John.* In PG 59:23–482. Translated by Philip Schaff, *Homilies on the Gospel of St. John.* In NPNF 1.14:6–500; Sister Thomas Aquinas Goggin, *St. John Chrysostom: Commentary on Saint John the Apostle and Evangelist,* 1–88. 2 Vols. New York: Fathers of the Church, 1960.

———. *Homiliae In Matthew.* In PG 57:13—58:794. Translated by W. R. W. Stephens, *Homilies on the Gospel of St. Matthew.* In NPNF 1.10:3–717.

———. *Homiliae In Philippians.* In PG 62:177–297. Translated by John A. Broadus, *Homilies on Paul's Epistle to the Philippians.* In NPNF 1.13:249–350.

————. *Homiliae In Romans*. In PG 60:392–681. Translated by J. B. Morris, et al., *Homilies on Paul's Epistle to the Romans*. In NPNF 1.11:452–753.

————. *Homiliae In Thessalonians Primam*. In PG 62:391–467. Translated by John A. Broadus, *Homilies on Paul's First Epistle to the Thessalonians*. In NPNF 1.13:439–511.

————. *Homiliae In Thessalonians Secundam*. In PG 62:467–500. Translated by John A. Broadus, *Homilies on Paul's Second Epistle to the Thessalonians*. In NPNF 1.13:511–40.

————. *Homiliae In Timothy Primam*. In PG 62:502–600. Translated by Philip Schaff, *Homilies on Paul's First Epistle to Timothy*. In NPNF 1.13:540–634.

————. *Homiliae In Timothy Secundam*. In PG 62:601–61. Translated by Philip Schaff, *Homilies on Paul's Second Epistle to the Timothy*. In NPNF 1.13:634–95.

————. *Homiliae In Titus*. In PG 62:663–700. Translated by Philip Schaff, *Homilies on Paul's Epistle to Titus*. In NPNF 1.13:695–730.

————. *Oraciones Adversus Judeaos*. In PG 48:843–945. Translated by Paul W. Harkins, *St. John Chrysostom: Discourses against Judaizing Christians*. Washington, DC: Catholic University of America Press, 1979.

————. *Quod Nemo Laeditur Nisi a Seipso*. In PG 52:459–80. Translated by T. P. Brandram, *That No One Can Harm the Man Who Does Not Injure Himself*. In NPNF 1.09:290–309.

————. *Sermo De Eleemosuna*. In PG 51:261–72. Translated by Gus George Christo, *On Repentance and Almsgiving* (ORA), 131–51. Washington, DC: The Catholic University of America Press, 1998.

TRANSLATIONS

Barkley, Gary Wayne. *Origen: Homilies on Leviticus*. Washington, DC: The Catholic University of America Press, 1990.

Bettenson, Henry. *Saint Augustine: City of God*. London: Penguin, 2003.

Christo, Gus George. *St. John Chrysostom: On Repentance and Almsgiving*. Washington, DC: The Catholic University of America Press, 1998.

Goggin, Sister Thomas Aquinas. *St. John Chrysostom: Commentary on Saint John the Apostle and Evangelist 1–88*. 2 Vols. New York: Fathers of the Church, 1960.

Griffin, Miriam, and Brad Inwood. *Lucius Annaeus Seneca: On Benefits*. Chicago: University of Chicago Press, 2011.

Gummere, Richard M. *Ad Lucilium Epistulae Morales*. LCL 77. London: Heinemann, 1918.

Harbert, Bruce. *The Enchiridion on Faith, Hope, and Charity*. In *Saint Augustine: On Christian Belief*, edited by Boniface Ramsey, 265–344. Hyde Park, NY: New City Press, 2005.

Harkins, Paul W. *Fathers of the Church: St. John Chrysostom On the Incomprehensible Nature of God*. Washington, DC: The Catholic University of America Press, 1999.

————. *St. John Chrysostom: Discourses against Judaizing Christians*. Washington: Catholic University of America Press, 1979.

Hill, Robert Charles. *St. John Chrysostom: Commentary on the Psalms*. 2 Vols. Brookline, MA: Holy Cross Orthodox, 2007.

————. *St. John Chrysostom: Homilies on Genesis*. 2 Vols. Washington, DC: Catholic University of America Press, 2001.

——. *St. John Chrysostom: Old Testament Homilies.* 3 Vols. Brookline, MA: Holy Cross Orthodox, 2003.

Holmes, Michael W, editor. *The Apostolic Fathers: Greek Texts and English Translations.* 3rd ed. Grand Rapids: Baker, 2007.

Hunter, David G. *A Comparison between a King and a Monk/Against the Opponents of the Monastic Life. Two Treatises.* Lampeter, UK: Mellen, 1989.

Laistner, Max L. W. *An Address on Vainglory and the Right Way for Parents to Bring Up Their Children by John Chrysostom.* In *Christianity and Pagan Culture in the Later Roman Empire,* 75–122. 1951. Reprint. Ithaca, NY: Cornell University Press, 1967.

Maier, Paul L. *Eusebius: The Church History.* Grand Rapids: Kregel, 2007.

Mayer, Wendy, and Pauline Allen. *John Chrysostom.* London: Routledge, 2000.

Mayer, Wendy, and Bronwen Neil. *St. John Chrysostom: The Cult of the Saints.* New York: St. Vladimir's Seminary Press, 2006.

Meyer, Robert T. *Palladius: Dialogue on the Life of St. John Chrysostom.* New York: Newman, 1985.

Neville, Graham. *St. John Chrysostom: Six Books On the Priesthood.* Yonkers, NY: St. Vladimir's Seminary Press, 1996.

O'Sullivan, Jeremiah F. *The Writings of Salvian, the Presbyter.* New York: Catholic University of America Press, 2008.

Roth, Catherine P. *St. John Chrysostom: On Wealth and Poverty.* Yonkers, NY: St. Vladimir's Seminary Press, 1997.

OTHER PRIMARY SOURCES

Calvin, John. *La Forme Des Prieres.* Bärenreiter: Kassel, 1969.

Chemnitz, Martin. *On Almsgiving.* Translated by James A. Kellerman. St. Louis: LCMS, 2004.

Gutierrez, Gustavo. *Essential Writings.* Edited by James B. Nickoloff. Minneapolis: Fortress, 1996.

——. *Liberation and Change.* Atlanta: John Knox, 1977.

——. *A Theology of Liberation.* Maryknoll: Orbis, 1973.

——. *The Truth Shall Make You Free.* Maryknoll: Orbis, 1990.

Malthus, Thomas Robert. *The Works of Thomas Robert Malthus.* 8 Vols. Edited by E. A. Wrigley and David Sonden. London: Pickering and Chatto, 1986.

Mathews, Shailer. *The Gospel and the Modern Man.* New York: Macmillan, 1912.

——. *The Social Teaching of Jesus.* New York: Macmillan, 1900.

Rauschenbusch, Walter. *Christianity and the Social Crisis.* New York: Macmillan, 1907.

——. *Christianizing the Social Order.* New York: Macmillan, 1912.

——. *Prayers for the Social Awakening.* Boston: Pilgrim, 1909.

SECONDARY SOURCES

Alberto, Vicent Llorca. "El Socorro De Los Pobres: Libertad o Regulacion." D.Th., Universidad De Navarra, Spain, 1998.

Albertz, Rainer. "Die 'Antrittspredigt' Jesu im Lukasevangelium auf ihrem alttestamentlichen Hintergrund." *Zeitschrift für die Neutestamentliche Wissenschaft* 74 (1983) 182–206.

Allen, Pauline, Bronwen Neil, and Wendy Mayer. *Preaching Poverty in Late Antiquity: Perceptions and Realities.* Leipzig: Evangelische, 2009.

—————. and Wendy Mayer. "Through a Bishop's Eyes: Towards a Definition of Pastoral Care in Late Antiquity." *Augustinianum* 40 (2000) 345–97.

Ameringer, Thomas Edward. *The Stylistic Influence of the Second Sophistic on the Panegyrical Sermons of St. John Chrysostom: A Study in Greek Rhetoric.* Washington, DC: The Catholic University of America Press, 1921.

Anderson, Gary A. "Redeem Your Sins by the Giving of Alms: Sin, Debt, and the 'Treasury of Merit' in Early Jewish and Christian Tradition." In *Letter and Spirit: The Hermeneutic of Continuity—Christ, Kingdom, and Creation*, edited by Scott W. Hahn and David Scott, 39–70. Steubenville, OH: St. Paul Center for Biblical Theology, 2007.

Anderson, Graham. *The Second Sophistic: A Cultural Phenomenon in the Roman Empire.* London: Routledge, 1993.

Aquilina, Mike. *The Fathers of the Church.* Huntington, IN: Our Sunday Visitor, 2006.

Atherton, John, editor. *Christian Social Ethics: A Reader.* Cleveland, OH: Pilgrim, 1994.

Atkins, Margaret, and Robin Osborne, editors. *Poverty in the Roman World.* Cambridge: Cambridge University Press, 2009.

Avery-Peck, Alan. "Charity in Judaism." In *Encyclopedia of Judaism*, vol. 1, edited by Jacob Neusner et al., 50–63. New York: Continuum, 1999.

Bagnall, Roger. "Monks and Property: Rhetoric, Law, and Patronage in Apophthegmata Patrum and the Papyri." *Greek, Roman, and Byzantine Studies* 42 (2001) 7–24.

Barcelona, Ruby. "The Face of the Poor." *Patmos* 11 (1995) 3–5, 21.

Barnes, Timothy D. *Constantine and Eusebius.* Cambridge: Harvard University Press, 1981.

Bauer, Walter and Frederick Danker, editors. *A Greek-English Lexicon of the New Testament and Other Christian Literature.* 3rd ed. Chicago: University of Chicago Press, 1999.

Baur, Chrysostomus. *John Chrysostom and His Time.* 2 Vols. London: Sands, 1959.

Beeri, Emmanuel. "Communal Amenities." In *Encyclopaedia Judaica*, vol. 2, edited by Michael Berenbaum, 39–40. Detroit: Macmillan, 2007.

Bloch, R. Howard. "Medieval Misogyny." In *Misogyny, Misandry, and Misanthropy*, edited by R. Howard Bloch and Frances Ferguson, 1–24. Berkeley: University of California Press, 1989.

Blomberg, Craig. *Matthew.* Nashville: Broadman, 1992.

—————. *Neither Poverty Nor Riches: A Biblical Theology of Material Possessions.* Downers Grove, IL: InterVarsity, 1999.

Bolkestein, Hendrik. *Wohltätigkeit und Armenpflege im vorchristlichen Altertum.* Utrecht: Arno, 1939.

Bosch, David. *Transforming Mission.* Maryknoll, NY: Orbis, 1991.

Bosinis, Constantine. "Two Platonic Images in the Rhetoric of John Chrysostom: 'The Wings of Love' and 'The Charioteer of the Soul.'" *Studia Patristica* 41 (2006) 433–38.

Bowman, Matthew. "Sin, Spirituality, and Primitivism: The Theologies of the American Social Gospel, 1885–1917." *Religion and American Culture* 17 (2007) 95–126.

Brady, Judith Ann. "A Burning Desire for Social Justice." *Religious Education* 105 (Jan–Feb 2010) 8–11.

Bibliography

Brakke, David. "Care for the Poor, Fear of Poverty, and Love of Money: Evagrius Ponticus on the Monk's Economic Vulnerablity." In *Wealth and Poverty in Early Church and Society*, edited by Susan R. Holman, 76–87. Grand Rapids: Baker, 2008.

Brändle, Rudolph. *John Chrysostom: Bishop, Reformer, Martyr*. Australia: St. Paul's, 2004.

———. "This Sweetest Passage: Matthew 25:31–46 and Assistance to the Poor in the Homilies of John Chrysostom." In *Wealth and Poverty in Early Church and Society*, edited by Susan R. Holman, 127–39. Grand Rapids: Baker, 2008.

Breen, Mike. "Man of Peace." *Outreach Magazine* (Nov 2010) 1–3. Online: http:// www. churchleaders.com/outreach–missions/outreach–missions–articles/139684–man–of–peace.html.

Bremmer, Jan N. *The Apocryphal Acts of Paul and Thecla*. Leuven: Peeters, 1996.

Bremner, Robert H. *Giving: Charity and Philanthropy in History*. 2nd ed. New Brunswick: Transaction, 2000.

Britt, David. "From Homogeneity to Congruence." In *Planting and Growing Urban Churches*, edited by Harvie M. Conn, 130–50. Grand Rapids: Baker, 1997.

Broc-Schmezer, Catherine. "De l'aumône faite au pauvre à l'aumône du pauvre: Pauvreté et spiritualité chez Jean Chrysostome." In *Les Pères de l'Eglise et la voix des pauvres, Actes du IIe Colloque de la Rochelle*, 131–48, 2–4 septembre 2005. Histoire et Culture, Paris: Cerf, 2006.

———. *Les figures féminines du Nouveau Testament dans l'oeuvre de Jean Chrysostome*. Turnhout: Brepols, 2011.

Brooks, Roger. *Support for the Poor in the Mishnaic Law of Agriculture: Tractate Peah*. Chico, CA: Scholars, 1983.

———. "Peah." In *The Mishnah: A New Translation*, edited by Jacob Neusner, 14–35. New Haven: Yale University Press, 1988.

Brown, Peter. "Christianization and Religious Conflict." In *Cambridge Ancient History: The Late Empire, AD 337–425*, vol. 13, edited by Averil Cameron and Peter Garnsey, 632–64. Cambridge: Cambridge University Press, 1998.

———. "A Parting of the Ways: Wealth, Working, and Poverty in Early Christian Monasticism." Lecture given at the Library of Congress (Washington, DC, April 30, 2009).

———. *Poverty and Leadership in the Later Roman Empire*. London: Brandeis, 2002.

———. *Power and Persuasion in Late Antiquity: Towards a Christian Empire*. Madison, WI: University of Wisconsin Press, 1992.

———. "The Rise and Function of the Holy Man in Late Antiquity, 1971–1997." *Journal of Early Christian Studies* 6 (1998) 353–76.

———. *The World of Late Antiquity: AD 150–750*. 1971. Reprint. New York: Norton, 1989.

Brown, Robert Mcafee. *Gustavo Gutierrez: An Introduction to Liberation Theology*. Maryknoll: Orbis, 1990.

Cameron, Averil. *The Later Roman Empire: AD 284–430*. Cambridge: Harvard University Press, 1993.

———, and Peter Garnsey, editors. *Cambridge Ancient History: The Late Empire, AD 337–425*. Vol. 13. Cambridge: Cambridge University Press, 1998.

Caner, Daniel. *Wandering, Begging Monks: Spiritual Authority and the Promotion of Monasticism in Late Antiquity*. Berkeley: University of California Press, 2002.

————. "Wealth, Stewardship, and Charitable 'Blessings' in Early Byzantine Monasticism." In *Wealthy and Poverty in Early Church and Society*, edited by Susan R. Holman, 221–42. Grand Rapids: Baker, 2008.

Cardman, Francine. "Poverty and Wealth as Theater: John Chrysostom's Homilies on Lazarus and the Rich Man." In *Wealthy and Poverty in Early Church and Society*, edited by Susan R. Holman, 159–75. Grand Rapids: Baker, 2008.

Carras, Irmgard Elisabeth. "Who Cared? The Poor in Colonial New York City, 1628–1753." PhD diss., New York University, 1995.

Carson, D. A. "Church and Mission: Reflections on Contextualization and the Third Horizon." In *The Church in the Bible and the World: An International Study*, edited by D. A. Carson, 213–57. Grand Rapids: Baker, 1987.

————. *Matthew*. Grand Rapids: Zondervan, 1958.

Casey, R. P. "The Apocalypse of Paul." *Journal of Theological Studies* 34 (1933) 1–32.

Charry, Ellen T. "When Generosity is Not Enough." *Quarterly Review* 21 (2001) 266–78.

Christian Century, Religious News Service. "Federal Faith-Based Grands Doubled in 2004." *Christian Century* 122, May 3, 2005, 13.

Cole, Virginia Ann. "Royal Almsgiving in Medieval England: A Study in the Ritual and Administrative Construction of Kingship." PhD diss., State University of New York at Binghamton, 2002.

Coleman-Norton, P. R. *Palladii Dialogus de Vita Sancti Joannis Chrysostomi.* Cambridge: Harvard University Press, 1928.

Colish, Marcía L. *The Stoic Tradition from Antiquity to the Early Middle Ages: Stoicism in Christian Latin Thought through the Sixth Century.* 2 Vols. Leiden: Brill, 1990.

Compton, Bobby D. "Cooperation through Missions." *Baptist History and Heritage* 24 (Jan 1989) 4–12.

Conn, Harvie M., editor. *Planting and Growing Urban Churches: From Dream to Reality.* Grand Rapids: Baker, 1997.

————, and Manuel Ortiz. *Urban Ministry: The Kingdom, the City, and the People of God.* Downers Grove: InterVarsity, 2001.

Constantelos, Demetrios J. *Byzantine Philanthropy and Social Welfare.* 2nd ed. Athens: Caratzas, 1991.

————. "The Hellenic Background and Nature of Patristic Philanthropy in the Early Byzantine Era." In *Wealth and Poverty in Early Church and Society*, edited by Susan R. Holman, 187–210. Grand Rapids: Baker, 2008.

Conzelmann, Hans. *History of Primitive Christianity.* Translated by John E. Steely. Nashville: Abingdon, 1973.

Corbett, Steve and Fikkert, Brian. *When Helping Hurts.* Chicago: Moody, 2009; Rev. ed., 2012.

Cronbach, Abraham. "The Me'il Zedakah." *Hebrew Union College Annul* 11 (1936) 503–67.

Cross, Frank Leslie, editor. *St. Cyril of Jerusalem's Lectures on the Christian Sacraments: The Procatechesis and the Five Mystagogical Catecheses.* Text translated by R. W. Church. Yonkers, NY: St. Vladimir's Seminary Press, 1986.

Cunningham, Mary B., and Pauline Allen, editors. *Preacher and Audience: Studies in Early Christian and Byzantine Homiletics.* Leiden: Brill, 1998.

Dagron, Gilbert. *Naissance d'une capitale: Constantinople et ses institutions de 330 á 451.* Paris: University of Paris Press, 1974.

Daniels, Gene. "Personal Piety vs. Institutional Aid: A Case for a Return to Alms-giving." *Evangelical Missions Quarterly* 44 (2008) 450–56.

Davis, David. "St. John Chrysostom on Ministry, Discernment, and Call." *Theology Today* 62 (2005) 408–13.

De Vinne, Michael James. "The Advocacy of Empty Bellies: Episcopal Representation of the Poor in the Late Roman Empire." PhD diss., Stanford University, 1995.

De Wet, Christiaan R. "John Chrysostom's Use of the Book of Sirach in his Homilies on the New Testament." *Studia Historiae Ecclesiasticae* 32 (Oct 2010) 1–10.

Delmaire, Ronald. "Les 'lettres d' exil' de Jean Chrysostome. Études de Chronologie et de prosopographie." *Recherches Augustiniennes* 25 (1991) 71–180.

DeYmaz, Mark. *Building a Healthy Multi–Ethnic Church.* San Francisco: Jossey-Bass, 2007.

DeYoung, Curtiss Paul, Michael O. Emerson, George Yancey, and Karen Chai Kim. *United by Faith: The Multiracial Congregation as an Answer to the Problem of Race.* New York: Oxford University Press, 2004.

Diehl, Douglas Alan. "The Significance of Almsgiving in Primitive Christianity as a Means of Understanding New Testament Piety." PhD diss., SWBTS, 1991.

Dorn, Christopher. *The Lord's Supper in the Reformed Church in America: Tradition in Transformation.* New York: Lang, 2007.

Dorrien, Gary. *Social Ethics in the Making: Interpreting an American Tradition.* West Sussex, UK: Wiley, 2008.

———. *Soul and Society: The Making and Renewal of Social Christianity.* Minneapolis: Fortress, 1995.

Downey, Glanville. *A History of Antioch in Syria from Seleucus to the Arab Conquest.* Princeton: Princeton University Press, 1961.

Downing, F. Gerald. *Cynics and Christian Origins.* Edinburgh: T. & T. Clark, 1992.

Dragas, George Dion. *The Holy Sacraments of Baptism, Chrismation and Holy Communion: The Five Mystagogical Catechisms of St. Cyril of Jerusalem.* Rollinsford, NH: Orthodox Research Institute, 2008.

Dunn, Marilyn. *The Emergence of Monasticism: From the Desert Fathers to the Early Middle Ages.* Hoboken, NJ: Wiley-Blackwell, 2003.

Eadie, John W. "Constantine." In *Encyclopedia of Religion*, 2nd ed., vol. 3, edited by Lindsay Jones, 1966–67. Detroit: Macmillan Reference USA, 2005.

Ellis, Marc H., and Otto Maduro, editors. *The Future of Liberation Theology: Essays in Honor of Gustavo Gutierrez.* Maryknoll, NY: Orbis, 1989.

Eltester, Walther. "Die Kirchen Antiochias im IV. Jahrhundert." *Zeitschrift für Neutestamentliche Wissenschaft* 36 (1937) 251–86.

Escobar, Samuel. *Changing Tides: Latin America and World Mission Today.* New York: Orbis, 2002.

Ettlinger, Gerard H. "John Chrysostom: Christian History Timeline." *Christian History* 44 (1 Oct 1994) 22–23.

Fagan, Kevin. "New Panhandling Law—S.F. to Take It Easy: City Says It Will Use Persuasion Not Jail." *San Francisco Chronicle*, May 25, 2004.

———. "Success in the City of Brother Love." *San Francisco Chronicle,* June 13, 2004.

Ferguson, Everett. "Spiritual Sacrifice in Early Christianity and Its Environment." *Aufstieg und Niedergang der römischen Welt* 2.23.2 (1981) 1152–92.

Finn, Richard. *Almsgiving in the Later Roman Empire: Christian Promotion and Practice (313–450).* Oxford: Oxford University Press, 2006.

————. "Portraying the Poor: Descriptions of Poverty in Christian Texts from the Late Roman Empire." In *Poverty in the Roman World*, edited by Margaret Atkins and Robin Osborne, 130–44. Cambridge: Cambridge University Press, 2006.

Francis, James A. *Subversive Virtue: Asceticism and Authority in the Second-Century Pagan World*. University Park, PA: Pennsylvania State University Press, 1995.

Frend, W. H. C. *The Rise of Christianity*. Philadelphia: Fortress, 1984.

Garnsey, Peter, and Richard Saller. *The Roman Empire: Economy, Society, and Culture*. Berkeley: University of California Press, 1987.

Garrison, Roman. *Redemptive Almsgiving in Early Christianity*. Sheffield, UK: Sheffield Academic Press, 1993.

Geisler, Norman L. "Some Philosophical Perspectives on Missionary Dialogue." In *Theology and Mission*, edited by David. J. Hesselgrave, 241–58. Grand Rapids: Baker, 1978.

Gibbon, Edward. *History of the Decline and Fall of the Roman Empire*. Vol. 5. Edited by William Smith. London, 1788. Reprint. New York: American Book Company, 1856.

Gladden, Washington. *Working People and their Employers*. New York: Funk and Wagnalls, 1885.

González, Justo L. *Faith and Wealth: A History of Early Christian Ideas on the Origin, Significance, and the Use of Money*. San Francisco: Harper and Row, 1990.

————. *The Story of Christianity*. 2 Vols. San Francisco: Harper Collins, 1984.

Goodall, John A. A. *God's House at Ewelme: Life, Devotion, and Architecture in a Fifteenth-Century Almshouse*. Aldershot, UK: Ashgate, 2001.

Gordon, Barry. *The Economic Problem in Biblical and Patristic Thought*. Leiden: Brill, 1989.

Greenway, Roger S., editor. *Discipling the City*. 2nd ed. Grand Rapids: Baker, 1992.

Grissom, Fred Allen. "Chrysostom and the Jews: Studies in Jewish-Christian Relations in Fourth-Century Antioch." PhD diss., Southern Baptist Theological Seminary, 1979.

Guder, Darrell L., et. al. *Missional Church: A Vision for the Sending of the Church in North America*. Grand Rapids: Eerdmans, 1998.

Haarmann, Ulrich. "Islamic Duties in History." *Muslim World* 68 (Jan 1978) 1–24.

Hagner, Donald Alfred. *Matthew 14–28*. Dallas: Word, 1995.

Hall, Ron, Denver Moore, and Lynn Vincent. *Same Kind of Different as Me*. Nashville: Thomas Nelson, 2006.

Halton, Thomas. "Saint John Chrysostom on Education." *The Catholic Educational Review* 61 (1963) 163–75.

Hamel, Gildas. *Poverty and Charity in Roman Palestine: First Three Centuries C.E.* Berkeley: University of California Press, 1990.

Harmless, William. *Desert Christians: An Introduction to the Literature of Early Monasticism*. New York: Oxford University Press, 2004.

Harnack, Adolf von. *The Expansion of Christianity in the First Three Centuries*. Translated by James Moffatt. London: Williams and Norgate, 1908.

Harper, Keith. *The Quality of Mercy: Southern Baptists and Social Christianity, 1890–1920*. Tuscaloosa, AL: University of Alabama Press, 1996.

Harries, Jill. "Favor Populi: Pagans, Christians, and Public Entertainment in Late Antique Italy." In *Bread and Circuses: Euergetism and Municipal Patronage in Roman Italy*, edited by Kathryn Lomas and Tim Cornell, 125–41. London: Routledge, 2003.

Hartney, Aideen M. *John Chrysostom and the Transformation of the City*. London: Duckworth, 2004.

Bibliography

Hasselhoff, Görge K. "James 2:2–7 in Early Christian Thought." In *Wealth and Poverty in Early Church and Society*, edited by Susan R. Holman, 48–55. Grand Rapids: Baker, 2008.

Hays, Christopher. "Beyond Mint and Rue: The Implications of Luke's Interpretive Controversies for Modern Consumerism." *Political Theology* 11.3 (2010) 387–402.

Heayn, David A. "Urban Violence in Fifth Century Antioch: Riot Culture and Dynamics in Late Antique Mediterranean Cities." *Concept* (Nov 2008) 1–29. Online: http://concept.journals.villanova.edu/article/view/303.

Heim, Maria. "Almsgiving." In *Encyclopedia of Religion*, 2nd ed., edited by Lindsay Jones, 266–69. Detroit: Macmillan Reference USA, 2005.

Hesselgrave, David J. *Communicating Christ Cross-Culturally: An Introduction to Missionary Communication*. 2nd ed. Grand Rapids: Zondervan, 1991.

———. "Fitting Third-World Believers with Christian Worldview Glasses." *Journal of the Evangelical Theological Society* 30 (1987) 215–22.

Hillner, Julia. "Clerics, Property and Patronage: The Case of the Roman Titular Churches." *Antiquité Tardive* 14 (2006) 59–68.

Hoag, Gary, Andy Bales, and Ronald J. Sider. "Everyday Benevolence: Should Christians Always Give Money to Street People who Ask for It?" *Christianity Today* 55, Jan 2011, 60–61.

Holman, Susan R. "The Entitled Poor: Human Rights Language in the Cappadocians." *Pro Ecclesia* 9 (2000) 476–89.

———. *God Knows There's a Need: Christian Responses to Poverty*. Oxford: Oxford University Press, 2009.

———. *The Hungry are Dying: Beggars and Bishops in Roman Cappadocia*. London: Oxford, 2001.

———. "Patristic Christian Views on Poverty and Hunger." *Journal of Lutheran Ethics* 10 (June 2010) 15–18.

———, editor. *Wealth and Poverty in Early Church and Society*. Grand Rapids: Baker, 2008.

Honore, Tony. "Roman Law AD 200–400: From Cosmopolis to Rechtstaat?" In *Approaching Late Antiquity: The Transformation From Early to Late Empire*, edited by Simon Swain and Mark Edwards, 109–32. New York: Oxford University Press, 2004.

Hopkins, Keith. "Early Christian Number and its Implications." *Journal of Early Christian Studies* 6 (1998) 185–226.

Humphrey, John H. *Roman Circuses: Arenas for Chariot Racing*. Berkeley: University of California Press, 1986.

Ierodiakonou, Katerina, editor. *Byzantine Philosophy and its Ancient Sources*. New York: Oxford University Press, 2004.

Illert, Martin. *Johannes Chrysostomus und das antiochenisch-syrische Mönchtum. Studien zu Theologie: Rhetorik und Kirchenpolitik im antiochenischen Schrifttum des Johannes Chrysostomus*. Zürich: Pano, 2000.

Johnson, Kelly S. *The Fear of Beggars: Stewardship and Poverty in Christian Ethics*. Grand Rapids: Eerdmans, 2007.

Joslyn-Siemiatkoski, Daniel. *Christian Memories of the Maccabean Martyrs*. New York: Palgrave MacMillan, 2009.

Kalantzis, George. "Crumbs from the Table: Lazarus, the Eucharist and the Banquet of the Poor in the Homilies of John Chrysostom." In *Ancient Faith for the Church's*

Future, edited by M. Husbands and J. P. Greenman, 156–68. Downers Grove, IL: InterVarsity, 2008.

Kalleres, Dayna "Exorcising the Devil to Silence Christ's Enemies." PhD diss., Brown University, Providence, RI, May 2002.

Kelly, J. N. D. *Early Christian Creeds.* 3rd ed. London: Continuum, 1972.

————. *Golden Mouth: The Story of John Chrysostom—Ascetic, Preacher, Bishop.* Ithaca, NY: Cornell University Press, 1998.

Kim, Kyoung-Jin. *Stewardship and Almsgiving in Luke's Theology.* Sheffield, UK: Sheffield Academic Press, 1998.

Kinnaman, David. "Do We Give a Rip About the Poor?" *Rev,* May–June 2008, 15–17.

Koch, Mark Douglas. "The Economy of Beggary in English Literature from the Reformation to the Enlightenment." PhD diss., State University of New York at Buffalo, 1987.

Kohler, Kaufmann. "Alms." In *The Jewish Encyclopedia,* edited by Cyrus Adler et al., no pages. New York: Funk and Wagnall, 1906. Online: http:// jewishencyclopedia.com/ articles /1295-alms.

Kolbe, Matthias. "Nur eine Metapher?: Tetimími oder Wo badete die grosse Badende?" In *Zurück zum Gegenstand: Festschrift für Andreas E. Furtwängler,* vol. 2, edited by R. Einicke et al., 67–76. Langenweissbach: Beier un Beran, 2009.

Knight, George W. "Luke 16:19–31: The Rich Man and Lazarus." *Review and Expositor* 94 (1997) 277–83.

Krupp, R. A. *Shepherding the Flock of God: The Pastoral Theology of John Chrysostom.* New York: Lang, 1991.

Kucharek, Casimir. *The Byzantine-Slav Liturgy of St. John Chrysostom.* Allendale, NJ: Alleluia, 1971.

Labberton, Mark. "A Mighty River or a Slippery Slope? Examining the Cultural and Theological Forces behind the New Interest in Justice." *Leadership,* Summer 2010, 20–25.

Ladd, George Eldon. *The Presence of the Future.* Grand Rapids: Eerdmans, 1974.

Laistner, Max Ludwig Wolfram. *Christianity and Pagan Culture in the Later Roman Empire.* 1951. Reprint. Ithaca, NY: Cornell University Press, 1967.

Larkin, William J. "Mission in Luke." In *Mission in the New Testament: An Evangelical Approach,* edited by William J. Larkin and Joel F. Williams, 152–70. Maryknoll, NY: Orbis, 1998.

Lassus, J. "La ville d'Antioch á l'époque romaine d'aprés l'archéologie." *Aufstieg und Niedergang der Römischen Welt* 2 (1977) 54–102.

Latourette, Kenneth S. *A History of Christianity.* Vol. 1. San Francisco: Harper-Collins, 1975.

Leemans, Johan, Brian J. Matz, and John Verstraeten, editors. *Reading Patristic Texts on Social Ethics: Issues and Challenges for Twenty-First-Century Christian Social Thought.* Washington, DC: Catholic University of America Press, 2011.

Leithart, Peter J. *Defending Constantine: The Twilight of an Empire and the Dawn of Christendom.* Downers Grove, IL: InterVarsity, 2010.

Lewis, Andrew R. "Biblical Directives for Combating Hunger and Poverty." *ERLC,* 31 July 2007, no pages. Online: http://erlc.com/article/biblical–directives–for–combating–hunger–and–poverty.

Leyerle, Blake. "John Chrysostom on Almsgiving and the Use of Money." *Harvard Theological Review* 87 (1994) 29–47.

Bibliography

————. *Theatrical Shows and Ascetic Lives: John Chrysostom's Attack on Spiritual Marriage.* Berkeley: University of California Press, 2001.

Liebeschuetz, J. H. W. G. *Antioch: City and Imperial Administration in the Later Roman Empire.* New York: Oxford University Press USA, 1972.

————. *Barbarians and Bishops: Army, Church, and State in the Age of Arcadius and Chrysostom.* New York: Oxford University Press: 1992.

Lindenmeyr, Adele. "Public Poor Relief and Private Charity in Late Imperial Russia." PhD diss., Princeton University, 1980.

Little, Lester K. *Religious Poverty and the Profit Economy in Medieval Europe.* Ithaca, NY: Cornell University Press, 1978.

Lomas, Kathryn, and Tim Cornell, editors. *Bread and Circuses: Euergetism and Municipal Patronage in Roman Italy.* London: Routledge, 2003.

Lunn-Rockliffe, Sophie. "A Pragmatic Approach to Poverty and Riches: Ambrosiaster's *Quaestio* 124." In *Poverty in the Roman World*, edited by Margaret Atkins and Robin Osborne, 115–30. Cambridge: Cambridge University Press, 2006.

Lupton, Robert D. *Compassion, Justice, and the Christian Life: Rethinking Ministry to the Poor.* Ventura, CA: Regal, 2007.

————. *Toxic Charity: How Churches and Charities Hurt Those They Help (And How to Reverse It).* New York: HarperOne, 2011.

MacMullen, Ramsey. *Christianity and Paganism in the Fourth to Eighth Centuries.* New Haven: Yale University Press, 1999.

————. "The Preacher's Audience (AD 350–400)." *Journal of Theological Studies* 40 (1989) 503–11.

————. *The Second Church: Popular Christianity AD 200–400.* Atlanta: Society of Biblical Literature, 2009.

Maier, J. L. *Le Dossier Du Donatisme.* Berlin: Akademie, 1987.

Malosse, Pierre-Louis. "Jean Chrysostome a-t-il été l'évève de Libanios?" *Phoenix* 62 (2008) 273–80.

Mandryk, Jason. *Operation World: The Definitive Prayer Guide to Every Nation.* 7th ed. Colorado Springs: Biblica, 2010.

Marrou, H. I., and George Lamb. *A History of Education in Antiquity.* Madison, WI: University of Wisconsin Press, 1982.

Martin, Matthew. "Communal Meals in the Late Antique Synagogue." In *Feast Fast or Famine: Food and Drink in Byzantium*, edited by Wendy Mayer and S. Trzcionka, 135–46. Brisbane: Australian Association for Byzantine Studies, 2004.

Martin, Mike W. *Virtuous Giving: Philanthropy, Voluntary Service, and Caring.* Bloomington, IN: Indiana University Press, 1994.

Maston, T. B. *Biblical Ethics.* Waco, TX: Word, 1980.

————. *The Christian, the Church, and Contemporary Problems.* Waco, TX: Word, 1968.

Matthews, Alfred Warren. *The Development of St. Augustine, from Neoplatonism to Christianity, 386–391 A.D.* Lanham, MD: University Press of America, 1983.

Maxwell, Jaclyn L. *Christianization and Communication in Late Antiquity: John Chrysostom and His Congregation in Antioch.* New York: Cambridge University Press, 2006.

Mayer, Wendy. "Biography and Chronology." In *Chrysostomika II*, edited by Sever J. Voicu. Rome: Augustinianum, 2012.

————. "The Bishop as Crisis Manager: An Exploration of Early Fifth-Century Episcopal Strategy." In *Studies of Religion and Politics in the Early Christian Centuries*, edited by David Luckensmeyer and Pauline Allen, 159–71. Strathfield, Australia: St Paul's, 2010.

———, and Pauline Allen. *The Churches of Syrian Antioch (300–638 CE).* Leuven: Peeters, forthcoming.

———. "Constantinopolitan Women in Chrysostom's Circle." *Vigilae Christianae* 53 (1999) 1–24.

———. *The Homilies of St. John Chrysostom: Provenance. Reshaping the Foundations.* Rome: Institutum Patristicum Orientalium Studiorum, 2005.

———, and Pauline Allen. *John Chrysostom.* London: Routledge, 2000.

———. "John Chrysostom and His Audiences: Distinguishing Different Congregations at Antioch and Constantinople." *Studia Patristica* 31 (1997) 70–75.

———. "John Chrysostom as Bishop: the View from Antioch." *Journal of Ecclesiastical History* 55 (2004) 455–66.

———. "John Chrysostom: Extraordinary Preacher, Ordinary Audience." In *Preacher and Audience: Studies in Early Christian and Byzantine Homiletics,* edited by Mary B. Cunningham and Pauline Allen, 103–36. Leiden: Brill, 1998.

———. "John Chrysostom's Use of the Parable of Lazarus and the Rich Man (Luke 16:19–31)." *Scrinium. Revue de patrologie, d'hagiographie critique et d'histoire ecclésiastique* 4 (2008) 45–59.

———. "The Making of a Saint: John Chrysostom in Early Historiography." In *Chrysostomosbilder in 1600 Jahren: Facetten der Wirkungsgeschichte eines Kirchenvaters,* edited by M. Wallraff and Rudolph Brändle, 39–59. Berlin: de Gruyter, 2008.

———. "Monasticism at Antioch and Constantinope in the Late Fourth Century: A Case of Exclusivity or Diversity?" In *Prayer and Spirituality in the Early Church: Liturgy and Life,* vol. 1, edited by Pauline Allen et al., 275–88. Brisbane: Centre for Early Christian Studies, 1998.

———. "Patronage, Pastoral Care, and the Role of the Bishop at Antioch," *Vigilae Christianae* 55 (2001) 58–70.

———. "Poverty and Generosity toward the Poor in the Time of John Chrysostom." In *Wealth and Poverty in Early Church and Society,* edited by Susan R. Holman, 140–58. Grand Rapids: Baker, 2008.

———. "Poverty and Society in the World of John Chrysostom." In *Social and Political Archaeology in Late Antiquity,* edited by William Bowden et al., 465–84. Leiden: Brill, 2006.

———, and Bronwen Neil. *St. John Chrysostom: The Cult of the Saints.* New York: St. Vladimir's Seminary Press, 2006.

———. "What Does It Mean to Say That John Chrysostom Was a Monk?" *Studia Patristica* 41 (2006) 451–55.

———. "Who Came to Hear John Chrysostom Preach? Recovering a Late Fourth-Century Preacher's Audience." *Ephemerides Theologicae Lovanienses* 76 (2000) 73–87.

McCarthy, James G. *Talking with Catholic Friends and Family.* Eugene, OR: Harvest House, 2005.

McGavran, Donald. *Understanding Church Growth.* Grand Rapids: Eerdmans, 1970.

McGuckin, John Anthony. *Patristic Theology.* Louisville: Westminster John Knox, 2004.

McKee, Elsie Anne. "John Calvin on the Diaconate and Liturgical Almsgiving." PhD diss., Princeton Theological Seminary, 1982.

Bibliography

McKinley, E. H. *Marching to Glory: The History of the Salvation Army in the United States, 1880-1992*. Grand Rapids: Eerdmans, 1997.

Meeks, Wayne A., and Robert L. Wilken. *Jews and Christians in Antioch in the First Four Centuries of the Common Era*. Atlanta: Scholars, 1978.

Metzger, Bruce et al., translators. *The Apocrypha: New Revised Standard Version*. Cambridge: Cambridge University Press, 1992.

Miller, T. S. *The Birth of the Hospital in the Byzantine Empire*. Baltimore: Johns Hopkins University Press, 1985.

Minus, Paul M. "Rauschenbusch, Walter." In *Encyclopedia of Religion*, edited by Lindsay Jones, 7629-30. Detroit: Macmillan Reference USA, 2005.

Mitchell, Ben C. "The Samaritan Imperative: Southern Baptists Meeting Human Needs in Times of Crises." *Baptist History and Heritage* 29 (July 1994) 19-27.

Mitchell, Margaret Mary. *The Heavenly Trumpet: John Chrysostom and the Art of Pauline Interpretation*. Louisville: Westminster John Knox, 2002.

Morley, Neville. "The Poor in the City of Rome." In *Poverty in the Roman World*, edited by Margaret Atkins and Robin Osborne, 21-39. Cambridge: Cambridge University Press, 2006.

Moulton, Harold K., editor. *The Analytical Greek Lexicon*. 7th ed. Grand Rapids: Zondervan, 1972.

Mulheron, T. Greenan. "La opción por los pobres en las homilías de Monseñor Romero y de San Juan Crisóstomo: Análisis de la convergencias y de las peculiaridades en los presupuestos teológicos y en las orientaciones morales." PhD diss., Madrid, 2003.

Munzer, Stephen. "Heroism, Spiritual Development, and Triadic Bonds in Jain and Christian Mendicancy and Almsgiving." *Numen* 48 (2001) 47-80.

Murphy, F. X. "The Moral Doctrine of Saint John Chrysostom." *Studia Patristica* 11 (1972) 52-53.

Myers, Bryant L. *Walking with the Poor: Principles and Practices of Transformational Development*. Maryknoll, NY: Orbis, 1999.

Nagle, D. Brendan, and Stanley M. Burstein. *The Ancient World: Readings in Social and Cultural History*. Englewood Cliffs, NJ: Prentice Hall, 1995.

NAMB. "Annual Report" (2010), no pages. Online: http://www.namb.net/annualreport.

Neil, Bronwen. "Models of Gift-Giving in the Preaching of Leo the Great." *Journal of Early Christian Studies* 18 (2010) 225-59.

Neusner, Jacob. *Judaism and Christianity in the Age of Constantine: History, Messiah, Israel, and the Initial Confrontation*. Chicago: University of Chicago Press, 1987.

———. *The Mishnah: A New Translation*. New Haven: Yale University Press, 1988.

———. *Torah: From Scroll to Symbol in Formative Judaism*. Philadelphia: Fortress, 1984.

———. *Tzedakah: Can Jewish Philanthropy Buy Jewish Survival?* Atlanta: Scholars, 1990.

Newbigin, Lesslie *Foolishness to the Greeks*. Grand Rapids: Eerdmans, 1986.

Nicholls, Bruce J. *Contextualization: A Theology of Gospel and Culture*. Vancouver: Regent College, 1995.

Nida, Eugene A. *Message and Mission: The Communication of the Christian Faith*. Pasadena: William Carey, 1990.

Nolan, Albert. "Theology in a Prophetic Mode." In *The Future of Liberation Theology: Essays in Honor of Gustavo Gutierrez*, edited by Marc H. Ellis and Otto Maduro, 430-45. Maryknoll, NY: Orbis, 1989.

Noll, Mark A. *A History of Christianity in the United States and Canada*. Grand Rapids: Eerdmans, 1992.

Olejniczak, William John. "The Royal Campaign in France against Beggary and Vagrancy during the Eighteenth Century as Implemented in the Generalite of Champagne." PhD diss., Duke University, 1983.

Oliphant, Old Hughes. "Daily Prayer in the Reformed Church of Strasbourg." *Worship* 52 (Mar 1978) 121–38.

Osborne, Robin. "Roman Poverty in Context." In *Poverty in the Roman World*, edited by Margaret Atkins and Robin Osborne, 1–25. Cambridge: Cambridge University Press, 2009.

Osiek, Carolyn. *Shepherd of Hermas: A Commentary*. Minneapolis: Fortress, 1999.

———. "The Widow as Altar: The Rise and Fall of a Symbol." *The Second Century* 3 (1983) 159–69.

Parkes, James. *The Conflict of the Church and the Synagogue: A Study in the Origins of Antisemitism*. New York: Jewish Publication Society, 1934.

Parkin, Anneliese. "Poverty in the Early Roman Empire: Ancient and Modern Conceptions and Constructs." PhD, Cambridge, 2001.

———. "'You Do Him no Service': An Exploration of Pagan Almsgiving." In *Poverty in the Roman World*, edited by Margaret Atkins and Robin Osborne, 60–82. Cambridge: Cambridge University Press, 2009.

Patlagean, Evelyne. *Pauvreté économique et pauvreté sociale à Byzance, 4e-7e siècles*. Paris: Mouton, 1977.

Pipes, Paula F., and Helen R. F. Ebaugh. "Faith-Based Coalitions, Social Services, and Government Funding." *Sociology of Religion* 63 (2002) 49–68.

Pope, Stephen J. "Aquinas on Almsgiving, Justice and Charity: An Interpretation and Reassessment." *Heythrop Journal* 32 (1991) 167–91.

Princeton University, History Department. "Peter Brown." Online: http://www.princeton.edu /history/people/display_person.xml?netid=prbrown.

Rad, Gerhad von. *Genesis—A Commentary*. Rev. ed. 1961. Reprint. Philadelphia: Westminster, 1972.

———. *Old Testament Theology*. Vol. 1. San Francisco: Harper, 1967.

Ramsey, Boniface. "Almsgiving in the Latin Church: The Late Fourth and Early Fifth Centuries." *Theological Studies* 43 (1982) 226.

Rawlings, Annie. "Poverty, Truth and Reconciliation." *Church & Society* 92 (May–June 2002) 61–63.

Repp, A. C. "John Chrysostom on the Christian Home as a Teacher." *Concordia Theological Monthly* 22 (1951) 937–48.

Retzleff, Alexandra. "Near Eastern Theatres in Late Antiquity." *Phoenix* 57 (Spr–Sum 2003) 115–38.

Rhee, Helen. *Loving the Poor, Saving the Rich: Wealth, Poverty, and Early Christian Formation*. Grand Rapids: Baker Academic, 2012.

Roth, Catharine P. *St. John Chrysostom: On Wealth and Poverty*. Yonkers, NY: St. Vladimir's Seminary Press, 1997.

———, and David Anderson. *St. John Chrysostom: On Marriage and Family Life*. Crestwood, NY: St. Vladimir's Seminary Press, 1986.

Rothman, Flora. "Bad Girls/Poor Girls: A New York History of Social Control from the Alms House to Family Court." PhD diss., City University of New York, 1989.

Rousseau, Philip. "'The Preacher's Audience': A More Optimistic View." In *Ancient History in a Modern University*, vol. 2, edited by T. W. Hillard and E. A. Judge, 391–400. Grand Rapids: Eerdmans, 1998.

Bibliography

Sachs, Jeffrey. *The End of Poverty: Economic Possibilities for Our Time*. New York: Penguin, 2005.

Sandwell, Isabella. *Religious Identity in Late Antiquity: Greeks, Jews and Christians in Antioch*. Cambridge: Cambridge University Press, 2007.

Schaller, Lyle E., editor. *Center City Churches: The New Urban Frontier*. Nashville: Abingdon, 1993.

Schottroff, Luise, and Wolfgang Stegemann. *Jesus and the Hope of the Poor*. Translated by Matthew J. O' Connell. Maryknoll, NY: Orbis, 1986.

Schroeder, J. A. "John Chrysostom's Critique of Spousal Violence." *Journal of Early Christian Studies* 12 (2004) 413–42.

Schwartz, Seth. *Imperialism and Jewish Society 200 BCE to 640 CE*. Princeton: Princeton University Press, 2001.

Segal, Arthur. *Theatres in Roman Palestine and Provincia Arabia*. Leuven: Brill, 1997.

Serfass, Adam. "A Review of *Almsgiving in the Later Roman Empire: Promotion and Practice (315–450)*." *Bryn Mawr Classical Review* 7.50 (2007) 3.

Sider, Ronald J. *Just Generosity: A New Vision for Overcoming Poverty in America*. 2nd ed. Grand Rapids: Baker, 2007.

———. *Rich Christians in an Age of Hunger: Moving from Affluence to Generosity*. Rev. ed. Nashville: Thomas Nelson, 2005.

Simon, Marcel. *Verus Israel. Etude sur les relations entre chrétiens et juifs dans l' empire romain (135–425)*. Paris: de Boccard, 1964.

Sitzler, Silke. "Identity: The Indigent and the Wealthy in the Homilies of John Chrysostom." *Vigiliae Christianae* 63 (2009) 468–79.

Slater, William. *Roman Theater and Society*. Ann Arbor, MI: University of Michigan Press, 1996.

Smith, Adam. *An Inquiry into the Nature and Causes of the Wealth and Poverty of Nations*. London, 1776. Reprint. London: Methuen, 1904.

Smith, William, and Henry Wace, editors. *A Dictionary of Christian Biography, Literature, Sects, and Doctrines*. 4 vols. Boston: Little, Brown, and Co., 1877.

Speckman, McGlory Tando. "Alms or Legs?" DTh thes., University of South Africa, 1999.

Sterk, Andrea. *Renouncing the World Yet Leading the Church: The Monk-Bishop in Late Antiquity*. Cambridge: Harvard University Press, 2004.

Stetzer, Ed, and David Putman. *Breaking the Missional Code*. Nashville: Broadman & Holman, 2006.

Stowe, Connie Rae Stowe. "The Meaning and Justification of the Term, 'Option for the Poor.'" PhD diss, Vanderbilt University, 1999.

Strayer, Joseph R., editor. *Dictionary of the Middle Ages*. New York: Scribner's Sons, 1987.

Swain, Simon. "Sophists and Emperors: The Case of Libanius." In *Approaching Late Antiquity: The Transformation From Early to Late Empire*, edited by Simon Swain and Mark Edwards, 355–400. New York: Oxford University Press, 2004.

Sutton, Jerry. *A Matter of Conviction: A History of Southern Baptist Engagement with the Culture*. Nashville: Broadman and Holman, 2008.

Taft, Robert. "The Authenticity of the Chrysostom Anaphora Revisited. Determining the Authorship of Liturgical Texts by Computer." *Orientalia Christiana Periodica* 56 (1990) 5–51.

Talbert, Charles H. *Reading the Sermon on the Mount: Character Formation and Decision Making in Matthew 5–7*. Columbia: University of South Carolina Press, 2004.

Thayer, Joseph Henry, and Carl L. W. Grimm. *Greek-English Lexicon of the New Testament: being Grimm's Wilke's Clavis Novi*. Grand Rapids: Zondervan, 1970.

Thorsteinsson, Runar M. *Roman Christianity and Roman Stoicism: A Comparative Study of Ancient Morality*. New York: Oxford University Press, 2010.

Van Rheenen, Gailyn. *Contextualization and Syncretism: Navigating Cultural Currents*. Pasadena: William Carey, 2006.

———. "Contrasting Missional and Church Growth Perspectives." *Missiology* MMR 34 (2007) no pages. Online: http://missiology.org/mmr/mmr34.htm.

———. "Modern and Postmodern Syncretism in Theology and Missions" In *The Holy Spirit and Mission Dynamics*, edited by C. Douglas McConnell, 164–207. Pasadena: William Carey, 1997.

Vatican."Article 1434: The Many Forms of Penance in Christian Life." In *Catechism of the Catholic Church*, 322. Rev. Eng. ed. London: Continuum, 2002.

Verbeke, Gérard. *The Presence of Stoicism in Medieval Thought*. Washington, DC: Catholic University of America Press, 1983.

Viansino, Giovanni. "Aspetti dell'opera di Giovanni Crisostomo." *Koinonia* 25 (2001) 137–205.

Wagner, C. Peter. *Your Church Can Grow*. Glendale: Regal, 1976.

Wallace, Daniel B. *The Basics of New Testament Syntax*. Grand Rapids: Zondervan, 2000.

Wallace-Hadrill, Andrew. "Patronage in Roman Society: From Republic to Empire." In *Patronage in Ancient Society*, edited by Andrew Wallace–Hadrill, 63–87. New York: Routledge, 1989.

Walsh, Efthalia Makris. "Wealthy and Impoverished Widows in the Writings of St. John Chrysostom." In *Wealth and Poverty in Early Church and Society*, edited by Susan R. Holman, 176–86. Grand Rapids: Baker, 2008.

Wan, Enoch and Michael Pocock, editors. *Missions from the Majority World: Progress, Challenges, and Case Studies*. Pasadena: William Carey, 2009.

Whittaker, C. R. *Frontiers of the Roman Empire: A Social and Economic Study*. Baltimore: Johns Hopkins University Press, 1997.

Wilken, Robert Louis. *The Christians as the Romans Saw Them*. New Haven: Yale University Press, 1984.

———. *John Chrysostom and the Jews: Rhetoric and Reality*. Eugene, OR: Wipf and Stock, 2004.

Yéor, Bat. *The Decline of Eastern Christianity under Islam: From Jihad to Dhimmitude: Seventh-Twentieth Century*. Madison, NJ: Fairleigh Dickinson, 1996.

Young, Richard. *Intermediate New Testament Greek*. Nashville: Broadman and Holman, 1994.

Youngs, Susan Grinna. "A New Edition of 'Instructions for Christians.'" PhD diss, University of Wisconsin, 1995.

Scripture Index

Names Index

Names Index

Valens, 27
Valentinian I, 27
Valentinus (presbyter), 125–26

Walsh, Efthalia M., 52n, 60
Wilken, Robert L., 27, 52n, 59n

Zaccheus, 106n